D0879621

PINDAR

The greatest Lyric poet of ancient Greece. A native of Thebes in Boeotia. Born 518 B.C. Date of death uncertain, probably within a few years of 440 B.C.

The Odes of Pindar

Translated into English Verse
by

GEOFFREY S. CONWAY
M.C., T.D., M.A.

J. M. Dent & Sons Ltd, London

Made in Great Britain
at the
Aldine Press · Letchworth · Herts
for
J. M. DENT & SONS LTD
Aldine House · Bedford Street · London
First published 1972

No. 17 ISBN: (if a hardback) 0 460 00017 9
No. 1017 ISBN: (if a paperback) 0 460 01017 4

To My Wife

CONTENTS

Preface ix

Introduction xi

Sicily and Magna Graecia (map) xxvi
Greece and the Aegean (map) xxvii

Tables of Victors, Events and Myths
Olympian and Pythian Odes xxviii
Nemean and Isthmian Odes xxx

THE ODES OF PINDAR
Olympian I–XIV 1
Pythian I–XII 79
Nemean I–XI 169
Isthmian I–VIII 231

PREFACE

My aim in this book has been to provide an accurate and easily readable translation of the Odes of Pindar which would be intelligible and of interest to the general reader, whether or not he or she has been a student of ancient Greece and its literature. It was also hoped that the translation would be of use to the increasing number of students who study the Classics in translation, as well as to students of the Odes in the original Greek. To achieve this purpose it was essential to provide ample explanatory material, partly because of the abundant freedom of Pindar's vividly imaginative language and style, and especially because his poetry abounds in allusions which would be clear to readers of his own time, but which for the modern reader, and in many cases even for the Classical student, need adequate explanation. I hope that in the present work this need has been adequately met by the general introduction, forewords to each Ode and explanatory notes to the text.

Of the various authoritative works on Pindar which I have consulted in making this translation I especially wish to acknowledge my debt to the French Budé Edition of Pindar's works (1931), edited and translated by Aimé Puech, late Professor of Greek Poetry in the University of Paris, with introductory matter of especial interest.

Finally I wish to record the grateful thanks which I owe to my wife, not only for her encouragement during a lengthy task, but also for undertaking the typing of the script.

Cambridge, 1972 G. S. Conway

INTRODUCTION

The Odes of Pindar were written in honour of victors in the events of the four great national athletic meetings of ancient Greece, held at regular intervals at Olympia, at Delphi (the Pythian Games[1]), on the Isthmus of Corinth and at Nemea. These Games were in each case part of one of the four Panhellenic festivals, the most important of all the religious festivals of ancient Greece.

THE PANHELLENIC GAMES AND THE EPINICIAN ODE Competitive athletic meetings had from early times been a regular part of Greek life, and by the time of Pindar, whose working years covered the first half of the fifth century B.C., these were widespread amongst the cities of Greece. Such local festivals however were far surpassed in importance by the four Panhellenic meetings, and superlative honour attached to those who were successful in these most eagerly contested of all Greek athletic competitions. On their return to their native city the victors were abundantly fêted and given distinctions and privileges of various kinds, sometimes including a free table at the headquarters of the local government. The fête in honour of the victor's success was held in combination with religious rites, and often followed by a banquet. Where an Ode in honour of the victory, known as an 'epinician' Ode, had been commissioned, its performance was an important part of this celebration. The epinician Ode was written for accompaniment by music and a dance, and was performed by a chorus of singers and dancers. Little knowledge has come down to us of the music and dances, but their composition was undertaken by the writer of the Ode and was held to be of no less importance than the words. The writer was also responsible for the training of the chorus, and if he attended the celebration, though this might involve him in a lengthy journey to the victor's city, he would also direct the performance of the Ode. Sometimes a triumphal march or procession took the place of the dance. A few of Pindar's short Odes, on those occasions when he had himself been an onlooker at the Games, as he not infrequently was, were

[1] The name 'Pythian' derives from Pytho, the Serpent, who was worshipped as god of the Delphic oracle in early times before the introduction of the Olympic deities to Greece. Pytho was then ousted by Apollo, who became the tutelary god of Delphi. Snakes were always associated, both in earlier times and in the Classical era of Greece, with the powers of divination and prophecy.

written immediately on the victor's success and performed at the venue of the athletic meeting, at a fête, or procession to the temple, held on the evening of the contest or before the conclusion of the festival. Most of his Odes however were completed after an interval of time and delivered for performance at the home of the victor.

THE MYTHS Pindar was the author of many different kinds of lyric poetry —he is credited with the composition of seventeen books of various types of poem—but except for his four books of epinician Odes, corresponding with the four Panhellenic festivals, which have come down to us in nearly complete form, his other works now consist only of fragments, few of them of any length. A feature of his Odes, written in conformance with rules for lyric poetry well established by Pindar's time, is the inclusion in each Ode, except the few very short ones, of a myth, a story chosen from the vast stock of Greek mythological legends with which most Greeks were familiar from childhood onwards. We thus find expressed in lyrical form a combination of epic and lyric material which adds no little to the interest and attractiveness of these poems.

THE EPINICIAN ODE AND THE PANHELLENIC IDEAL The Panhellenic festivals and Games, which were open to all men of Greek birth, were attended by great numbers of pilgrims, competitors or onlookers drawn from all parts of the Greek world, including such distant places as the Greek cities in south Italy and Sicily, Cyrene in North Africa and the island of Rhodes in the eastern Aegean, as well as from all parts of the mainland of Greece and the Greek islands. They played an important part amongst those elements in Greek life which helped to foster the Panhellenic spirit, to strengthen the idea of a common Hellenic tradition and a unity of outlook in religious and cultural spheres. Other such elements were the bond of their common language, their common recognition of Delphi as the supreme oracle and centre of religious worship for all Greeks, and their common inheritance of the poems of Homer, held in veneration throughout the Greek world for many centuries both before and during the Classical era of Greece. The poems of Pindar can certainly be regarded as a further influence, by no means a small one, tending in the same direction. Though his Odes are concerned with particular achievements, his treatment of his subject-matter frees it from all local limitations, and his poetical genius raises the victor's achievement and the poem which celebrates it out of the sphere of every-day reality to the plane of the ideal. His myths, treating as they do of the legends of gods, heroes (demi-gods) and mortals of mythical antiquity and their more than human exploits, are in keeping with this idealizing tendency.[1] The

[1] It is thought by some scholars that the practice of including myths in epinician Odes was adopted not only with a view to increasing the decorative

competitors in the 'Great Games', for whom his Odes were written, were for the most part drawn from members of wealthy and aristocratic families who took pride in tracing their descent from the heroes of antiquity, and through them, often enough, from the gods themselves. It need not surprise us that his Odes became the treasured possessions of the families to whom they were delivered, or that one of his best-known Odes (Ol. VII), written in honour of Diagoras of Rhodes, is said to have been set up in letters of gold in the temple of Pallas Athene in Lindus, one of three main cities of the island.

The connection of the myth with the victory which the Ode celebrates is not always a close one, deriving sometimes from the reputed ancestral descent of the victor's family, sometimes from the mythical figures associated with the early legends of the victor's city, sometimes from some similarity in the nature or circumstances of the victory with the legendary tale. In some Odes the connection is more subtle and less easily defined. Pindar's handling of his myths appears to have been a special target for the criticisms of his rivals or adversaries, often jealous of the high reputation which his poetry achieved from fairly early in his career. His myths are rarely told in a conventional way, though they are no less effective for this, sometimes consisting of briefly told references rather than the full story, and on occasion telling the story back to front, the final outcome announced first, followed by the preceding incidents, e.g. the stories of Castor and Pollux (Nem.X.str.4–ep.5), and of Perseus and Medusa (Pyth.XII). To a Greek audience, to whom those legends were familiar, this would be of little account.

RELIGION AND ETHICS The content of Pindar's Odes makes it quite clear that their purpose was much more than that of providing an attractive record of a joyful event. Descriptions of the victor's actual athletic achievement are not given, but the Odes find their main theme in extolling the fine qualities—the *aretê* or excellence of spirit—which have enabled the victor to rise to the heights of supreme skill; and the hard work of the preliminary training is frequently included as an additional mark of that merit. The Greek word *aretê*, in other contexts often translated 'virtue', has a much wider meaning than that English word, and can apply to high merit in almost any activity that is praiseworthy or skilful. It is also used by Pindar, more often in the plural than the singular, to mean the actual deeds, usually deeds of courage or heroism, which exemplify the spirit of the doer:

> Brave deeds, high merits are ever rich in story
> (*Pyth.IX.str.4.1.*)

---

effect of the poems but also to give to the Odes, and to the men in whose honour they were written, some share in the *aura* of timeless immortality which these legends enjoyed in the minds of the Greeks of those times.

This quality of excellence which has now proved itself in action, thus earning the praises which will give it immortality, 'For words live longer down the years than deeds' (Nem.IV.str.1.8.), is the prevailing *motif* of the Odes, and this is combined with the theme that such qualities, and the successes they bring, derive from the will of heaven:

For from the gods comes every skilled endeavour
Of mortal quality (*Pyth.I.str.3.1.*)

This path of glory where his sandals tread
Is given of heaven (*Ol.VI.ant.1.2.*)

Reverence for the gods is constantly emphasized, and that a man's aims, however great his capabilities, should be in keeping with divine law:

God achieves all his purpose and fulfils
His every hope (*Pyth.II.str.3.1.*)

But if a man shall hope in aught he does
To escape the eyes of god, he makes an error
(*Ol.I.str.3.8.*)

The need for humility in a man's outlook and the avoidance of acts of pride and insolence is equally stressed:

Seek not to become Zeus . . .
For mortals mortal gifts are fitting.
(*Isth.V.ep.1.3.*)

But violence brings to ruin even
The boastful hard-heart soon or late
(*Pyth.VIII.ep.1.1.*)

Many of his myths exemplify the theme of the punishment which attends failure to comply with the eternal laws, e.g. the myths of Tantalus (Ol.I.), of Ixion (Pyth.II.), and of Asclepius and his mother Coronis (Pyth.III.). It will be clear to readers of the Odes that Pindar regarded his function as that of a preacher as well as that of a poet. His poems give forceful and clear expression to the traditional beliefs and moral or ethical standards which over many centuries had helped the Greek people to reach the position they enjoyed by the beginning of the fifth century B.C., a position which enabled them, not without justification, to regard the Hellenic race as the possessor of gifts of a special kind, and encouraged them to look on other races as people of quite a different order.

In general however Pindar does not attempt any analysis or close definition of what constitutes right or wrong action. He was a man of conservative mind and his poems were composed for people of a similar outlook. They assume that the principles of right and wrong are generally recognized and that the individual conscience will not have difficulty in deciding what actions are or are not in keeping. In these respects his poems have no direct share in the great outburst of liberalizing ideas which found its zenith in the latter half of the fifth century and the ensuing years of the fourth. Though the origin of many of these new ideas can be traced to the influence of writers of Pindar's time, notably to Aeschylus, Pindar's exact contemporary, and to Sophocles, his junior by twenty-five years, we cannot look to Pindar for an expression of the more considered philosophies and the attitude of enquiry and rational analysis which found their place in the world after his time. But his poems throw a bright light, probably more clearly than any other writer, on the beliefs and standards prevalent amongst the Greeks of his own earlier age. The Greek achievement and its pre-eminent influence on future civilizations is sometimes apt to be remembered mainly in respect of its later more intellectually diversified period. Pindar's poetry is a reminder of the splendid foundation on which that later development rested.

PINDAR'S POETRY It is not however to Pindar's thought or philosophy that we look to find the qualities that have given his poems their unique reputation. It is as a master of language and a poet of supreme lyrical merit that his name has won such well-deserved fame. His poems show, amongst their more obvious characteristics, superb qualities of vigour and vividness and a mastery of metre and imaginative diction. Expressing, as has been suggested, much of what lay at the root of the Hellenic spirit, often in terms of impressive weight, they display a mind of marked individuality whose engaging idiosyncrasies are constantly felt, whether in his methods of expression or in the skill with which he laces together the various elements, often numerous and differing in kind, of a particular poem. In the choice and order of his words and in the magnificent sound of his lines Pindar reveals himself as a superb craftsman at the height of his technique, unfolding a lyrical beauty which a translation cannot reproduce. Nor can we reconstruct the music or the melodies and dances which were an integral part of the composition and production of the Ode.

It may be useful however to make brief mention of a few basic features of Pindar's style and method. His poems are marked by the swiftness of his transition from image to image and from thought to thought, and by an abundant and strikingly imaginative use of metaphor—it was Aristotle in his 'Poetics', written in the fourth century B.C., who referred to the use of metaphor as 'the token of genius'. Poetry becomes in Pindar's phrases:

. . . the fine flower
Of music's utterance (*Ol.I.ant.1.4.*)

A pillar . . . whiter than Parian marble
(*Nem.IV.str.10.2.*)

. . . this gift
Of milk and honey blended,
And the cream of the mixing crowns the bowl,
A draught of song
Borne on the breath of flutes of Aeolis.
(*Nem.III.ant.4.8.*)

Many of man's activities contribute to the picture of poetry and its inspiration:

Many a swift arrow my quiver holds
. . . . speaking to men of wisdom (*Ol.II.str.5.4.*)

. . . my Muse in her array
Nurses her strongest dart of all. (*Ol.I.ep.4.4.*)

Listen, I plough the meadow
Of Aphrodite of the glancing eyes, or of the Graces
(*Pyth.VI.str.1.1.*)

. . . that my hand may till
The precious beauty of the Graces' garden.
(*Ol.IX.ep.1.7.*)

Or the poem becomes a ship, while Pindar rebukes himself for straying off course:

Oh heart of mine,
To what far foreign headland
Lead you my sail astray? (*Nem.III.str.2.7.*)

About, my ship: to Europe's mainland
Turn once again your sail (*Nem.IV.str.8.11.*)

Sometimes his metaphors are mixed:

Hold now your oar, and quickly from the prow
Cast anchor to the deep sea-bed, to hold
Our ship from the rocky reef.
For like a bee flitting from flower to flower,
The rich strain of my songs of triumph
Lights now on one tale now upon another.
(*Pyth.X.ep.3.3.*)

In another passage Pindar suggests:

. . . maybe to souls below the earth
Great deeds are known,
Sparkling in the soft dew of flowing songs of triumph
(*Pyth.V.str.4.5.*)

Another feature of interest, one which again makes the meaning of some passages less easy to grasp at first sight, is his frequent habit of interspersing, at appropriate places in his text, comments or 'asides', usually quite briefly expressed, related more or less directly to the passage in which they occur. These 'asides' are always phrased in general terms and are of a general validity, as are our own proverbs; they usually serve to point the moral, briefly and pithily, to the theme or story which is being handled. Sometimes they appear to have the further purpose of providing a useful link passage to bridge over a change in the subject matter or in the flow of thought. In a few cases, where the 'aside' seems to be introduced with almost surprising abruptness, it is usually a sign that the passage which is to follow it is one on which Pindar wishes to throw special emphasis. The main interest however of these 'asides' is that they contribute with much else in Pindar's poetry to furnish us with a clearly cut picture of his lively convictions, whether on ethical or moral themes, or on various other aspects of human behaviour, or on topics such as the poet's inspiration and the importance of his art:

> Yet only of god's giving
> In a poet's heart is born the flower of song.
> (*Ol.X.ant.1.3.*)

> The songs inspired of heaven (*Ol.III.ant.1.10.*)

On occasion they supply us with forcibly expressed comments on his critics and rivals, amongst whom were often to be found, though they are never mentioned by name, the poets Simonides and Bacchylides, who were also composers of epinician Odes and other lyrical poetry. In two such passages he likens himself to an eagle compared with lesser birds:

> . . . taught skills, rough-hewn,
> Gross-tongued, are like a pair
> Of ravens vainly chattering
> Before the divine bird of Zeus. (*Ol.II.str.5.8.–ant.5.1.*)

And with an apology for the late delivery of a poem:

> Though it comes late. Yet of all birds on wing
> Swift is the eagle, from the deep sky afar
> Spying his mark,
> Lo, suddenly hath he seized, swooping,
> His tawny-dappled prey.
> But chattering daws have a lowly range.
> (*Nem.III.ep.4.1.*)

Pindar makes clear his firm belief that the true poet was divinely inspired, and does not conceal his own justifiable pride in the excellence of his own art:

> Inborn of nature's wisdom
> The poet's truth (*Ol.II.str.5.7.*)

> . . . the task divinely given (*Ol.III.ant.1.3.*)

In a metaphor from the long-jump, with another rapid change of image, he writes:

. . . rake a long landing-pit
Straightway for me; my limbs can muster
A nimble spring; even o'er the main
Eagles can wing their way. (*Nem.V.str.2.2.*)

Through all Hellas pride of the poet's art.
(*Ol.I.ep.4.12.*)

An aristocrat himself, and one whose work and friendships lay largely amongst people of his own kind, Pindar was fittingly a great believer in the value of inherited qualities. Many of his most forceful comments are intended to point the superiority of inborn genius over acquired or instructed skills, not only in the sphere of poetry but in many other of man's activities:

. . . let him follow straight
The paths appointed, striving with the skill
That nature's gift endowed him.
(*Nem.I.str.2.9.*)

His inborn fate decrees each man's achievement
(*Nem.V.str.3.6.*)

. . . By worth
Of inborn talent a man
Wins rich repute. Whose art is but instructed,
An obscure feather-brain he (*Nem.III.ep.2.6.*)

Pindar's conservative inclinations made him a respecter of established authority and of wealth and possessions, provided their possessors were aware of the responsibilities these entailed and used them with justice and generosity.

The best that fate can bring
Is wealth joined with the happy gift of wisdom.
(*Pyth.II.str.3.13.*)

. . . Wealth too,
Be it with noble deeds inwrought,
Brings gifts of many a kind,
Sustaining deep and troublous cares,
A shining star, light of sure trust for man
(*Ol.II.ant.3.7.*)

This is followed by a warning that in the next world

Hearts that were void of mercy
Pay the due penalty (*Ol.II.ep.3.4.*)

Frequently featured in his Odes are short and vividly expressed warnings to the victors whom he is praising against the dangers of pride and excessive ambition. The theme that success can only derive from the favour of heaven also finds frequent repetition:

. . . Therefore forget not
. . . to ascribe
This glory to none other but the hand of god.
(*Pyth.V.ep.1.3.*)

. . . For from thee,
Great Zeus, only may mortal souls be given
Worth of true excellence (*Isth.III.str.1.6.*)

But success lies not in the power of men;
It is a deity bestows it,
Exalting one man now, another
Crushing beneath strong hands. (*Pyth.VIII.ep.4.3.*)

On occasion Pindar addresses remarks to himself, sometimes by way of an apology for a digression, or to explain a change in his theme:

Be still my tongue; here profits not
To tell the whole truth with clear face unveiled.
Often is man's best wisdom to be silent.
(*Nem.V.ep.1.8.*)

After a digression, Pindar tells himself to return to his proper theme:

Search nearer home. There you have fitting glory,
Rich theme for song. (*Nem.III.ant.2.2.*)

STRUCTURE OF THE ODES The normal arrangement of the Pindaric Ode, though many Odes vary from this, is not difficult to follow. The athletic contest celebrated by the poem is not directly described, but it often colours the metaphors and similes used. Starting with a short invocation to one of the gods, or to the Muse or Muses, or some other appropriate deity, the poem proceeds to praise of the victor and his success, often including eulogies of his family and ancestors or of his native city. Then follows the myth, usually occupying the central and longest section of the poem, after which the Ode concludes with further eulogies of the victor. A due tribute to the tutelary god of the Games in which the victory was won—to Zeus, Apollo or Poseidon as the case may be—was always included by Pindar, often with repeated emphasis. Mention by name of the victor's father and of any other athletic successes gained by the victor appears also to have been a *sine qua non*, and it is clear from some of the Odes that the commission given to Pindar frequently included instructions for the mention of this or that relative or ancestor, and of any athletic successes, or sometimes other distinctions, gained by members of the family.

Of the forty-five[1] Odes of Pindar which have come down to us, a minority, seven in all, consist of a succession of stanzas, known as strophes, of identical length and metre in any one Ode. This form appears to have been more suitable for performance in company with a triumphal march or procession, rather than a dance. The remaining thirty-eight Odes are made up of triads, each triad consisting of three stanzas, the strophe, antistrophe and epode.[2] In any one poem the strophe and antistrophe are of identical length and metre, the epode slightly different. Subject to this arrangement of stanzas, each Ode has its own metre differing from that of any other. This is also the case in the seven Odes made up of a succession of strophes. The present translation conforms in these respects with the original Greek, but the English metres adopted are necessarily quite different from the Greek, which were governed by entirely different and far stricter rules of metrical scansion. The Odes vary considerably in length; those made up of strophes vary between two strophes and twelve; those made up of triads consist mainly of three, four or five triads; a few shorter Odes have only one triad, and one exceptional Ode Pythian IV, a notably fine one, has thirteen triads, i.e. thirty-nine stanzas.

ORDER OF THE ODES Editions of Pindar's Odes, both of earlier years and of more recent publication, maintain the traditional order of the Odes in each book, though this is not the order of their dates of composition. The present translation keeps to the same arrangement.[3]

Readers will notice that the last three Nemean Odes do not refer to victories won at the Nemean Games. The ninth Ode celebrates a victory won at the games of Sicyon, the tenth a victory at Argos, and the eleventh is not in honour of any athletic success, but celebrates the appointment of a Greek named Aristagoras to the presidency of the island of Tenedos, though, as the Ode mentions, he had won successes at various unnamed athletic meetings. The reason for this is that in the earliest manuscripts of Pindar's Odes, the four books were no doubt arranged in the order of importance in which the four festivals were regarded, that is, with the Isthmian book third and the Nemean book last. These three Odes, as they have a closer resemblance to epinician Odes than to any other category of lyric poetry, were no doubt tacked on as an appendix to the last book of the four. At some later date, in copies made of the earlier manuscripts, the Isthmian and Nemean books changed places, and as the earlier manuscripts disappeared, that has remained the traditional order of the books through later editions, leaving the three Odes to appear under the Nemean title.

[1] Or forty-four, depending on whether the third and fourth Isthmian Odes are counted as one Ode or two, a debated point.

[2] The literal meaning of these terms is: strophe, a turning; antistrophe, a turning back; epode, the song that follows; appropriate terms for poems set to a dance.

[3] Except in the case of Ol. X and Ol. XI. See Foreword, p. 59.

THE PANHELLENIC FESTIVALS The Panhellenic festivals and Games, and the order of importance in which they were held, were as follows:

1. The Olympian festival was founded, according to the earliest historical records which have come down to us, in the year 776 B.C. This year came to be adopted by Greek historians as the first in the Greek calendar, from which all subsequent events were dated. Olympia lies in the district of Elis in the north west of the Peloponnese, and was situated beside the river Alpheus not far from the city of Pisa. The festival was held every four years in honour of Zeus, king of the gods, and the prize awarded to victors in the Games was a wreath of wild olive.

2. The next in importance were the Pythian Games, held at Delphi once in every four years, two years after those of Olympia, in honour of Apollo, god of music, poetry and the arts, and of prophecy. The prize for victors was a wreath of laurel. The festival was founded (or put on a firmer footing in place of an earlier existing one) in the year 582 B.C.

3. The Isthmian Games were held every two years on the Isthmus of Corinth, in honour of Poiseidon, god of the sea and of subterranean powers. Their establishment, or revival, is attributed to the year 582 B.C. The prize awarded was a wreath of wild parsley or of pine.

4. The Nemean Games were held every two years at Nemea, near the small town of Cleonae in the north-eastern part of the Peloponnese, about twenty miles south of Corinth. They were held in honour of Zeus and the prize was a wreath of wild parsley. The date of their foundation or revival was 573 B.C.

Greek legend attributed the foundation of the Panhellenic festivals to much earlier periods; the Olympian Games, for example, are pictured as founded by Heracles, and the Nemean Games by Adrastus, a legendary king of Argos, in times anterior to any historical records. It is significant of the importance in which the Panhellenic festivals were held throughout Greece, that on their approach a sacred truce was proclaimed by heralds sent to all Greek states. Even in a period of constant inter-state warfare the truce was rarely if ever broken, and the safety of travellers to the festival was assured. In the district of Elis in which Olympia lies, any soldier-in-arms who crossed the border of that state during the festival was treated as a prisoner of war who could not return to his own state until he had been ransomed.

THE GAMES The competitive events which made up the Panhellenic Games were chariot-races, horse-races, foot-races (including the race for men in armour), the long-jump, boxing, wrestling, the pankration (a combination of boxing and wrestling, probably with a wide licence of rules), javelin-throwing, hurling the discus, and the pentathlon, an event combining the foot-race, the long-jump, the javelin, the discus, and a wrestling match. The four-horsed chariot-race enjoyed the highest prestige, and entailed the highest honour for the victor.

At Delphi, where musical programmes had been a feature of the earlier festival reorganized in 582 B.C., two competitions were added: singing to the flute and a solo on the flute. Playing on the lyre was added in 558 B.C. At Olympia a mule-chariot-race existed for a period of about fifty years until discontinued in 444 B.C.

The competitor whose name appeared as the official entrant for an event, and to whom in case of his victory the epinician Ode was addressed, did not always compete himself in the horse or chariot-races, but could delegate this to a subordinate. The powerful Sicilian rulers, Hieron and Theron, for whom several of Pindar's Odes were written, did not themselves ride in the races which gave them their victory, though Theron's young nephew Thrasybulus acted as charioteer for his father Xenocrates, the brother of Theron, in the race celebrated in Pindar's sixth Pythian Ode, in 490 B.C. The majority of the victors addressed in Pindar's Odes were however actual participants in the events. The expense of entry, which involved not only the cost of training, the supply of horses and equipment etc., but sometimes of lavish contributions to the religious rites of the festival, was considerable.

There were three classes of event: for grown men, for youths (the 'beardless' class) and for boys. Professional trainers were employed, particularly for boy competitors, during the arduous training which preceded the competitor's entry. The Games and the religious rites were open only to males. Women were strictly excluded, even from participation as spectators. Only one noteworthy exception is recorded to this rule. A famous wrestler, Diagoras of Rhodes, celebrated in Pindar's seventh Olympian Ode, won victories at all four Panhellenic festivals. His three sons were also Olympian victors, and two grandsons were successful at Olympia and Delphi. His daughter Callipateira was accorded the exceptional privilege of attendance at the Games, in virtue of her being the mother, the daughter, the sister or the aunt of six Olympian victors.

AEGINETAN ODES No less than eleven of Pindar's forty-five Odes were written in honour of victors whose home was on the island of Aegina, where it is clear that Pindar had many friends and found a society sympathetic to his poetical and musical interests. For the subjects of his myths in the Aeginetan Odes Pindar drew naturally enough from the famous stories of the clan of Aeacus, the first mythical king of Aegina, whose descendants included such great names as Peleus, Telamon, Ajax and not least Achilles. Although the Aeacid clan became dispersed to other parts of Greece these mythical heroes continued to be regarded as part of the great heritage of Aegina. The following is a family tree of the clan of Aeacus.

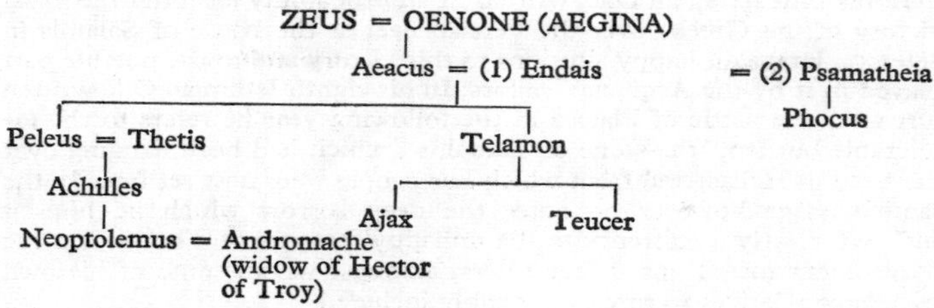

PRONUNCIATION The pronunciation of Greek names in their English form should not offer difficulty to the reader. It should be noted however that the names Neméa and Aégina should be pronounced with the stress on the second and first syllables respectively, as here indicated.

PINDAR'S LIFE Of the details of Pindar's life little knowledge has come down to us. He was born in 518 B.C. in the village of Cynoscephalae, about half a mile from Thebes in Boeotia, and lived most of his life in that city. He had an early training in music and poetry, spending a few of his earlier years in Athens for this purpose. His first Ode, the tenth Pythian, was written in 498. The fame of his poetry was not long in spreading abroad. In 490 he was in Delphi to witness the victory in the chariot-race, referred to in a previous paragraph, of Thrasybulus, the nephew of Theron, the powerful ruler of the Sicilian city of Acragas, a victory commemorated in the sixth Pythian. His contacts with Sicily brought him in the year 476 to perhaps the most important period of his life, when three Olympian victories won in that year were celebrated in his Odes. This was the year of his visit to Sicily as the guest of Hieron of Syracuse and Theron of Acragas, the two most powerful rulers at that time of the Greek cities in the west. The first, second and third Olympian Odes were written during this visit and also the first Nemean, commemorating an earlier victory of Chromius, one of Hieron's chief lieutenants. Pindar's close and friendly relations with Hieron are also exemplified in the first, second and third Pythian Odes, written during the ensuing years.

The invasion of Greece by the Persians in 480–479 B.C. found him greatly troubled by the conflict between his feelings for Hellas, menaced so severely by the invasion, and his loyalty to his native city of Thebes, who had thrown in her lot with the Persians—a decision for which she was to suffer dearly at the hands of the Greek allies after the final defeat of the Persians at the battle of Plataea in 479 B.C., in which the Theban forces suffered heavily.

In his fifth Isthmian Ode, written in all probability just after the naval victory of the Greeks over the Persian fleet at the battle of Salamis in 480 B.C., he makes happy allusions to this victory and to the notable part played in it by the Aeginetan sailors. In his eighth Isthmian Ode written just after the battle of Plataea in the following year he refers to the intolerable burden, 'the stone of Tantalus', which had been hanging over the head of Hellas, and from which her people were now set free. In the same passage however he notes the deep sorrow which he himself suffered, clearly a reference to the unhappy fortunes of Thebes and the punishment meted out to her rulers, amongst whom some of his own friends or relatives were very probably included.

Pindar did not as far as we know take any part in politics. As a Theban, and Thebes was in long-standing enmity with Athens, and as an admirer of the 'Dorian' aristocracy and of the established authority of the 'Dorian' type of government, he was likely to be less in sympathy with the more democratic types of rule which had emerged or were emerging in Athens and other parts of Greece. As a realist however he could not fail to give honour where honour was due, and while he objects to the 'milling crowd' of Sicilian revolutionaries, he makes more than one complimentary reference to Athens, 'city of noble name and sunlit splendour' (Nem.V.str.3). In a dithyramb of 474 B.C. of which a famous fragment remains (Fragment 76), he eulogized Athens for the part she played in the Persian War, and refers to her as the 'bulwark of Hellas'. For this the Theban government is said to have imposed a fine on Pindar, but the Athenians are believed to have repaid him by a gift of 10,000 drachmas, twice the amount of the fine.

There is evidence, however, particularly in Pindar's ninth and eleventh Pythian Odes, that for some little time after his return from his visit to Sicily, that is in the years immediately following 475 B.C., he was not in favour in some quarters, very possibly in governmental circles, in Thebes, and that he was anxious to put this right and to demonstrate his loyalty to the city. The punishment meted out to Thebes after 479 B.C. by the Athenians and Spartans involved the death or banishment of many of the former aristocratic governing class and the establishment of a more representative type of government. The new leaders of the city may well have regarded Pindar with suspicion or dislike, as an aristocrat by birth and one whose preference for governments of aristocratic or oligarchic type must have been well-known, if only from many passages in his Odes. His close friendship with the autocratic Sicilian rulers was no doubt a mark in his disfavour amongst leaders of the new Theban government, and his dithyramb, referred to above, and other expressions in honour of Athens were not likely to make his position any easier. It is believed, though there is no clear evidence to this effect, that during the Persian invasion of 480–479 B.C. Pindar spent a good deal of his time in Aegina. He was certainly absent from Thebes while in Sicily in 476–475, and lines in his ninth Pythian Ode written in 474 suggest that he is answering criticisms that he had not taken a fair share of the burdens of the citizens of Thebes in the troubled and painful times which must have been their portion in those years (Pyth.IX.ant.4.). The lines are part of a longer passage, the fourth triad of that Ode, in which he goes out of his way to pay a compliment to Thebes, no doubt with a view to dispelling suggestions that he was wanting in loyalty to his own city. In his eleventh Pythian Ode written at about the same time Pindar again seems to have taken real trouble to demonstrate his approval of government of a less autocratic type, and his dislike of 'tyrannies' (Pyth.XI.str.4.).

We have only this indirect evidence of these difficulties between Pindar and his native city, and no detailed knowledge has come down to us of what actually occurred. As nothing further is recorded of this matter, or of his having been in any way prominent in public affairs, it may be assumed that he continued to follow his customary mode of life as a private citizen.

PINDAR'S DEATH, AND STORIES ATTACHED TO HIS NAME Pindar's latest Odes, the eighth Pythian and probably the eleventh Nemean, are attributed to the year 446 B.C. He is said to have attained the age of eighty, but the exact date of his death is unknown; probably it was shortly before or after the year 440 B.C.

Many stories and legends are told of Pindar, some probably true, others clearly later inventions. In his student days he is said to have composed a poem without myths and showed it to his fellow-student the poetess Corinna. Admonished by her for the omission, he crowded his next poem with mythological figures. Her response to this—the fragment is still preserved—was 'You should sow with the hand, not with the whole sack'. Pindar, as we know from historical evidence, was elected to a priesthood of Apollo at Delphi and had a place at the annual Theoxenia there, a religious feast at which the gods were reputed to be the guests. Pindar's iron chair is said to have been kept with reverence, and the priest of Apollo was said to have cried nightly as he closed the temple 'Let Pindar the poet go unto the supper of the gods'. We need not believe the story, told also of other poets, that while he was asleep in the open air during his childhood, a bee alighted on his lips and placed honey there. Another story tells that in his old age he dreamt that Persephone, the queen of the underworld, came to him and said that of all the deities she alone had not received a poem from him in her honour, but that he should write a song for her also when he came to her; and that within ten days Pindar's life came to an end. After his death he is said to have appeared in a vision to an aged kinswoman and to have repeated to her a poem on Persephone, which she wrote down after she awoke. The existence of such stories is evidence of the widespread admiration and affection in which his poems were held in ancient times.

G.S.C.

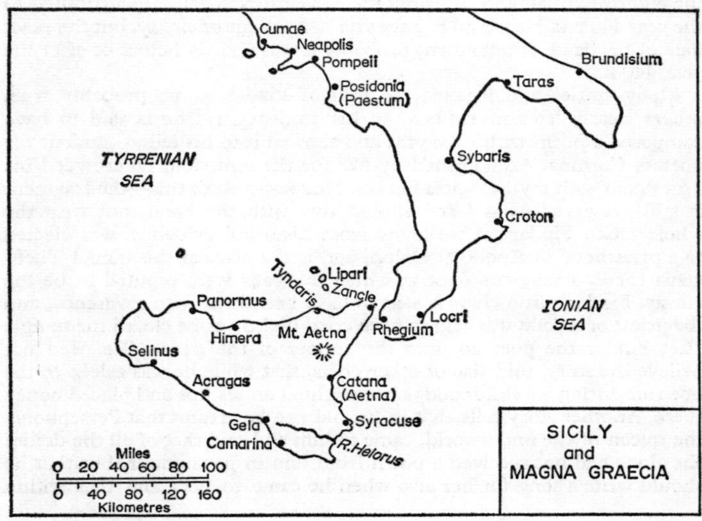

GREECE and the AEGEAN
Miles
0 50 100
0 80 160
Kilometres
Chalcidice
Epirus
Corcyra
Thessaly
Leucas
Aetolia
Ithaca
Cephallenia
Zacynthus
Elis
Euboea
Euripus
Skyros
Andros
Tenos
Mykonos
Keos
Delos
Paros
Naxos
Ios
Thera
Laconia
1. Ambracian Gulf
2. Mt. Pindus
3. Ionian Sea
4. Dodona
5. Mt. Olympus
6. R. Peneius
7. Mt. Ossa
8. Lakereia
9. Lake Boibias
10. Iolcus
11. Mt. Pelion
12. Phthia
13. R. Cephissus
14. Opous
15. Orchomenus
16. Lake Copais
17. Mt. Parnassus
18. Delphi
19. Krisa
20. Onchestus
21. Mt. Helicon
22. R. Asopus
23. Thebes
24. Plataea
25. Marathon
26. Athens
27. Eleusis
28. Salamis
29. Megara
30. Aegina
31. Isthmus
32. Corinth
33. Sicyon
34. Aigae
35. Phlious
36. Stymphalus
37. Cleonae
38. Nemea
39. Argos
40. Tiryns
41. Nauplion
42. Lerna
43. Epidaurus
44. Mt. Cyllene
45. Pheneos
46. Pyrgos
47. Pisa
48. Olympia
49. Elis
50. R. Alpheus
51. R. Eurotas
52. Sparta
53. Amyclae
54. Gytheum
55. Mt. Taygetus
56. Thyrea
57. Megalopolis
58. Mantinea
59. Tegea
60. Taenaros
61. Messene
62. Pylos

VICTORS, EVENTS AND MYTHS

Some of the dates given in these tables cannot, owing to lack of evidence, be determined with certainty. In most cases, where there is no reason for thinking that the composition of the ode was delayed, the date given is that of the victory and of the composition of the ode. In a few cases where it is known that the ode was written at a date later than that of the victory, the date is that of the composition of the ode. These cases are marked *.

OLYMPIAN ODES

Page	*Ode*	*Date*	*Victor*
1	I	476	Hieron of Syracuse
8	II	476	Theron of Acragas
17	III	476	Theron of Acragas
22	IV	456 or 452	Psaumis of Camarina
26	V	456 or 452	Psaumis of Camarina
29	VI	468 or 472	Agesias of Syracuse
38	VII	464	Diagoras of Rhodes
47	VIII	460	Alcimedon of Aegina
52	IX	466*	Epharmostus of Opous
59	X	476	Agesidamus of Epizephyrian Locri
61	XI	after 476*	Agesidamus of Epizephyrian Locri
67	XII	470*	Ergoteles of Himera
69	XIII	464	Xenophon of Corinth
77	XIV	488	Asopichus of Orchomenus

PYTHIAN ODES

Page	*Ode*	*Date*	*Victor*
79	I	470	Hieron of Aetna
88	II	475 or 474	Hieron of Syracuse
96	III	474 or 473	Hieron of Syracuse
104	IV	462	Arcesilas of Cyrene
125	V	462	Arcesilas of Cyrene
132	VI	490	Xenocrates of Acragas
136	VII	486	Megacles of Athens
138	VIII	446	Aristomenes of Aegina
145	IX	474	Telesicrates of Cyrene
153	X	498	Hippocleas of Thessaly
158	XI	474	Thrasydaeus of Thebes
165	XII	490	Midas of Acragas

Event	Myth
Horse-Race	Pelops
Chariot-Race	Isles of the Blest
Chariot-Race	Heracles' journey to Hyperboreans
Chariot-Race with mules	Erginus at Lemnos
Chariot-Race with mules	None
Chariot-Race with mules	Iamus
Boxing-Match	Tlepolemus and origin of Rhodes
Boys' Wrestling Match	Aeacus and walls of Troy
Wrestling-Match	Deucalion and Pyrrha
Boys' Boxing-Match	None
Boys' Boxing-Match	Founding of Olympian Games
Long Foot-Race	None
Short Foot-Race and Pentathlon	Bellerophon and Pegasus
Boys' Foot-Race	None

Event	Myth
Chariot-Race	Typhon and Mount Aetna
Chariot-Race	Ixion
Horse-Race	Asclepius
Chariot-Race	Medea and the Argonauts
Chariot-Race	Battus
Chariot-Race	Antilochus and Nestor
Chariot-Race	None
Wrestling-Match	Prophecy of Amphiaraus
Foot-Race in Armour	Apollo and Cyrene
Boys' Long Foot-Race	Perseus and the Hyperboreans
Boys' Short Foot-Race	Orestes and Clytemnestra
Flute-Playing	Perseus and Medusa

VICTORS, EVENTS AND MYTHS

NEMEAN ODES

Page	*Ode*	*Date*	*Victor*
169	I	476*	Chromius of Aetna
174	II	487 or 485	Timodemus of Acharnae
176	III	474–3*	Aristocleides of Aegina
184	IV	about 473	Timasarchus of Aegina
191	V	about 489	Pytheas of Aegina
196	VI	about 470	Alcimidas of Aegina
201	VII	before 460?	Sogenes of Aegina
210	VIII	after Ode VII	Deinis of Aegina
215	IX	475–471*	Chromius of Aetna
220	X	uncertain	Theaius of Argos
227	XI	about 446	Aristagoras of Tenedos

ISTHMIAN ODES

Page	*Ode*	*Date*	*Victor*
231	I	458	Herodotus of Thebes
238	II	after 472	Xenocrates of Acragas
245	III	477 or 475	Melissus of Thebes
246	IV	478 or 476*	Melissus of Thebes
251	V	480 or 478	Phylakidas of Aegina
255	VI	484 or 482	Phylakidas of Aegina
260	VII	uncertain	Strepsiades of Thebes
264	VIII	478	Cleandrus of Aegina

Event	*Myth*
Chariot-Race	Infant Heracles and the Snakes
Pankration	None
Pankration	Aeacids and Achilles
Boys' Wrestling-Match	Aeacids, Peleus and Thetis
Youths' Pankration	Peleus, Hippolyta and Thetis
Boys' Wrestling-Match	Aeacids, Achilles and Memnon
Boys' Pentathlon	Neoptolemus
Foot-Race	Death of Ajax
Chariot-Race	Seven against Thebes
Wrestling-Match	Castor and Pollux
Inauguration as Prytanis	None
Chariot-Race	Eulogies of Castor and Iolaus
Chariot-Race	None
Chariot-Race (Nemea)	None
Pankration	Heracles and Antaeus
Pankration	Aeacids and Achilles
Pankration	Heracles' prophecy to Telamon
Pankration	None
Pankration	Zeus, Poseidon and Thetis

For this it is gives to the path of song
Immortal life, if on the poet's tongue
Fair praise is fairly set.

Isthmian IV. Str. 3.

OLYMPIAN I

For HIERON OF SYRACUSE

Winner of the Horse-Race

HIERON was the second of the four sons of Deinomenes of Gela, in Sicily. His elder brother Gelon, ruler of Gela from 491 B.C., had subdued and made himself master of Syracuse also in 485. Hieron took over the rule of Gela in that year, and on Gelon's death in 478 succeeded him as tyrant of Syracuse. By the date of the present Ode (476), Hieron was approaching the summit of his power, and together with Theron of Acragas, related to him by marriage, was virtually master of all those parts of Sicily which had been colonized by the Greeks. His court was noted throughout the Greek world for its wealth and lavish magnificence and for the patronage given to the arts, in particular to poetry and architecture. An observer of the Mediterranean scene at this period might well have thought that Syracuse, rather than Athens, was destined to become the political and cultural leader of the fifth-century world.

Other victories won by Hieron are celebrated in Pindar's first three Pythian Odes. The present Ode begins with tributes to the glory of the Olympian Games, to the virtues of Hieron, and the victory of his horse Pherenikos. The greater part of the Ode is then devoted to the legend of Tantalus and his son Pelops. The poem concludes with a further short tribute to Hieron, and a prayer that he may succeed in his highest ambition, that of winning the chariot-race at Olympia. Some years later this ambition was fulfilled at the Olympian Games of 468 B.C., but this victory was not celebrated by an Ode of Pindar, but by Bacchylides in his Ode 3.

In telling the legend of Tantalus and Pelops, Pindar is at pains, as in some of his other Odes, to dissociate himself from the idea that the gods are capable of criminal or sacrilegious acts—in this case the eating of human flesh. The generally accepted legend was that Tantalus, when preparing a banquet at which the gods were to be guests, in a fit of insane pride killed and cut up his young son Pelops in order to serve up his flesh for the gods to eat. Clotho, one of the three Fates, rescued Pelops from the cauldron and put his body together again; but a part of his shoulder was missing, and this was replaced by a piece of ivory. Pindar dismisses this story as a false tale inspired by envy. He gives a different reason for the disappearance of Pelops from his father's banquet, and maintains that the sin of Tantalus, which brought him eternal punishment, was that of giving ambrosia and nectar, the food and drink of the gods, to some of his mortal friends.

The lesson to be drawn from this legend is clearly that of the need for moderation in one's conduct, and of respectful obedience to the laws of the gods. It was no strange thing for Pindar to 'point the moral', as is shown by numerous passages throughout the Odes, and since he could hardly have failed to be aware of the many faults and excesses in Hieron's method of rule, capable though it was, he shows in this Ode—as he does to an even more marked extent in his first Pythian Ode, also addressed to Hieron—that he was by no means deterred by that ruler's high position from addressing to him words of precept and advice as well as of praise.

In the section which follows, telling of Pelops' proposed challenge to Oenomaus for the hand of his daughter, Pindar has no room for the full story of the resulting chariot-race and its related events, but in the prayer of Pelops to Poseidon Pindar gives himself, as so often, the opportunity of emphasizing the heroic qualities necessary to those who aspire to victory in the Games.

str. 1 Best blessing of all is water,
And gold like a fiery flame gleaming at night,
Supreme amidst the pride of lordly wealth.
But if you seek, beloved heart,
To sing of the great Games,
Then neither in the lonely firmament
By day, look for another star more bright
And gladdening than the sun, nor can we praise
A greater contest than Olympia;
Whence the bright arrows of renownéd song
Play round the minds of poets,
In hymns to honour
The son of Cronos, as our steps approach
The rich and blessed hearth of Hieron,

str. 1 *The son of Cronos:* Zeus, king of the gods, patron god of the festival and Games of Olympia.
The hearth of Hieron: this indicates that Pindar was present in Syracuse to take part in the performance of this Ode. There is other evidence to show that he visited Sicily in the year 476/75 B.C.

ant. 1 Who wields his rod of justice
In Sicily, land of rich flocks, and culls
Of all things excellent the noblest fruit;
Made glorious too by the fine flower
Of music's utterance—
Such strains as men will often blithely sing
Where we sit round the table of a friend.
Come then, take from its peg the Dorian lyre,
If a sweet spell of thought's delight the grace
Of Pisa and of Pherenikos bred
Within your heart, when, speeding
By Alpheus' bank,
His lovely limbs ungoaded on the course,
He brought his lord to victory's embrace,

ep. 1 That master who delights in horsemanship
King of great Syracuse;
And in the colony of Lydian Pelops,
That land of noble souls, his fame is bright;
Pelops, who stirred Poseidon's love,
The god of mighty strength, the earth-holder,
When Clotho drew him from the untainted bowl,
His shoulder shod with gleaming ivory.
True, there are many marvels; here or there
Maybe the tongues of men
O'er-riding truth's sure word, deceive
With false-spun tales, the embroidery of lies.

ant. 1 *The Dorian lyre:* the music to which this Ode was set was in the Dorian 'mode'. No exact knowledge has come down to us of the music which accompanied Pindar's Odes.

Pherenikos: the name of the horse which won this race for Hieron. The same horse had already won two races for Hieron at the Pythian Games of 482 and 478 B.C.

Alpheus' bank: the river Alpheus runs past Olympia.

The last six lines of this antistrophe seem to suggest that Pindar was a spectator at Olympia when this race was run.

ep. 1 *Lydian Pelops:* according to legend, Pelops and his father Tantalus derived from Lydia in Asia Minor. The 'colony' means that part of the Peloponnese, the district of Elis, in which Olympia lies—where Pelops settled. He was soon to give his name to the whole of the Peloponnese.

Clotho: one of the three Fates associated with birth, life and death—Clotho, the spinner of the thread of life, Lachesis who apportions or assigns each man's fate, and Atropos, the Fate who cannot be turned aside.

The untainted bowl: in place of the usual story (see foreword) of the rescue of Pelops from the cauldron, Pindar substitutes this picture of his being washed as a new-born child in purifying water and of his being born with an ivory shoulder.

str. 2 For Beauty, goddess who fashions
All things that lovely are for mortal men,
Her shower of glory many a time enriched
That which deserves no firm belief
To be a trusted tale.
But days to come will prove the surest witness.
Right is it a man speak well of the immortals,
Less then will be his blame. Tantalus' son,
Unlike to bards of old, my tongue shall tell
How when your father gave the all-seemly banquet,
On Sipylus that he loved,
To make return
Of hospitable gift to the immortals,
Then he of the Bright Trident seized upon you,

ant. 2 His heart mad with desire,
And brought you mounted in his glorious chariot
To the high hall of Zeus whom all men honour,
Where later came Ganymede, too,
For a like love, to Zeus.
But when you were thus vanished with no sign,
And the wide search of men had brought you not
Back to your mother, then quickly was heard
Some secret voice of envious neighbours, telling
That for the seething cauldron's fiery heat
Your limbs with a knife's blade
Were cut asunder,
And at each table, portioned to the guests,
The morsels of your flesh became their meal.

ep. 2 Senseless, I hold it, for a man to say
The gods eat mortal flesh.
I spurn the thought. A slanderer's evil tongue
Often enough brings him to no good end.

str. 2 *Right is it . . . , etc.:* here Pindar maintains his refusal, as in many other passages in the Odes, to allow that the gods are guilty of criminal acts. (See foreword.)

Sipylus: a mountain in Asia Minor.

He of the Bright Trident: Poseidon, god of the sea and of subterranean powers.

ant. 2 *Ganymede:* the beautiful youth who was appointed cup-bearer to the gods by Zeus.

But if indeed any man ever
Won honour from Olympus' lords, that man
Was Tantalus. Yet could he not stomach
His high fortune, but earned for his excess
A doom o'erwhelming, when the Father poised
A mighty stone above him,
Which with its ever-threatening blow
To strike his head, robs all his days of joy.

str. 3 Thus bound within an endless
Prison of toil and tortured pain, his life
Is set, fourth penalty with other three,
For that he stole from the immortals,
And gave to his companions
In revelry, ambrosia and nectar,
Whereby the gods gave him undying life.
But if a man shall hope in aught he does
To escape the eyes of god, he makes an error.
Thence was it the gods sent his son down again
To share the short-lived span
Of mortal life.
But when the flower of rising youth shaded
His cheek with down, then for a speedy marriage

ant. 3 He counselled in his mind,
From her father of Pisa to win the maid
Hippodamia, of glorious fame. And coming
Near to the salt sea's edge, alone
At night, he called aloud
To the loud-roaring Wielder of the Trident,
Who came, and stood before him. Then spoke Pelops,
And said 'Lo, great Poseidon, if in your count
The Cyprian goddess' gifts find aught of favour,

ep. 2 The legend of Tantalus includes other punishments not mentioned by Pindar here: that he was placed in a lake tormented by thirst, but whenever he stooped to drink the water drew away from his lips; or that he was tied beneath a tree loaded with fruit, but whenever he tried to pluck it, it was drawn away from his hand.

str. 3 *Fourth penalty:* this probably means the 'endless prison', i.e. punishment throughout his immortal life—the other three penalties being hunger, thirst, and the stone over his head. Some commentators read into the words a reference to Ixion, Tityos and Sisyphus, three evildoers who were also given eternal punishment by the gods.

His son: Pelops.

ant. 3 *Her father of Pisa:* Oenomaus, who ruled at Pisa, the capital city of Elis.

The Cyprian goddess: Aphrodite, goddess of love, whose traditional residence was at Paphos in Cyprus.

Then shackle Oenomaus' brazen spear, and bring me
On speeding chariot wheels
To the land of Elis,
And grant me victory. For thirteen souls
Now has he slain, her suitors, and holds back

ep. 3 The marriage of his daughter. Great danger
Calls to no coward's heart;
But for man, who must die, why should he nurse
A nameless old age through, in vain, in darkness,
And of all deeds that glorious are
Have not a share? But for me shall this contest
Lie for my challenge. Do thou but grant fair issue
My heart's desire.' So he spoke, and his prayer
Uttered no words that failed of their achievement.
But for his glory's honour,
The god gave him a gleaming chariot,
And steeds that flew unwearied upon wings.

str. 4 And mighty Oenomaus
He slew, and took the maiden for his bride;
Six sons she bore, chieftains leading the field
In valorous deeds. By Alpheus' ford
He lies now, closely joined
To the great feast of glorious sacrifice,
His tomb oft visited, beside the altar
Where many a stranger treads. And the great fame
Of the Olympiad Games shines far afield,
In the course known of Pelops, where are matched
Rivals in speed of foot
And in brave feats
Of bodily strength. Thence, all his life, around him
The victor knows a sunlit day's delight,

Thirteen souls: Oenomaus promised the hand of his daughter to any suitor who could defeat him in a chariot-race, for which his own chariot was equipped with invincible horses. But the penalty for a suitor, if defeated, was death.

str. 4 *Six sons:* these included Atreus, father of Agamemnon and Menelaus. *His tomb:* modern archaeology has confirmed the existence at Olympia, to the south of the temple of Hera, of the large sanctuary of Pelops, known to the ancients as the Pelopion, one of the oldest of the monuments of Olympia. In the centre of this precinct stood the statue of Pelops, his altar and a pit for the sacrificial remains.

ant. 4 Prize of the contest's struggle.
Yet for all men the blessing of each day
Is the best boon. My task is now to crown
My hero in the horseman strain,
And the Aeolian mode.
And well I know that of all living men
No host, both of more heart for noble ends
And more power to achieve them, shall by me
Be enriched in glorious harmonies of song.
Over your labours, Hieron, a god
Keeps watch, bearing your cares
Close to his thought;
And if he leave you not too soon, I trust
That a still sweeter glory I may proclaim,

ep. 4 Finding thereto a path ready for song
To honour your swift chariot,
When I am come to Cronos' sunlit hill.
For I know well, my Muse in her array
Nurses her strongest dart of all.
In various enterprise, various men
Ascend to greatness, but the highest crown
Is given to kings. Further seek not to glimpse.
Be it yours through all your life to tread the heights
And mine no less to share
Friendship with victors in the Games,
Through all Hellas pride of the poet's art.

ant. 4 *The blessing of each day:* it is not easy to be sure of Pindar's purpose in this sentence. Two interpretations seem possible: (1) that the blessings of each day compensate us, through our life, for our daily troubles; but by contrast, the happiness derived from a victory in the Games lasts a man, as the preceding lines have suggested, without interruption throughout his life. (2) That this is Pindar's way of saying to himself, as he does not infrequently in other Odes, that it is time for him to stop generalizing and to get down to the pleasant task of this Ode, i.e. to sing the praises of Hieron.

ep. 4 *Swift chariot:* prior to the victory which this Ode celebrates, won in the Olympian Games of 476 B.C., Hieron had gained two victories, also in the horse-race, at the Pythian Games of 482 and 478 B.C. He was to win another Olympic horse-race in 472 and a chariot-race at Pythia in 470. The hope which Pindar expresses here, that he will win the chariot-race at Olympia (Cronos' sunlit hill), the event which was held in the highest prestige of all, was not fulfilled until his chariot victory in the Olympian Games of 468 B.C. This victory was not however celebrated in an Ode by Pindar, but by the poet Bacchylides in his Ode 3.

OLYMPIAN II

For

THERON OF ACRAGAS

Winner of the Chariot-Race

THERON became ruler of Acragas, one of the larger Greek cities on the south coast of Sicily, about the year 488 B.C. He allied himself closely with his son-in-law Gelon ruler of Gela, who in 485 made himself master of Syracuse and left the rule of Gela to his younger brother Hieron. Under these leaders the Greek forces inflicted a severe defeat on the Carthaginians at the battle of Himera in 480. This victory brought Acragas and Theron to the summit of their wealth and power. When Gelon died in 478 he left the rule of Syracuse to Hieron, and the hand of his wife Damareta, the daughter of Theron, to another younger brother Polyzelus. The harmony of relations between Hieron and Theron was soon however to fall into disarray, increased no doubt by the complicated marital connections of the two families. Theron had married the daughter of Polyzelus, and Hieron a niece of Theron. Hieron fell out with Polyzelus, who joined forces with Theron's son Thrasydaeus, who had been installed as ruler of Himera. The people of Himera, discontented with the rule of Thrasydaeus, took sides with Hieron. By the year 476 there seemed every possibility that war would break out between Hieron and Theron, who between them were by now masters of almost all the Greek cities of Sicily. This catastrophe was however averted, largely it is believed through the intervention of the poet Simonides, who acted as negotiator between the two parties.

Only the barest outline of these events has now come down to us, and we have no knowledge of the details of this complicated scene. Lasting peace between the two rulers was however restored in the year 476, and Polyzelus was pardoned. This was probably in the early part of that year, since Theron's victory in the chariot-race celebrated in the present Ode, and Hieron's victory in the horse-race, celebrated in Olympian I, both took place at the Olympian Games of 476. Both these Odes were written during Pindar's visit to Sicily in 476/75. Pindar's connection with the family of Theron was already of long standing. In 490 B.C. he had been an onlooker at the Pythian Games when the chariot-race was won by Theron's brother Xenocrates, whose young son Thrasybulus was the charioteer. A close friendship sprang up between Thrasybulus and Pindar, who was at that time a young man of twenty-eight. Pindar's sixth Pythian Ode was written to celebrate this victory of Xenocrates, and the poem is in fact a warm tribute to Thrasybulus, who is said to have been a charming young man. That this friendship lasted is made clear by Pindar's second Isthmian Ode, celebrating another victory won by Xenocrates in the year 477, though the poem was written a few years later. Here again Pindar speaks of Thrasybulus in terms of warm affection.

Against this background of his friendship with members of Theron's family, and a close knowledge, which his presence in Sicily must have afforded him, of the dangers and stresses which had so recently threatened his friends, it is not surprising that the present Ode shows unmistakable signs of Pindar's concern. 'Man's deeds,' as he says in epode 1, 'Be they done rightly or unrightly' cannot be 'undone again'. He was no doubt anxious lest a similar situation should recur, a recurrence which in the turbulent state of Sicilian politics of that period may well have seemed possible, or even very likely. Pindar was a man of strong feelings, not one, as he often shows, who found it easy to conceal what he felt called upon to say. Indeed he makes it clear towards the end of this Ode that for those who can read between the lines, his Ode contains many pointed references—'many a swift arrow . . . speaking to men of wisdom. But for the throng they need interpreters' (str. 5). To what particular persons or events Pindar may have intended these allusions to refer we are prevented from knowing, owing to our lack of any detailed knowledge of what had transpired.

On the other hand we need have no difficulty in judging from the general trend of this Ode, its subject-matter and treatment—in which it differs markedly from other Odes of Pindar—that it was written under the influence of factors which were of deep concern to Pindar. In parts of the Ode (the fourth triad) where we should normally expect to find the myth, Pindar speaks of the life to come and gives a description of the Isles of the Blest, or Elysium. There are close resemblances between this passage and two fragments of Pindar's Dirges, or Laments, addressed to Theron (Fr. 129–130; Fr. 131). That an Ode celebrating the happy event of an Olympian victory should adopt this melancholy vein is surprising, but the same tone is found throughout the Ode, and suggests very strongly that Pindar's visit to Sicily brought into his view many things of a sad and anxious nature.

After a brief introductory passage the Ode follows convention in expressing the praise of Theron and of his ancestors who founded the city of Acragas. But a note of anxiety makes itself felt in the latter half of antistrophe 1, with the prayer to Zeus that Acragas may always remain the home of this family. The Ode then embarks on the two related themes which, except for the picture of the Isles of the Blest in the fourth triad, remain with it throughout—the alternation of good fortune and ill fortune in human life and the insecurity of man's lot under an inscrutable Fate. Theron, and the Emmenid clan to which he belonged, claimed descent from Cadmus, the first legendary king of Thebes, and from Oedipus, the son of Laius, king of Thebes in a later generation. Thus, ready to Pindar's hand as illustration of his themes were these well-known stories, first those of Semele and Ino, the daughters of Cadmus, who both met with death at the hands of the gods but were afterwards made immortal (str. 2 and ant. 2), and secondly (ep. 2 and str. 3), the tragic history of the family of Oedipus, including that of his two sons Eteocles and Polyneices. It was through Thersander (str. 3) the son of Polyneices that the line continued and became the ancestry from which Theron claimed descent.

In the third triad, the poem returns to the present, acclaiming Theron's victory at Olympia and the previous victories of his brother Xenocrates (referred to above) at the Pythian and Isthmian Games. A short tribute follows to Theron's wealth, and the benefits which wealth can bestow, a by no means infrequent subject for Pindar's praise, but almost invariably accompanied, as here, by the proviso that to be praiseworthy it must be 'with noble deeds inwrought'—aware, in fact, of the responsibilities which it entails. This leads (ep. 3) to a warning of the penalties which await this earth's sinners in the next world, followed in the fourth triad by Pindar's picture of the Isles of the Blest. In this he follows the Pythagorean theory of the next world, and quotes the names of Peleus, Cadmus and Achilles as examples of those who, after the three necessary periods of trial in this world and the next, have succeeded in winning the reward of eternal life.

In strophe 5, after the lines indicating that this poem contains many pointed allusions, Pindar then voices his proud claim to inspired truth, a claim expressed in similar terms in more than one of his other Odes, often accompanied, as here, by a scornful reference to his inferior rivals who are compared to ravens matched with an eagle. This spirited passage is probably intended to reinforce the point of the lines which immediately precede and follow it.

In antistrophe 5 we return to generous expressions of approbation for Theron, but the note of anxiety creeps in again in the epode before the final lines of renewed praise.

str. 1 Lords of the lyre, ye hymns, what god,
What hero, what man shall we honour? Zeus
Holds Pisa; the Olympiad feast
Heracles founded, the first-fruits of war;
Now for his four-horsed chariot victory
Let Theron's name be praised, who to all strangers
Shows the true face of justice,
Of Acragas the staunch pillar,
Upholder of his city,
Of famous fathers the fine flower;

ant. 1 They after many a labour, took
Beside this river bank their sacred dwelling,
And were the eye of Sicily;
And an age sent of heaven attended them,
Bringing them wealth and honour, to crown their inborn
Merit. O son of Cronos, Rhea's child,
Who rules Olympus' seat
And the great Games by Alpheus' ford,
Gladdened with songs, be gracious
To grant this soil be still their homeland

ep. 1 For all their race to come. But of man's deeds
Be they done rightly or unrightly,
Not even Time, father of all,
Can make accomplishment
Undone again. Yet if good fortune wills,
Forgetfulness may come;
Quelled by the charm of noble joys, grief dies,
Thrown to the ground again,

str. 1 *Lords of the lyre:* the rhythms of Pindar's music, he implies, are dependent on the rhythms of his poetry.
Zeus holds Pisa: the name of Pisa, the capital city of the district of Elis, near to Olympia, is used here as elsewhere to mean Olympia. Zeus was the patron god of the religious festival of Olympia of which the Games were a part.
Heracles founded: the legendary story of the founding of the Olympian Games by Heracles is told in Pindar's eleventh Olympian Ode.
Famous fathers: Theron's ancestors were among early Greek colonists of Sicily who founded the city of Gela about the year 689 B.C. A century later his family moved on to found the neighbouring city of Acragas.

ant. 1 *This river bank:* Acragas was situated by a river of the same name.
Son of Cronos: Zeus.

str. 2 When Fate brings from the hand of heaven
Happiness rich and wide. Such is the tale
Told of the fair-throned maids of Cadmus,
Who suffered mightily, but heavy woe
Falls before greater good. With the immortals
Semele of the flowing locks lives still
—Who died in the roar of thunder—
And Pallas loves her ever, and Zeus
No less, and dearly too
The ivy-bearing god, her son.

ant. 2 The tale runs too, that in the ocean
With the sea-maidens, Nereus' daughters, Ino
Was given undying life for ever.
Verily no term of death is set for mortals,
Who know not even if some peaceful day,
Child of the sun, shall bring us to its end
Midst happiness still unfailing.
This way and that the currents run
—Be they the tides of joy
Or toil—that make the lot of man.

ep. 2 For as Fate, who accords our mortal race
Their heritage of happy fortune,
To their heaven-sent prosperity
Brings at another hour

str. 2 *Maids of Cadmus:* Semele and Ino, daughters of Cadmus the first legendary king of Thebes, from whom Theron claimed descent. Their story is used by Pindar (see foreword) to illustrate the vicissitudes of human life.

Semele: was loved by Zeus, and was induced, through the jealousy of Hera, to ask Zeus to come to her in his true form so that she could be certain who he was. He therefore appeared to her in the shape of thunder and lightning, and she was consumed. She was six months pregnant by Zeus, but the infant was preserved in the thigh of Zeus until the time of his birth, when he became the god Dionysus, 'the ivy-bearing god'. Later he went down to the Underworld to rescue Semele, and gave her immortal life in heaven.

Pallas: the goddess Athene; her full name was Pallas Athene.

ant. 2 *Ino:* Semele's sister, who also incurred the wrath of Hera for various reasons, amongst them because she had nursed the infant Dionysus. Hera drove her mad so that she threw herself into the sea. She was preserved however to live an immortal life with the sea-nymphs, the Nereids, daughters of Nereus, the Greek 'Old Man of the Sea'.

An opposite load of ill, so, long ago,
The fated son of Laius,
Slaying his father on the road, fulfilled
Pytho's old oracle.

str. 3 This saw Erinys, fierce avenger,
And by their own hands slew that warrior race
Of brothers. Polyneices felled,
Was left Thersander, in new contests honoured
And in war's battles; this scion of the line
Stayed up the house of dead Adrastus' sons.
Bred from that seed's descent,
Right is it Ainesidamus' son
Should win triumphant songs
Of revel, and music of the lyre.

ep. 2 *Son of Laius:* Oedipus. The full story, too long for these notes, of the disastrous tragedy of Oedipus, who unknowingly killed his father Laius and married his mother Iocasta, is the subject of the well known tragedies of the playwright Sophocles, *Oedipus Rex* and *Oedipus at Colonus.*

str. 3 *Erinys:* the goddess of vengeance. Better known in the plural form, the Erinyes were the avenging spirits who plagued men who had committed grave crimes, and drove them mad. Orestes who killed his mother Clytemnestra is a well known example.

Polyneices: after Oedipus left Thebes, his sons Eteocles and Polyneices shared the rule of the city. They quarrelled and Polyneices was banished. With the help of Adrastus king of Argos, Polyneices took part in the unsuccessful expedition of the 'Seven against Thebes', where he and Eteocles were both killed in single combat with each other.

Thersander: the son of Polyneices. He was the sole survivor of the line of Oedipus. The 'new contests' are a reference to the second, successful, expedition against Thebes of the 'Epigoni' (Successors) led by Thersander and his generation. Some editors however prefer to interpret the phrase as referring to new athletic contests such as the Nemean Games, whose foundation was attributed by legend to the time of Adrastus. This interpretation connects more easily with the point that follows, that Theron as a descendant of Thersander can fittingly be awarded the honours of an athletic triumph.

War's battles: a reference to the Trojan war, in which Thersander also took part. According to one account he was one of the Greeks who hid in the Wooden Horse.

Stayed up the house, etc.: Adrastus with his son Aegialeus took part, again, in the second expedition against Thebes. On hearing that Aegialeus had been killed in the conflict, he died of grief. His line was saved from extinction by Thersander, who was the son, by Polyneices, of Adrastus' daughter.

Ainesidamus' son: Theron.

ant. 3 For he received Olympia's prize
And for his brother alike, the impartial Graces
At Pytho and the Isthmus gave
His four-horsed chariot on the twelve-lap course
Their crown of flowers. Victory, for a man
Who braves the contest's struggle, sets at rest
All discontent. Wealth too,
Be it with noble deeds inwrought,
Brings gifts of many a kind,
Sustaining deep and troublous cares,

ep. 3 A shining star, light of sure trust for man,
If but who holds it, knows what is
To come—that straightway, when they die
Hearts that were void of mercy
Pay the due penalty, and of this world's sins
A judge below the earth
Holds trial, and of dread necessity
Declares the word of doom.

str. 4 But the good, through the nights alike,
And through the days unendingly, beneath
The sun's bright ray, tax not the soil
With the strength of their hands, nor the broad sea
For a poor living, but enjoy a life
That knows no toil; with men honoured of heaven,
Who kept their sworn word gladly,
Spending an age free from all tears.
But the unjust endure
Pain that no eye can bear to see.

ant. 4 But those who had good courage, three times
On either side of death, to keep their hearts
Untarnished of all wrong, these travel
Along the road of Zeus to Cronos' tower.

ant. 3 *His brother:* Xenocrates, who won the chariot race at the Pythian Games in 490 B.C. and at the Isthmian Games in 477, celebrated by Pindar in his sixth Pythian and second Isthmian Odes.

The impartial Graces: the three Graces were Euphrosyne, representing wisdom or talent, particularly poetic talent; Thalia, beauty; and Aglaia, glory. It was no doubt in virtue of their function of enhancing the beauty of everything that gives delight to man that Pindar pictures them here as giving their 'crown of flowers' to the victor.

ant. 4 *The road of Zeus:* perhaps the Milky Way.
Cronos' tower: the entrance to Heaven.

There round the islands of the blest, the winds
Of ocean play, and golden blossoms burn,
Some nursed upon the waters,
Others on land on glorious trees;
And woven on their hands
Are wreaths enchained and flowering crowns,

ep. 4 Under the just decrees of Rhadamanthus,
Who has his seat at the right hand
Of the great father, Rhea's husband,
Goddess who holds the throne
Highest of all. And Peleus and Cadmus
Are of that number, and thither,
When her prayers on the heart of Zeus prevailed,
His mother brought Achilles,

str. 5 He who felled Hector, Troy's pillar
Invincible, unyielding, and brought death
To Cycnus, and the Ethiop son
Of Dawn. Many a swift arrow my quiver holds
Beneath my arm, speaking to men of wisdom,
But for the throng they need interpreters.

ep. 4 *Rhadamanthus:* one of the judges of the Underworld, who, with Cronos, tried the souls of the departed.

The great father: Cronos, father of Zeus.

Peleus: a noted hero, one of the sons of Aeacus, the first legendary king of the island of Aegina. By the order of Zeus, the immortal sea-nymph Thetis, one of the daughters of Nereus, was allotted to Peleus as his bride. Their son was Achilles. After his death in the Trojan war Zeus granted the prayer made to him by Thetis, that Achilles might become an immortal.

str. 5 *Hector:* the son of Priam, king of Troy, and the most famous warrior on the Trojan side in the Trojan war. Homer's *Iliad* tells his story, including his death at the hands of Achilles.

Cycnus: a son of Poseidon, who was living on the island of Tenedos and was killed by Achilles when the Greek army landed on the island while on their way to Troy.

The Ethiop son of Dawn: Memnon, the leader of the Ethiopians who came to Troy to fight on the Trojan side in the Trojan war. He was a famous warrior, but succumbed to Achilles. His father was Tithonus, a half-brother of Priam, and his mother was Eos, the goddess of Dawn.

Many a swift arrow, etc.: see foreword.

Inborn of nature's wisdom
The poet's truth; taught skills, rough-hewn,
Gross-tongued, are like a pair
Of ravens vainly chattering

ant. 5 Before the divine bird of Zeus.
Come, set your bow, my soul, upon its mark;
From a soft-spoken heart again,
On whom do we now launch our shafts of honour?
It shall be Acragas that holds my aim,
Telling on oath, no falsehood, that this city
Not for a hundred years
Has bred a man, who for his friends
Wrought goodness with more kind
A heart, and a more bounteous hand

ep. 5 Than Theron. Yet is high praise trampled down
By envy, against all right confronted
By madmen's hands, scheming in whispers
To shroud in secret blame
Good deeds of noble men. Yet the sea-sands
Are fled beyond all count,
And of the joys this man has given to others,
Who could declare their number?

A pair of ravens, etc.: an uncertainty of the Greek text in this passage makes it possible that the translation should not be the dual 'a pair of ravens' but simply the plural 'ravens' or a 'flock of ravens'. If the first reading is adopted, Pindar's remark must almost certainly have been directed against the rival poets Simonides and his nephew Bacchylides, of whose strained relations with Pindar there is no lack of evidence. Some editors prefer to adopt the second alternative, because no facts are known which would seem to justify the appearance at this date and in this particular Ode of an attack by Pindar against these two poets. The superiority of natural talent over acquired or instructed skill is a theme which recurs constantly in Pindar's Odes, and it would not be out of place to couple it here with an expression of scorn for all inferior poets generally. It would then serve to give added strength to what Pindar is saying, particularly to the renewed praise of Acragas and Theron which follows. On the other hand it was not long after this date that the influence of Simonides and Bacchylides seems to have done Pindar harm at the court of Hieron at Syracuse, and if Pindar was already aware that this was happening, it would account for such a reference to this pair of poets.

ant. 5 *The divine bird of Zeus:* the eagle was regarded as the king of birds, the emblem of Zeus, king of the gods. In Pythian I. str. 1. Pindar speaks of the eagle asleep on the sceptre of Zeus, and in the present passage Pindar likens himself, as compared with other poets, to an eagle compared with ravens, and in Nemean III. ep. 4 an eagle compared with jackdaws.

Not for a hundred years: the date of this poem is just over a hundred years later than the founding of the city of Acragas by Theron's ancestors, in or about the year 582 B.C.

OLYMPIAN III

For

THERON OF ACRAGAS

Winner of the Chariot-Race

THIS Ode celebrates the same victory as the preceding second Olympian, but whereas that Ode was probably performed at Theron's palace, the present Ode was written for performance at the festival of the Theoxenia in Acragas. The Theoxenia was a religious festival found in many cities of Greece, which took the form of a banquet at which the gods were supposed guests. In this Ode Heracles, the legendary founder and first president of the Olympian Games, is represented as coming to take charge of the ceremony and act as host to the divine guests ('to rule this feast' str. 3), together with the Dioscuri, the legendary twins Castor and Pollux. The short invocation at the opening of the Ode is addressed to these twin brothers and their sister Helen, the famous cause of the Trojan war, who were children of Tyndareus, king of Sparta. Pollux was in fact the son of Zeus and Leda, the wife of Tyndareus, and so immortal. The story of the death of the mortal Castor and of the prayer of Pollux and the answer given by Zeus, is finely told at the end of Pindar's tenth Nemean Ode.

The structure of this Ode is more straightforward and its tone less unusual than that of the preceding Ode. In the first and second strophes Pindar speaks of having invented for this Ode a new type of music, combining the lyre and the flute with the chorus of human voices. We have not enough knowledge of Greek music to understand what this novelty implies. The myth, which begins in epode 1, tells the story of the second journey of Heracles to the land of the Hyperboreans, undertaken in order to transplant to Olympia the olive trees which he had admired on his previous journey to those lands. The Hyperboreans, the 'Men-beyond-the-North-Wind', were the inhabitants, according to the rather vague geographical knowledge of the Greeks of the fifth century B.C., of the areas to the north of Greece and west of the Black Sea, roughly equivalent to the modern Balkan countries. They were worshippers of Apollo.

In epode 2 and strophe 3 Pindar, who here as elsewhere does not tie himself to chronological order in unfolding his stories, goes back to the first journey of Heracles to the lands of the north in pursuit of the hind of golden horns, which he had been ordered to bring back alive. This task, 'the bidding of Eurystheus' (ep. 2), was one of the Twelve Labours of Heracles imposed on him by Eurystheus king of Mycenae. The version of the story followed by Pindar is that the maiden Taygeta had dedicated this hind to the goddess Artemis in gratitude for having been temporarily disguised as a hind and thus escaping the embraces of Zeus. Heracles captured the hind after a long pursuit which took him to Istria, a country thought by the Greeks to lie round the sources of the Danube. Artemis, Leto's daughter (ep. 2), who is also known by the name of Orthosia, came to rebuke Heracles for misusing her holy beast, but he pleaded necessity and put the blame on Eurystheus. It is possible that this legend derives from the existence in north Europe of the reindeer, the only species of deer whose hinds have horns.

The third triad pictures Heracles and the Dioscuri attending this feast of the Theoxenia, and records that when Heracles departed from this earth and became immortal, he handed over to these twin brothers the presidency of the Olympian Games. Castor and Pollux were noted in legend for athletic qualities, particularly horsemanship and boxing, and were credited with having won victories in these events in the Olympian Games of previous times. After suggesting that it is to the Dioscuri that Theron and his family owe their high success (ant. 3), the Ode returns to the praise of Theron and ends on a warning note, typical of Pindar, against excessive ambition.

str. 1 Great sons of Tyndareus, dear to your guests,
        And Helen of the lovely tresses,
    I pray your pleasure, when my voice rings out
    To honour famous Acragas, and raise
            On high the name of Theron,
    And his Olympian victory, in proud song
    To match the steps of his untiring steeds.
        And the Muse, surely, stood beside me
    Unveiling new and sparkling paths of music,
            In Dorian cadence linked,

str. 1 *Sons of Tyndareus:* the Dioscuri. See foreword.

ant. 1 To voice the songs of our triumphant revel.
For the wreaths bound upon our locks
Command me to the task divinely given,
Worthily for Aenesidamus' son
To join in harmony
The sweet strains of the richly-varied lyre
With the notes of the flute, and the due setting
Of words; and Pisa too enjoins
My speech, for from her bidding come to men
The songs inspired of heaven,

ep. 1 For every man on whom the unswerving eye
Of the Hellenic judge,
Man of Aetolian breed,
Who guards the rites long years ago established
By Heracles, sets on his brow aloft
That shining glory, wreathed upon his hair,
Of the green olive leaf; which once
From Ister's shady streams
Amphitryon's son brought hither, to be
The fairest emblem of Olympia's Games.

str. 2 For the Hyperborean folk, Apollo's servants,
He so persuaded with fair words,

ant. 1 *The wreaths bound upon our locks:* it was customary for those attending the Theoxenia to wear wreaths in honour of the gods' attendance at the banquet.

Aenesidamus' son: Theron.

Pisa: the name of the neighbouring city is used here, as in the second Olympian Ode and elsewhere, for Olympia.

The songs: i.e. the Odes celebrating the victors at the Games.

ep. 1 *The Hellenic judge:* the judges at the Olympian Games were known by this title because only Greeks, Hellenes, were allowed to compete in the Games.

Man of Aetolian breed: an early king of Elis came from Aetolia in the north of Greece at the time of the Dorian invasions. The judges of the Olympian Games seem to have always been considered descendants of this king, or of the Aetolians who came with him.

Established by Heracles: Heracles was the legendary founder of the Olympian Games.

Olive leaf: the prize for victors in the Olympian Games was a wreath of olive leaves.

Ister: the river Danube.

Amphitryon's son: Heracles. He was in fact the son by Zeus of Alcmene, the wife of Amphitryon king of Thebes.

When, for the all-hospitable grove of Zeus,
His loyal heart begged for the tree, to make
Shade for all men to share,
And for brave deeds of valorous spirits, a crown.
For he had seen long since his father's altars
Sanctified, and the light of evening
Smiling at mid-month to the golden car
Of the full-orbéd moon;

ant. 2 And of the great Games had set up the contest
And sacred judgment, with the rites
Of the four-yearly feast, on the high banks
Of Alpheus' holy river. But the land
Of Pelops, and the vales
By Cronos' hill nourished no lovely trees,
And his eyes saw a garden spread defenceless
Beneath the fierce rays of the sun.
Then at length did his heart bid him begone,
To journey to the land

ep. 2 Of Istria, where, long since, Leto's daughter,
Lover of horsemanship,
Received him. For he came
From Arcady's high peaks and winding glens,
By constraint of his father, to perform
The bidding of Eurystheus, and bring back
The Hind of golden horns, which once
Taygeta had vowed
To Orthosia, a sacred gift,
And on it wrote the sign of consecration.

str. 2 *The grove of Zeus:* the precinct of Olympia, 'all-hospitable' because of the crowds which flocked there to attend the festival and the Games.

His father's altars: the altars of Zeus, set up by Heracles when he founded the Olympian Festival.

ant. 2 *The land of Pelops:* the kingdom of Elis, in which Olympia lay. Pelops became king of Elis after overthrowing Oenomaus, as related in the first Olympian Ode.

Cronos' hill: the hill beside Olympia.

ep. 2 *Leto's daughter:* the goddess Artemis, sister of Apollo. Her name is often associated with horsemanship and hunting.

By constraint of his father: the Twelve Labours of Heracles imposed on him by Eurystheus had behind them the authority of Zeus the father of Heracles, though his consent had been reluctantly given under pressure from Hera; however he made it a condition that when the Labours were finished Heracles should become an immortal.

Orthosia: the goddess Artemis, who was sometimes known by this name.

str. 3 And in that search he saw, too, the famed land
That lay behind cold Boreas
Of bleak and frozen breath; and standing there
Marvelled to see the trees. And in his heart
A dear resolve was born,
To set them planted there, where ends the course
Twelve times encircled by the racing steeds.
So comes he now with kind intent
To rule this feast, with the twin sons divine
Of Leda's generous breast.

ant. 3 For to these he gave charge, when he departed
To high Olympus, to preside
Over that glorious contest, where are matched
The prowess of brave hearts, and the swift-wheeling
Race of the charioteers.
Thus, then, my heart bids me declare this glory
Was given of Tyndareus' sons, those famous horsemen,
To Theron and the Emmenid clan,
Who of all mortals give them greatest welcome
With tables richly spread,

ep. 3 And guard with reverent loyalty the rites
Of the blest gods of heaven.
Is water best of all,
And gold of man's possessions the most worthy?
Yet for his valorous deeds Theron treads now
The highest peak, touching from hence the far
Pillars of Heracles. Beyond
Is pathless, for the wise
Or the unwise. That road shall I
Never pursue; name me a madman else.

str. 3 *Boreas:* the north wind.
The twin sons: Castor and Pollux, the Dioscuri.

ant. 3 *He gave charge:* see foreword.

ep. 3 *Is water best of all?:* compare the opening line of the first Olympian Ode.
The pillars of Heracles: the straits of Gibraltar, representing to the Greeks the end of the known world. This phrase was in common use to denote the summit of possible achievement.

OLYMPIAN IV

For

PSAUMIS OF CAMARINA

Winner of the Mule Chariot-Race

CAMARINA was a small city on the south-west coast of Sicily, of much less renown than Syracuse or Acragas. It had had chequered fortunes in the fierce internal conflicts of the island. Founded by emigrant Syracusans in 599 B.C., it was destroyed, following a revolt, in 553. Rebuilt in 492 by Hippocrates tyrant of Gela, it was destroyed again by his son Gelon in 484, and again reoccupied by the people of Gela in 461/60.

There is some uncertainty whether this Ode celebrates a victory in a chariot-race with horses, or in a chariot-race with mules. In the latter case the Ode may or may not be celebrating the same victory as Ode V which follows, and which was definitely written for a race with mules. There is some evidence in favour of the view that Ode IV celebrates a chariot-race with horses, but this is not conclusive, and neither Ode mentions another victory by Psaumis in addition to the one it celebrates. As it was Pindar's practice always to mention in an Ode any other successes won by the same victor, there is a strong presumption that both Odes celebrate the same victory. If so Ode IV was probably sung in the festal procession, and Ode V at the banquet which followed.

The chariot-race with mules ceased to be an event in the Olympian Games in 444 B.C. and thereafter. The date of the present victory must therefore lie between 461/60, when Camarina was refounded, and 444. It seems from the evidence available that it was probably won at the Games of 456 B.C., but 452 is also a possible date.

Psaumis was not the ruler of Camarina, but a wealthy private citizen, whose generous help had made possible the rebuilding of the city, a point to which Pindar refers in antistrophe 2 of Ode V. That a private citizen of a small city such as Camarina should have the means not only to stage a success at Olympia but also, as we shall see in Ode V, to compete in two other events at the same Games, probably caused surprise, and there is a suggestion in epode 2 of Ode V that the ambitious aims of Psaumis for success at Olympia may have been a matter for envy and disapproval amongst some of the citizens of Camarina, until justified by his victory.

The short myth at the end of this Ode is a legend whose concluding remark had become proverbial amongst the Greeks. Erginus the son of Clymenus was one of the Argonauts who sailed to Colchis on the Black Sea to bring back the Golden Fleece. Breaking their voyage at the island of Lemnos, they took part in the funeral games organized by Hypsipylia, the queen of Lemnos, in honour of her dead father Thoas. Erginus, entered for the race in armour, had grey or white hair, probably prematurely. When the competitors were lined up for the start, the onlooking Lemnian women jeered at him for attempting such a race at his age. He won the race however, defeating amongst others the sons of Boreas, the North Wind, who were supposed to be invincible in fleetness of foot. The remarks of Erginus which end the story are quoted by Pindar at the close of this Ode. The relevance of the story is presumably that Psaumis was also prematurely grey-haired or white-haired.

str. 1 Great Zeus, the thunder's charioteer
On its unwearied path
In the height of heaven, hear me. For thine
The swiftly circling seasons
Have sent me now with song,
And the lyre's rich embroidery,
To be the herald of the Games,
Greatest contest of all.
When friends have won success
A generous heart is quick with praise
To greet the happy tidings.

str. 1 The name of Zeus to whom Pindar here addresses a short invocation never fails of mention in the Olympian Odes. Later in the strophe he is addressed as 'lord of Aetna'. Camarina is by no means close to Mount Aetna, but the chief religious cult of Zeus in Sicily was that of 'Zeus of Aetna'.

The swiftly circling seasons: the phrase indicates that the time of the four-yearly Olympiad has come round again.

O son of Cronos, lord of Aetna,
That windswept mount where Typhon
The monster hundred-headed
Is held in thrall, receive, I pray thee,
For the Olympian victor's honour,
And for the Graces' favour,
This my triumphant song,

ant. 1 Bringing a light will long endure
On famous deeds of strength.
For Psaumis' chariot shall I sing,
Who at Pisa has won
The crown of olive, and now
Burns to raise high the glorious name
Of Camarina. May the hand
Of heaven give gracious issue
To all his further prayers.
Mine now to praise his ready skill
Nursing his gallant steeds,
And that with hospitable joy
He welcomes many a guest;
And with a heart unsullied
Labours for Peace, the city's friend.
No strain of falsehood will my songs
Admit. Trial by deed
Gives proof to all mankind.

ep. 1 As when the son of Clymenus,
Facing the Lemnian women,

That windswept mount: an echo of the fine description of Mount Aetna which occurs in Pindar's first Pythian Ode written in 470 B.C., many years before this Ode.

Typhon: the mythical monster who attacked Zeus and the other gods. He was overthrown by the thunderbolt of Zeus and imprisoned beneath Mount Aetna, and was credited with being the cause of the volcano and earthquakes in the vicinity.

ant. 1 *May the hand of heaven, etc.:* this prayer for Psaumis' further success, coupled with the phrase 'nursing his gallant steeds' in the lines which follow, could be taken to indicate that Psaumis was hoping to enter for the chariot-race with horses at some later Olympian Games. Some editors however find in this phrase part of the evidence implying that the victory celebrated in this Ode was in the chariot-race with horses.

ep. 1 *The son of Clymenus:* Erginus. See foreword.

Staved off dishonour's threat;
When he had won the race for men
In full bronze armour clad.
Thus spoke he to Hypsipylia
As he stepped forth to take the crown;
'Such then, for speed, am I,
In strength of hand and heart no less;
Even on men whose years are few,
White hairs do often grow,
Despite of flowering youth
Its natural season.'

OLYMPIAN V

For

PSAUMIS OF CAMARINA

Winner of the Mule Chariot-Race

THE date of this Ode and its connection with Ode IV have been discussed in the foreword to that Ode.

Ode V makes it quite clear that the victory it celebrates was that of the chariot-race with mules (str. 1), and also that Psaumis had competed in the same Games, though unsuccessfully, in the chariot-race with horses and in the horse-race (ep. 1). The structure of the Ode is simple. There is no myth. After a short passage of invocation to Camarina, which as a maritime city is addressed as 'Daughter of Ocean', the Ode proceeds to eulogies for the achievement of Psaumis and the honour and benefits he has brought to Camarina and her people.

The third triad expresses a prayer to Zeus that he will enrich Camarina with men of noble spirit, and grant happiness throughout his life to Psaumis, with his family around him. The Ode concludes, as does the third Olympian, with a brief warning against excessive ambition.

str. 1 Daughter of Ocean, pray you
Accept with a glad heart this song, the sweet
And choice reward for brave exploits
Of lofty spirits, and for the crowns
Won at Olympia,
The gifts of Psaumis and his team
On their untiring course.

ant. 1 He has raised up your city
Camarina, the mother of his people,

str. 1 *His team:* the Greek word used here is the one regularly applied to a chariot drawn by mules.

Honouring in splendid festivals
The six twin altars of the gods,
With oxen sacrifice,
And in the five-day games and contests,
In well-matched rivalry

p. 1 Of four-horsed chariots and the race
Of the mules' car, and in the contest
Of single horsemen. To you
His victory brought the peerless grace of fame,
And for his father Acron
And for his new-built city-seat,
Has bidden the herald's voice proclaim their honour.

str. 2 Leaving that lovely land,
Where Oenomaus and Pelops dwelt of old,
His song honours your sacred precinct,
Pallas, protectress of his city,
And Oanis your river
And the lake of his country's name;
The holy channels too

ant. 2 Of Hipparis whose streams
Give water to his people. And he builds
Well-founded mansions, grown with speed
Like to a forest's lofty branches,
Bringing his city's folk
From the harsh bonds of their distress
Into the light of day.

ant. 1 *In splendid festivals:* the religious rites, including the sacrifice of oxen, which took place before the start of the athletic contests, and to which it appears that Psaumis made a notable contribution.

The six twin altars: these were the altars at Olympia of Zeus-Poseidon, Hera-Athene, Hermes-Aphrodite, The Graces-Dionysus, Artemis-Alpheus, Cronos-Rhea.

str. 2 *That lovely land:* Elis, the land of Olympia, of which Pelops became king after ousting Oenomaus, as related in the first Olympian Ode.

Pallas: the Ode turns to address Pallas Athene, worshipped as the guardian goddess of the city.

Oanis and Hipparis: the two rivers of Camarina.

The lake: one of the features of Camarina was a large lake known by the same name.

ant. 2 *He builds:* Psaumis had made generous use of his wealth in rebuilding Camarina.

ep. 2 Toil and expense, for deeds of courage,
Must ever be the cost of valour's
Accomplishment, hidden
Within the veil of danger. But to those
Who win the victory,
Even amidst their citizens
Comes the reward of wisdom's reputation.

str. 3 O guardian Zeus, who dwellest
In the high clouds of heaven, and on the hill
Of Cronos, honouring the stream
Of Alpheus and the holy cave
Of Ida's name, to thee
With song and the flute's Lydian strain
I bring a suppliant's prayer,

ant. 3 Begging thee to enrich
This city with the glory of brave spirits;
And you, Olympia's victor, may
A long life and a happy heart,
Rejoicing in your steeds,
The gift of great Poseidon, bring you
Blessings through all your days,

ep. 3 And may you see your sons, Psaumis,
Standing beside you. If a man
Makes of his wealth a stream
Of healthful purpose, and of his possessions
Lacks not a bounteous store,
And adds thereto repute's good name,
Then let him not seek to become a god.

ep. 2 *Toil and expense, etc.:* this stanza suggests that the lavish expense to which Psaumis must have been put to enter for three events at Olympia and to cover his notable contribution to the religious rites may have roused the surprise or even envy of his fellow-citizens; but that his victory put such feelings to rest.

str. 3 *The hill of Cronos:* the hill beside Olympia.

The cave of Ida's name: according to legend, Zeus spent his early years with shepherds, living in a cave on Mount Ida in Crete. The reference here is probably to a cave near Olympia, which was given the same name.

Lydian strain: the music for this Ode was in the Lydian 'mode'.

ant. 3 *The gift of great Poseidon:* horses were always associated with and sacred to Poseidon, the god of the sea and subterranean powers. In the stables of his underwater palace he was credited with keeping white chariot horses and a golden chariot. He is said to have boasted of creating the horse and to have instituted horse-racing.

OLYMPIAN VI

For

AGESIAS OF SYRACUSE

Winner of the Mule Chariot-Race

AGESIAS was a citizen of Syracuse and also of Stymphalus in Arcadia. He was a member of the clan of Iamus, a family who claimed descent from Apollo and Poseidon and were noted in Greece and in Sicily as priests of divinatory powers. They were in the first rank of the priesthood at Olympia and held as a hereditary right the oracular service at the Olympian altar of Zeus. The principal theme of this Ode is the eulogy of this family, and the myth is devoted to the legend of the birth of Iamus and his appointment to the high altar of Zeus at Olympia.

Instead of the usual invocation the Ode begins by proclaiming through an architectural metaphor that the poem must have a noteworthy opening. Then follows praise of Agesias, including a reference to his descent from one of the Greek colonists who founded Syracuse in the eighth century B.C., and comparing him to the legendary Amphiaraus, the famous warrior and prophet who took part in the unsuccessful expedition under Adrastus of the 'Seven against Thebes'. In strophe 2 Pindar does not forget to mention Phintis, the charioteer who won the race for Agesias, asking him to conduct the Ode to the point where it can embark on the eulogy of the Iamid clan from its origin in the nymph Pitane, the mother by Poseidon of Evadne, who was the mother by Apollo of Iamus. It is possible that Pindar gives this rather unusual emphasis to the charioteer and to the mules he drove in order to encourage his audience to forget that the chariot-race with mules enjoyed far less glamour and prestige than the race with horses. The story of Iamus takes us to antistrophe 4, after which Agesias is reminded that he owes his success to the help of the gods, to Hermes who is president of the Olympian Games, and to Zeus their tutelary deity.

Pindar then mentions his own connection, as a Theban, with Arcadia, through the legendary nymph Metope, who was the daughter of the river Ladon, which rises not far from Lake Stymphalus in Arcadia. Metope married Asopus, the river near Thebes, and became the mother of Thebe, from whom the people of

Thebes might claim descent. In strophe 5 Pindar makes complimentary references to Aeneas, to whom he had delegated the training of the chorus and the direction of the Ode at its first performance in Stymphalus. Pindar was not present himself. He describes Aeneas as the 'unerring tally of the . . . Muses'—a true interpreter of the poem's meaning. The writing-tally or letter-stick was used in Greece for messages of which the contents were to be kept secret. In order to read the message the recipient needed a tally of exactly the same shape as that round which the writer had composed it. He also refers to Aeneas as a 'rich-filled bowl of sounding song', using this metaphor of the wine-bowl, in which the wine was mixed with water before serving, to imply that Aeneas will produce the right harmony of words, music and dance when the Ode is performed.

A second performance of this Ode was to be held at Syracuse on the return of Agesias to Sicily. As Agesias was one of the lieutenants of Hieron of Syracuse, this is no doubt the reason for the compliments to Hieron expressed in antistrophe 5, together with the hope that he will give a friendly reception to Agesias after his Olympian victory. Hieron's family held a hereditary priesthood of Demeter and her daughter Core, whose name became Persephone after her marriage to Hades, when she became queen of the Underworld. This accounts for Pindar's reference to these deities in this antistrophe.

At the date of this Ode, 468 B.C. (though 472 is also possible but perhaps less likely), Hieron was nearing the end of his reign in Syracuse. He died in 467. The last years of his life were seriously troubled with illness, and with anxiety, which events proved to have been justified, that his end would be fatal to the dynastic rule of his family, the Deinomenids. This is no doubt reflected in the hope expressed towards the end of antistrophe 5 that the 'tides of time' will not 'cast aside His days of fortune'. A further note of anxiety, this time on behalf of Agesias, is found in the final epode, in the lines recommending that a ship should rely on two anchors 'in the winter's storm, at night'. The two anchors mean his two homes, one in Syracuse, one in Arcadia. The 'winter's storm' however was not long in overtaking Agesias, since on the death of Hieron he lost his life in the disturbed times that followed shortly afterwards in Sicily.

str. 1 Pillars of gold, as for a stately palace,
Let us upraise, to build a strong-walled forecourt
Fronting the chamber of our song.
For to a growing work we needs must set
A rich entablature, seen from afar.
But he who won Olympia's crown,
Steward appointed to the prophetic altar
Of Zeus in Pisa, who shares the ancient fame
Of glorious Syracuse' foundation,
For such a man, what hymns shall not encompass
His path, unenvied of his citizens,
In strains of long-desiréd song?

ant. 1 Then let this son of Sostratus know well
This path of glory where his sandals tread
Is given of heaven. Noble deeds
Untried of danger, be it upon land
Or ships at sea, no honour win. But widespread
The records of a valorous act
Sternly encountered. Fitting for you that praise,
Agesias, which from Adrastus' tongue
In days of old most justly sprang,
Crying aloud to Oikleus' son, the prophet
Amphiaraus, when the split earth engulfed him,
His chariot and gleaming steeds.

ep. 1 For when on seven burning pyres were laid
Their warrior dead, then spoke at Thebes, in sorrow,
The son of Talaus this word,

str. 1 *Steward appointed:* in virtue of his membership of the Iamid clan. *In Pisa:* as frequently, the name Pisa is used for Olympia.

ant. 1 *Son of Sostratus:* Agesias.
Adrastus: legendary king of Argos who led the expedition of the 'Seven against Thebes'. *Amphiaraus* met his end when the 'Seven' were defeated and he fled from the battle-field in his chariot, pursued by one of the defenders of Thebes. To save him from the disgrace of being hit in the back by his enemy's spear, Zeus opened a chasm in the earth in front of him in which he was swallowed up.

ep. 1 *The son of Talaus:* Adrastus.

Saying 'Woe is me for the eye
Of all my host, at once a mighty prophet
And alike matchless in the fray of spears'.
Thus, too, behoves this man of Syracuse
And master of this revel, a like praise.
I am no man of strife, nor prone
To envy's quarrels, but on oath
Due sworn, my voice to this his honour
Shall clearly witness, and the honey-sweet
Song of the Muses shall affirm the word.

str. 2 Come then, Phintis, yoke for me now the power
Of your strong mules, that we may ride our car
With all speed on the clear-lit road,
To bring me to the source at last, where sprang
This race of men. Better than other steeds
They know well where to lead me
Along this road, who at Olympia
Have won the crowns of victory. Fitly
Must we now open wide for them
The gateway of our songs. Today must we
Begone beside Eurotas' stream, to journey—
Timely the hour—to Pitane.

ant. 2 She, so they tell, was loved of great Poseidon,
Son of Cronos, and bore the babe Evadne,
Child of the crown of violet tresses,
Hiding the pains of maiden motherhood
Beneath her robe. But when the month was come
Of labour's term, she sent her handmaids
And bade them give the child for watch and ward
To Eilatus' hero son at Phaisana,
Who ruled in Arcady, and dwelt
By Alpheus' stream. There was the young babe nursed
And grown, and by Apollo's love first knew
The touch of Aphrodite's joy.

This man of Syracuse: Agesias.
Envy's quarrels: see note on ant. 4.
This his honour: that he is worthy of the same praise as Amphiaraus, as a warrior, and in virtue of being an Iamid, as a prophet.

str. 2 *Phintis:* Agesias' charioteer. See foreword.
Pitane: the nymph Pitane lived by the river Eurotas in the south of the Peloponnese.

ant. 2 *Eilatus' son:* Aepytus, king of Arcadia.

ep. 2 Yet could she not from Aepytus keep hidden
Through all her time the divine seed she bore.
And he, struggling in bitter strain
To hold within his heart a wrath
Unbearable, to Pytho straight departed,
To seek a ruling of the oracle
For this most grievous woe. But she laid by
Beneath a thicket's shade her silvered urn,
And she let fall her crimson girdle
And bore a son, inspired of heaven.
And to serve at her side Apollo,
God of the golden locks, sent Eleithuia
The kindly goddess, and the Fates divine.

str. 3 And from her body's travail and the pains
That were but sweet delight, was born Iamus,
Sped forth to the bright light of day.
And she in her soul's anguish left the babe
There on the ground. But by the will of heaven
There came to him two snakes grey-eyed,
And gave to nourish him, with gentle care,
The sweet and harmless venom of the bees.
Then came the king, riding in haste
From rocky Pytho, and from all the household
Demanded of the child Evadne bore,
Saying he was the son begotten

ant. 3 Of Phoebus, and should be beyond all others
A peerless prophet for the race of man,
And that his seed should last for ever.
So he declared it to them. But all vowed
They had nor heard nor seen aught of the babe,
The five days of his infant being.
For in a deep brake had he lain concealed,
A pathless waste, and o'er his tender limbs
Flowers of gold and purple splendour,
Iris and Pansy shed their rays upon him;
Thence was it his mother for all time proclaimed
That he be called of men Iamus,

ep. 2 *Pytho:* the oracle at Delphi.
Eleithuia: the goddess of child-birth.

str. 3 *Two snakes:* snakes were always associated with divination. So too was honey, with which the snakes fed Iamus.

ant. 3 *Phoebus:* Phoebus Apollo is his full name.
Thence was it: the Greek word for iris or pansy (sometimes also it means violet) is 'ion', from which his mother made the name Iamus.

ep. 3 This his immortal name. And when he won
Youth's joyous fruit, fair Hebe's gleaming crown,
He went to the midwaters down
Of Alpheus' stream, and called aloud
To the god of far-spreading might, Poseidon
His ancestor, and to the archer god
Ruler of heaven-built Delos, and this prayer
He spoke, at night, beneath the starlit sky:
That on his brow be laid the honour
To be the shepherd of his people.
Brief and clear called his father's voice,
Answering 'Rise my son, hence to the place
Where all men meet, bearing my bidden word'.

str. 4 And they came to the lofty rock, where rules
The high-throned son of Cronos. There he gave him
Of the seer's art this two-fold treasure;
First that he hear the voice that knows no lie;
And when that Heracles, brave heart and hand,
Revered son of Alcides' seed,
Should come to establish to his father's name
The feast where many a countless foot shall tread,
With the ordinance of games and contests
Greatest of all, then shall the second honour,
His oracle, high on the supreme altar
Of Zeus be set. Thus he ordained.

ant. 4 Thenceforth for all the sons of Iamus' seed
Through all Hellas their race holds high renown;
And fortune's day attended them;
To deeds of noble grace paying due honour
They tread their way of light. Witness shall be
Their each achievement. Calumny
But from the hearts of others' envy, threatens
Those who came first, driving the twelve-lap course,

ep. 3 *Hebe:* the goddess of youth.
The archer god: Apollo.
Delos: the birthplace of Apollo; the sacred island in the Aegean sea.
The place where all men meet: Olympia.

str. 4 *The lofty rock:* the 'hill of Cronos' beside Olympia, where Zeus the 'son of Cronos' is the ruling deity.
The feast, etc.: the festival and Games of Olympia, founded by Heracles.
Greatest of all: the Olympian Games enjoyed the highest prestige of all the four Panhellenic festivals.

ant. 4 *Calumny, etc.:* this sentence appears to mean that winners of the chariot-race at Olympia, the event of the greatest honour, need fear no opposition

On whom the divine grace of Beauty
Has shed the dewdrops of her fame most fair.
Truth tells, Agesias, that your mother's kin,
Dwelling beneath Kyllene's height,

ep. 4 Often and yet again the sanctities
Of prayer and sacrifices rich presented
To Hermes, herald of the gods,
Who of the Games is president,
And shares the contests' glory, honouring
That land of noble souls, Arcadia.
Then surely, son of Sostratus, it is
That god, who with his father, lord of thunder,
Decrees you now your glad success.
Methinks a whetstone on my tongue,
Clear-sounding, brings me, nothing loth,
A sweet-flown breath of song. From Stymphalus
My mother's mother came, that maid of flowers,

str. 5 Metope, who bore Thebe, famous rider
Of horse. Her lovely waters shall I drink
Weaving the rich refrains of song
To honour famous men of arms. Come then,
Aeneas, rouse the chorus of your singers
First to praise Hera, the fair Maid,

except possibly that which derives from envy. Some editors think that these lines imply that in some quarters at Syracuse there might be envy of Agesias' victory amongst people jealous of the position he enjoyed under Hieron. If so the same comment probably applies to the phrase in epode 1 where Pindar declares that he is not 'prone to envy's quarrels', implying that some others may be.

Kyllene's height: Kyllene is a dominating mountain in Arcadia, the highest mountain in the Peloponnese except Mount Taygetus near Sparta.

ep. 4 *Lord of thunder:* Zeus, the father of Hermes.

A whetstone on my tongue: it was a common idiom in Greece to speak of the tongue being sharpened on a whetstone when it had something noteworthy to say. Compare the English 'whetting the appetite'.

Stymphalus: Lake Stymphalus in Arcadia.

My mother's mother: not literally, but a legendary ancestress of the Theban people through the nymph Thebe. See foreword.

str. 5 *Metope:* see foreword.

Aeneas: see foreword.

Hera, the fair Maid: Hera, the wife of Zeus, was worshipped both in her unmarried and in her married state. There was a special cult of Hera at Stymphalus.

Then to know well whether in very truth
We make of no account that sorry taunt,
  The old-worn slight 'Boeotian swine'.
For you give to my words their true report,
Unerring tally of the fair-tressed Muses,
  A rich-filled bowl of sounding song.

ant. 5 Bid them not spare to tell of Syracuse
And of Ortygia, where Hieron
  Rules with his rod of justice. Wise
And clear the counsels of his mind, who worships
The red-strewn carpet where Demeter treads,
  And the feast of her daughter, goddess
Of the white horses, and the lofty power
Of Zeus of Aetna. Him the sweet-sung notes
  Of lyre and voices know full well.
And may the tides of time not cast aside
His days of fortune, but with happy welcome
  And friendly heart may he receive

ep. 5 This triumph of Agesias, as he rides
From home to second home, leaving the walls
  Of Stymphalus his motherland,
  And the rich flocks of Arcady.
Well is it in the winter's storm, at night,
Two anchors to make fast to the ship's prow.
To the men then of his race, or here or there,
May friendly heaven bestow a path of glory.

'Boeotian swine': the people of Boeotia had a reputation, particularly amongst the quick-witted Athenians, for being slow and stupid, and this phrase was not uncommonly used by them. Pindar, no doubt half jestingly, implies that his poetry serves to refute this idea.

ant. 5 *Ortygia*: a small island on which the early Greek colonists first founded Syracuse. By Pindar's time this had grown into the much larger city on the mainland of Sicily, while the island of Ortygia was joined to it by a causeway.

Demeter: Hieron was the holder of a hereditary priesthood of Demeter. The 'red-strewn carpet' is a phrase to suggest her association, as the goddess of fertility, with the ripened corn.

Her daughter: Persephone, whose worship was given special attention by the Greeks of Sicily. (Cf. Nem. I. ant. 1.)

Zeus of Aetna: the chief religious cult of Zeus in Sicily was that of 'Zeus of Aetna'.

ep. 5 *From home to second home*: from Arcadia to Syracuse.

The winter's storm, etc. See foreword.

A straight-run sail free from all toil
Grant him I beg, great god of ocean,
Husband of Amphitrite, goddess
Of the gold spindle, and to the air on high
Raise up the joyful blossom of my songs.

Great god of ocean: Poseidon.

Of the gold spindle: Amphitrite, whom Poseidon married, was one of the sea-nymphs, the Nereids, who are traditionally represented as carrying golden spindles.

OLYMPIAN VII

For

DIAGORAS OF RHODES

Winner of the Boxing-Match

DIAGORAS belonged to one of the leading families in the island of Rhodes, the Eratidae, who in earlier times had exercised kingly power in the city of Ialysus. Though this power was now extinct, the family still enjoyed a pre-eminent position, and Damagetus, the father of Diagoras, to whom Pindar makes a complimentary reference in epode 1 of this Ode, is thought to have been 'prytanis', or president of the council which directed the affairs of the island.

Diagoras with his sons and grandsons won unique distinction in the athletic field in boxing contests and the pankration. Diagoras, who was a man of exceptional stature, won victories at all the four Panhellenic Games including four at the Isthmian and two at the Nemean Games, and at many other local athletic contests mentioned in the fifth strophe and antistrophe of this Ode. His three sons won between them five victories at Olympia, and his two grandsons were successful at Olympia and Delphi. The historian Pausanias, writing in the second century A.D., records that statues of Diagoras and of his sons and grandsons were to be seen displayed at Olympia. Modern archaeology has discovered the bases of these statues. The present Ode, written in 464 B.C., was widely esteemed. It was said to have been set up in letters of gold in the temple of Athene at Lindus in Rhodes. In the year 406 B.C., fifty-eight years after this victory of Diagoras, when the Athenians were engaged in the final and bitter stages of their long and disastrous war with Sparta, the eldest son of Diagoras, Dorieus, who had himself won three victories at Olympia, was captured by the Athenians in a sea-battle. Although at that period it was customary either to release prisoners of war for a ransom or to put them to death, the Athenians asked for no ransom for Dorieus but set him free immediately.

The structure of the Ode follows the normal pattern, except that for the usual lines of invocation to a deity or the Muses Pindar substitutes the attractive simile found in the opening strophe. Then follows praise of the victor's family and of the island of Rhodes and the ancestry of her people. The myth then occupies the middle section of the Ode (ant. 2 to ep. 4) and the last triad returns to eulogy of the victor.

The mythical section has features of special interest. It is in fact made up of three stories, with a passing reference also to a fourth, the legend of the birth of Athene. Pindar uses these stories to illustrate three main features of Rhodian life in his day: firstly that the religion of the Rhodian people centred round the worship of Helios, the god of the sun, and of Athene; secondly that the Rhodians were noted for skilled craftsmanship—their pottery and other works of art had from early times enjoyed a high reputation, which to a certain extent still exists today; and thirdly that they took pride in considering themselves descendants of genuine Greek ancestors of Dorian stock. History records the colonization of Rhodes by immigrants from Argos, a city of Dorian tradition. Pindar, and probably the people of Rhodes, preferred to look to the earlier legendary story told in this Ode of the coming of the Argives under the leadership of Tlepolemus, the son of Heracles. Their Dorian origin was one of the reasons which led the Rhodians, in the latter part of the fifth century, to take sides with the Spartans in the long struggle of the Peloponnesian War, which led to the downfall of Athens at the end of the century.

Modern readers should note that in relating the three mythical stories of this Ode, Pindar, as in some other Odes, reverses their chronological order. The more recent in time, the story of Tlepolemus, is placed first (ant. 2 and ep. 2). Then follows (str. 3 to ep. 3) the story of the command given by Helios, god of the sun, to his descendants, the early inhabitants of Rhodes, to set up the worship of Zeus and Athene. Finally (ep. 3 to ep. 4) comes the story of how the island of Rhodes grew from out of the sea to become the special charge of Helios, who took as his bride the maiden Rhodes, daughter of Aphrodite, and from their union were derived the ancestors of the Rhodian people.

These three stories have a noteworthy common feature. Each of them tells how wrong-doing or mischance led ultimately to a happy issue. Tlepolemus killed his relative Licymnius in Tiryns (an Argive city), and his consequent exile brought about his colonization, with his Argive followers, of the island of Rhodes. The early inhabitants of Rhodes, the Heliadae (sons of Helios) failed through negligence to carry out adequately the bidding of Helios, and founded 'a precinct without holy fire'; but they were nevertheless rewarded by the shower of gold sent to them by Zeus, and by the gift of skilled craftsmanship awarded to them by the goddess Athene. Helios, the sun, suffered the mischance of being absent from the allotment, made by Zeus to the other gods, of the various lands of the earth. This resulted however in his acquiring the island of Rhodes, newly risen from the depths of the sea, 'to hold in his dominion' . . . 'as for a crown of honour'.

The similarity which these three stories share cannot be accidental, but must have been part of Pindar's design. This seems the more certain because of the words with which Pindar prefaces his relation of the three stories. The sentence which begins in the latter part of strophe 2, and refers to the 'net of countless riddles' which besets the thoughts of men and prevents their foreseeing what the upshot of their actions may turn out to be, seems a clear indication that Pindar had in mind some event or events, unknown to us but no doubt recognizable by his audience, to which the three stories, told in this way, would have a pertinent meaning and perhaps a lesson to teach. Of what these events were we have now no knowledge. Here we have again 'arrows' from Pindar's quiver 'speaking to men of wisdom, but for the throng they need interpreters' (Ol. II. str. 5). One editor has supposed that the explanation lies in some fault or negligence on the part of Diagoras in winning his victory, and has gone so far as to suggest that, as is recorded occasionally of other athletes, he had injured an opponent so badly in the contest as to cause his death. There is no mention however in any ancient commentator of any such incident in connection with Diagoras, and as the notes on the Eratid family which have come down to us from ancient commentaries are full and varied, it seems highly unlikely that such an incident would not have been recorded.

The legend of the birth of Athene, well known to the Greeks, was that she was conceived in the mind of Zeus, and when released from within his head by the blow of an axe made by Hephaestus, the god of the forge and metalwork, she rose to the air in her full panoply of armour, spear and 'aegis', the shield commonly associated with her name.

The final lines of the Ode turn suddenly to a brief and typically Pindaric comment. The mutability of human fortunes and the warning that high success must not be allowed to turn a man's head are themes frequently found in Pindar's comments or 'asides'. It is in keeping that such a warning should be included in an Ode which records the unique distinctions won by Diagoras. But the sudden change here from the main theme of the poem to this brief general comment is unusually abrupt even for Pindar, and suggests that there may have been other factors, either in the life of Diagoras and his family or in current events affecting the fortunes of the people of Rhodes, which prompted Pindar to end the Ode on this note of warning. Once again our lack of knowledge must leave us without an answer to this question.

str. 1 As when a man raises a cup
Brimmed with the sparkling dewdrops of the vine, and drinks
Toast to a young bridegroom, wishing him joy
From one home to another,
And from his wealthy hand presents him
The cup, of pure gold, pride of his possessions;
To his kith and kin and to the banquet's grace
Paying due honour, there amidst his thronging friends
He sets him envied, who has won
A marriage of true minds.

ant. 1 So I too, for the men who honour
The athletes' field, proffer this draught of flowing nectar,
The Muses' gift, the sweet fruit of the mind,
Paying my homage due
To those who at Olympia,
And at Pytho have won the victor's crown.
He has true wealth, whom good reports encompass.
Now on one, now to another, Beauty's refreshing grace
Shines with the rich notes of the lyre
And the far-echoing flute.

ep. 1 Thus then, set to this twofold strain, my sail rides in
Diagoras to honour, and to praise
The ocean maid, daughter of Aphrodite,
Bride of the Sun, this isle of Rhodes.
Here shall my songs bring sweet reward
To him whose giant limbs, striding the fray,
By Alpheus' stream and at Castalia
Won him the boxer's crown, and to his father
Damagetus, whom Justice loves to honour.

str. 1 These opening lines appear to indicate that this Ode was to be chanted at the banquet to be held in Rhodes as part of the celebration of Diagoras' Olympic victory.

ep. 1 The first lines of this epode could possibly, but by no means certainly, mean that Pindar himself went to Rhodes to direct the performance of the Ode.

By Alpheus' stream: i.e. at Olympia.

Castalia: i.e. at the Pythian Games at Delphi, where the fountain of Castalia still exists.

Three cities crown their island home, near to the tongue
Of wide-spread Asia,
Amidst their folk of Argive warrior breed.

str. 2 Gladly shall I tell o'er their race,
And point their ancient seed, sprung from Tlepolemus,
And from great Heracles' broad-shouldered stock
In common ancestry.
From Zeus their father's line can boast
Descent, and from Amyntor by their mother
Astydamia. Yet for the race of man
Ever about his struggling thought hangs there a net
Of countless riddles, whence indeed
Is it most hard to tell

ant. 2 What fortune shall be best, or now
Or in the final hour, for any man to win.
For did not once the founder of this land,
In Tiryns long ago,
With his staff of hard olive wood,
In anger strike Alcemene's bastard brother,
Licymnius, and slew him as he came
From Midea's chamber? Troubled thoughts confound even
The wise. But he went to the god
To ask the oracle.

Three cities: Camirus, Lindus and Ialysus, the three main cities of the island of Rhodes.

The tongue of wide-spread Asia: The long promontory of the mainland of Asia Minor, not many miles to the north of Rhodes.

Argive warrior breed: The first colonization of Rhodes from the mainland of Greece, according to the legend which Pindar follows, was by Tlepolemus and his followers from Tiryns in the Argolid. History records the colonization of Rhodes from Argos in later times.

str. 2 *Tlepolemus:* The son of Heracles by Astydamia, daughter of Amyntor, king of Ormenium near Mount Pelion.

From Zeus: Heracles was the son of Zeus and Alcmene.

ant. 2 *The founder of this land:* Tlepolemus.

Alcmene: Grandmother of Tlepolemus. She was the daughter of Electryon, an early king of Mycenae, and his wife Anaxo.

Licymnius: Son of Electryon by a Phrygian woman, Midea. He was thus the great-uncle of Tlepolemus. The commonly accepted legend of the death of Licymnius was that it was an accident, and that the anger of Tlepolemus was directed against a servant whom he was beating with a cudgel. Licymnius, old and half blind, stumbled between them and received a blow on the head. Pindar seems to have changed the story to one of deliberate killing, probably to give greater emphasis to the theme which runs through the myths of this Ode, of misdeed or mischance resulting finally in good fortune.

The god: the temple of the Delphic oracle of Apollo.

ep. 2 Then to him from his temple of sweet incense spoke
The god of golden hair, and bade him launch
From Lerna's shore, and sail his ships straight-run
To the land circled by the sea,
Where once the great king of the gods
Showered upon the city snowflakes of gold;
In the day when the skilled hand of Hephaestus
Wrought with his craft the axe, bronze-bladed, whence
From the cleft summit of her father's brow
Athene sprang aloft, and pealed to the broad sky
Her clarion cry of war.
And Heaven trembled to hear, and Mother Earth.

str. 3 Then was it too that the great god
Hyperion's son, giver of light to mortal men,
This task to his beloved sons enjoined
To ensure well hereafter:
That they first to the goddess build
A shining altar, and founding holy rites
Of sacrifice, make glad the heart of Zeus,
And the maid of the sounding spear. Now Reverence,
Daughter of Forethought, gives to men
Virtue and valour's joy.

ant. 3 And yet comes too, on stealthy wing, that
Cloud of forgetfulness, drawing our baffled minds
Off from the straight road of their acts' intent.
For they mounted aloft,
But carried in their hands no seed
Of burning flame, but on the city's height
Founded a precinct without holy fire.

ep. 2 *Sweet incense:* The priestess of Delphi, while issuing the prophetic utterances, sat on the stone of the oracle, which lay in a rocky hollow or cave. Smoke of volcanic origin, rising round her from a fissure in the rock, was believed to inspire her with the divine answers.

The god of golden hair: Apollo, traditionally so described.

Sail his ships, etc.: Apollo's command is in keeping with the ancient tradition that the killing of a man, whether purposely or by accident, must be punished by exile.

Snowflakes of gold: the stories of the shower of gold, and of Athene's birth, were legends well known to the Greeks.

str. 3 *Hyperion's son:* Helios, the god of the sun.

His beloved sons: the earlier inhabitants of Rhodes, before the incursion of the Argives, were known as Heliadae.

The goddess: Athene. The worship of Athene, and of Helios, the sun, was the most important element in the religion of the people of Rhodes.

Maid of the sounding spear: Athene. She is traditionally represented as carrying her spear, and her shield, the aegis.

Yet for these men Zeus brought the saffron cloud, and rained
A flood of gold, and the grey-eyed
Goddess herself endowed them

ep. 3 The gift of skill, that of all men on earth, their hands
In craft excelling have the mastery.
And the roads carried their worked images
Of life and movement, and widespread
Was their renown. To men of knowledge
Wisdom grows freely, innocent of guile.
Now on the tongues of men are told the stories
Of ancient days, that when Zeus and the immortals
Made a division of the lands of earth,
Not yet to see was Rhodes, shining upon the waves
Of ocean, but the isle
Lay hidden deep within the salt sea's folds.

str. 4 But for the Sun no lot was drawn;
For he was absent, and they left him of broad earth
No heritage, that holy god. And when
He made known his mischance,
Zeus was in mind to portion out
The lots again; but he allowed him not,
For he said that beneath the surge of ocean
His eyes had seen a land growing from out the depths,
Blessed with rich nourishment for men
And happy with teeming flocks.

ant. 4 And straightway then the god commanded
Lachesis of the golden fillet to raise aloft
Her hands, and swear, not on her lips alone,
The great oath of the gods,

ant. 3 *The grey-eyed goddess:* another traditional epithet of Athene.

ep. 3 *Innocent of guile:* the earliest legendary inhabitants of Rhodes, before the Heliadae, were the Telchines, reputed for craftsmanhip and wizardry. Pindar wants to make the point that the art of the Heliadae was free from the latter imputation.

str. 4 *Rich nourishment for men, etc.:* Rhodes was famous for its grain and pasture-land.

ant. 4 *Lachesis:* one of the three Fates—Clotho who spins the thread of life, Lachesis who apportions it, and Atropos the Fate who cannot be avoided. The name Lachesis is derived from a Greek word meaning to 'receive by lot', and it is therefore appropriate for her to be called upon in reference to the allotment, as described, of Rhodes to Helios.

The great oath of the gods: to swear by the river Styx, the river of Hades, was the greatest oath of all, mentioned by Homer and Hesiod.

Promising with the son of Cronos
This land once risen to the light of heaven
Should be thenceforth as for a crown of honour
His own awarded title. The great words spoken, fell
In truth's rich furrow. And there grew
Up from the watery wave

ep. 4 This island, and great Helios who begets the fierce
Rays of the sun, holds her in his dominion,
That ruler of the horses breathing fire.
There long ago he lay with Rhodes
And begot seven sons, endowed
Beyond all men of old with genius
Of thoughtful mind. And of these one begot
His eldest Ialysus, and Camirus
And Lindus; and in three parts they divided
Their father's land, and of three citadels the brothers
Held each his separate share,
And by their three names are the cities called.

str. 5 Here then, to make him rich amends
For piteous misfortune, for Tlepolemus,
That ancient leader of the men of Tiryns,
Are set, as for a god,
These flocks, a rich-fed sacrifice,
And the high seat of judgment of the Games.
Whence have their flowers twice crowned Diagoras;
And the famed Isthmus saw him four times victorious,
Nemea once and again, crowned too
In Athens' rock-built city.

ant. 5 And in Argos he knew the prize
Of bronze, and in Arcadia won their awards,
And in Thebes too, and in the Games which honour
Men of Boeotian breed.

str. 5 *These flocks:* the sacrifice would be part of the ceremony at which Pindar's Ode was to be performed.

The high seat of judgment of the Games: Tlepolemus was regarded as the tutelary hero who presided over the Rhodian national games. Ancient commentators aver however that Pindar was here in error, and that these games were celebrated in honour of the Sun.

ant. 5 The many local games of Greek cities awarded prizes of various kinds. At Megara the victors' names were inscribed on a pillar or tablets of stone.

At Pellene and in Aegina
Six times he won; at Megara the pillar
Of stone inscribes a like tale. Ah, great Zeus,
Dwelling on Ataburion's broad shoulder, I pray thee
Honour my song, which sings the rite
Due to Olympia's victor;

ep. 5 And to Diagoras, whose boxing skill proclaims him
A man to valour born, grant him the joy
Of honour in the hearts of his own people,
And strangers too. Straight is the road
He treads, to insolent pride sparing
No mercy. Well he knows the part bequeathed him
Of upright minds from noble ancestry;
Whose seed, forget not, stems from Callianax.
Then in rich honour for the Eratid clan
Small wonder that the city festals ring. And yet,
In one brief breath of time,
Or here or there the changing breezes blow.

Ataburion: the highest mountain in Rhodes, a dominating ridge, on which there is said to have been a temple of Zeus.

ep. 5 *Callianax:* a distinguished ancestor of Diagoras.
The Eratid clan: Eratus was another ancestor, from whom the family of Diagoras took their name.

OLYMPIAN VIII

For

ALCIMEDON OF AEGINA

Winner of the Boys' Wrestling-Match

THIS victory was won in the year 460 B.C., and this Ode was probably composed and performed immediately after the victory. The place of its performance was either at Olympia or at Aegina after Alcimedon's return to his native city. Lines in the first antistrophe suggest the former place, but the references to Aegina in strophe 2 ('this sea-girt land') and in strophe 3 ('this isle') seem to point to Aegina as the place where the Ode was performed. It is perhaps easier to put a broad interpretation on the wording of antistrophe 1 than on the other two passages, and to suppose that, taken in conjunction with the initial invocation to Olympia, the lines express a prayer that the Ode may find favour in the eyes of the deity of Olympia.

The myth, as in other Odes celebrating Aeginetan victors, deals with one of the legends of the clan of Aeacus, the first legendary king of Aegina; in this case the story of the building of the walls of Troy by Apollo and Poseidon, helped by Aeacus.

The prayer with which the Ode concludes, for the continued prosperity of Aegina, reflects the increasing danger to Aegina of the hostility of Athens, which by the date of this Ode had become a severe threat and was shortly to lead to the downfall of the island's independence.

str. 1 O mother of the gleaming crowns of contest,
Olympia, queen of truth,
Where men of prophets' power, proven consultants
Of sacrificial fires, their questioned answer
Demand of Zeus, lord of the lightning flash,
Whether for men who thirst
To win the highest guerdon of true valour,
There be a word to grant their hearts' desire,
And respite from their toils.

str. 1 *Men of prophets' power:* the descendants of Iamus, whose story is told in the sixth Olympian Ode, held the hereditary rights of divination at the altar of Zeus in the Olympian precinct. These lines suggest that Alcimedon had consulted the oracle on his chances of success before entering the contest.

ant. 1 For to the grace of reverent minds is given
The answer to men's prayers.
Then look with favour, Pisa's tree-clad precinct
By Alpheus' stream, on this our song of triumph
And crowned procession. Great fame has he for ever
Who wins your honoured prize.
To one man hence, and to another thence
Are blessings given; many the roads that lead
With heaven's help to good fortune.

ep. 1 For you, Timosthenes, destiny has
Decreed that Zeus be guardian of your race,
Who at Nemea made your name renowned,
And by the hill of Cronos
Gave to Alcimedon Olympia's crown.
Fair was he to behold, and in his deeds
Belied not beauty's form;
King of the wrestlers' ring, he has proclaimed
Aegina his country, land of long-oared galleons,
Where Saviour Themis, throned beside great Zeus
God of the host and guest,

str. 2 Is given abundant worship. For in matters
Of many a purport, veering
On every wind that blows, fitly to make
Due disposition with an upright mind
Is hard indeed. Yet have the immortals ruled
This sea-girt land shall be
For strangers of all race a god-sent pillar
Of true justice; and may the rolling years
Uphold them in this task.

ant. 1 *To one man hence, etc.:* these lines seem to be intended by way of consolation to Alcimedon's elder brother Timosthenes, in that he had won only a Nemean victory while his younger brother had won the greater prestige of an Olympian victory. It was probably Timosthenes who had commissioned this Ode since Iphion, the father of the two brothers, was no longer alive.

ep. 1 *Timosthenes:* see foregoing note.

Zeus was the patron god both of the Nemean and the Olympian Games.

The hill of Cronos: the hill which overlooks Olympia and the temple precincts.

Themis: the goddess of Right.

God of the host and guest: Zeus, amongst his other attributes, was the protector of the laws of hospitality. These lines, together with strophe 2 which follows, are a tribute to the high reputation which Aegina enjoyed for just dealing. Owing to her widespread maritime commerce, traders from many other parts of Greece and the Mediterranean were constant visitors to the island.

ant. 2 Their isle is by a Dorian people governed,
The stock of Aeacus,
Whom long ago the son of Leto summoned
With wide-ruling Poseidon, to join with them
To build a crown of walls for Ilium.
For it was so ordained,
That in the surge of war and battles, wrecking
The pride of cities, then from Troy should pour
Billows of angry smoke.

ep. 2 And when the work was newly built, three serpents
Of fierce grey eyes leapt up to mount the wall,
And two fell back and in a stupor stunned,
Breathed out their spirit's life.
But one sprang over with a mighty cry.
Straightway Apollo pondering on the sign
Spoke and proclaimed it thus:
'Where your hands, hero Aeacus, have laboured
There shall this city Pergamos be taken,
So tells this portent sent by Cronos' son,
Zeus the loud thunderer.

str. 3 'And not without your seed, but to the first
And the fourth generation
The city's rule shall yield.' So spake the god,

ant. 2 *A Dorian people:* the 'Dorian' invasion is the name which came to be given to the movement of Greek-speaking peoples from the north of Greece and beyond, which in the twelfth century B.C. caused the downfall of the Mycenaean civilization and the three hundred years or more of the 'dark ages' of Greece. The Peloponnese received a large share of the invaders, who also spread to the island of Aegina. In later times it became a source of pride to the people of many Greek cities, as it did in the case of Aegina, to be able to claim that they were of 'Dorian' stock.

Aeacus: the first, mythical, king of Aegina and founder of the clan of heroes whom the Aeginetans held in high honour, and from whom several of their leading families claimed descent. The clan included such names as Telamon, Peleus, Ajax and Achilles.

The son of Leto: Apollo. As a punishment for their taking part in the revolt of the gods against himself, Zeus assigned Apollo and Poseidon to be servants to Laomedon, king of Troy, who gave them the task of building the walls of Troy. The two gods, knowing that the walls, if built entirely by divine hands, would be impregnable, called in the mortal Aeacus to help in the work.

Ilium: the original name of Troy, which is also known as Pergamos.

str. 3 *The first and fourth generation:* Telamon the son of Aeacus took part in the destruction of Troy with Heracles, who thus took his revenge upon Laomedon for failing to pay him the reward promised to him for killing a monster who was ravaging the land of Troy. The 'fourth

A word most clear, and sped away to Xanthus,
Driving to meet the Amazons richly horsed,
And to the streams of Ister.
Poseidon with his golden mares bore Aeacus
Home to this isle, and drove his flying chariot
To the Isthmus overseas,

ant. 3 Visiting the hills of Corinth, where are offered
The festals in his honour.
Now one joy cannot please all men alike,
And if I for Melesias raise high
My songs of praise for his young pupil's deeds,
May no sharp stone of envy
Be flung at me. For at Nemea he too
Won a like prize, and again in the struggles
Where grown men match their limbs

ep. 3 In the Pankration. The teacher's skill
Must be of knowledge bred; foolish indeed
Who has not well and truly learnt; a mind
Is but a poor lightweight
Lacking the proof of trial. But here stands one
Who, best of all men, from his own achievements
Can point the forward way
Whence from the sacred games a man may win
That prize the most desired of all. And now
To him Alcimedon's honour has given
His thirtieth victory.

generation' is a reference to Neoptolemus, the son of Achilles and great-grandson of Aeacus, who was one of the Greeks who entered Troy inside the Wooden Horse and thus brought about the second capture and destruction of Troy and the end of the Trojan War.

Xanthus: another name for the river Scamander, close to Troy.

Ister: the river Danube.

This isle: Aegina.

ant. 3 *Melesias:* Alcimedon's trainer. He was an Athenian and appears to have been a trainer of high repute. His name is mentioned in two other Odes, the fourth and sixth Nemean. At the date of this Ode, 460 B.C., the enmity between Athens and Aegina had already reached an acute stage, and this accounts for the cautionary word of self-defence with which Pindar preludes his praise of Melesias in this stanza and the next. Pindar makes it clear that Melesias has been a practising athlete, having, as a boy, won 'a like prize', i.e. as Alcimedon has now done, in the wrestling match at Nemea, and as a grown man in the pankration. As we learn from the last line of epode 3, Alcimedon's victory was the thirtieth gained by one of Melesias' pupils.

ep. 3 *The Pankration:* a combination of boxing and wrestling probably with a wide licence of rules.

str. 4 For this young boy by favour of kind heaven
And his own manly prowess,
Has on four vanquished rivals shed the fear
Of mocking tongues, and a return most hateful,
Flitting in secret through the back-door home;
And on his father's father
Has breathed a vigour to make naught of age;
For in good fortune a man may forget
Thoughts of the world to come.

ant. 4 But I must wake old memories and tell
The flowers of victory
Won by the strong hands of the Blepsiad clan;
Whose brows have now with six crowns been adorned
At the Games where the woven wreath is prized.
Those too who are no more,
Of offerings duly paid them take their share,
And the dust of the grave cannot keep hidden
Their kinsmen's honoured grace.

ep. 4 From Hermes' daughter, the maid Messenger,
Iphion shall hear and to Callimachus
Tell the rich lustre of Olympia's glory,
That Zeus has now bestowed
Unto their race; and may he favour them
With honour upon honour, and ward off
The bitter pains of sickness.
I pray that to their share of noble fortunes
He send no Nemesis of jealous will,
But in prosperity and free from ills,
Exalt them and their city.

str. 4 *Four vanquished rivals:* it seems clear from this phrase that the wrestling contest was a 'knock-out' competition, in which Alcimedon had had to overcome four other competitors.

ant. 4 *The Blepsiad clan:* the name of the family to which Alcimedon belonged.

ep. 4 *Hermes:* the messenger of the gods. The Greek word for 'message' or 'report' is here personified by Pindar to become the daughter of Hermes.

Iphion: probably the father, and *Callimachus* the uncle of Alcimedon; both were no longer alive.

Pains of sickness: the family had presumably suffered losses through illness.

Nemesis: the deity of revenge.

OLYMPIAN IX

For

EPHARMOSTUS OF OPOUS

Winner of the Wrestling-Match

EPHARMOSTUS was a citizen of Opous, a city of Eastern Locris in central Greece to the north of Boeotia. Epharmostus was a noted wrestler, having won victories at all the four Panhellenic Games and at many other local festivals as this Ode records. The date of this Olympian victory was 468 B.C. but the reference to 'Pytho' in the first sentence of antistrophe 1 and later in the same stanza to 'Castalia'—the well known spring at Delphi—indicate that when this Ode was written Pindar knew of the victory which Epharmostus won at the Pythian Games in 466 B.C. This Ode must thus have been not less than two years late in delivery, and this delay is probably connected with the opening lines in which Pindar refers to the chorus of praise, 'the melody of Archilochus', with which the friends of Epharmostus had accompanied him in the victor's procession at Olympia on the evening of his victory. This 'melody of Archilochus' was a short refrain with a repeated chorus, perhaps equivalent to the modern 'See the conquering hero comes' or 'For he's a jolly good fellow'. Pindar's reference to this hardly amounts to an apology, but could perhaps be regarded as at least an acknowledgment of the late arrival of this Ode. 'But now,' Pindar continues, this Ode, 'with a far-ranging flight', will celebrate the occasion really worthily, with a dedication to Zeus the patron god of Olympia and to 'revered Elis' where Olympia lies.

In antistrophe 1 Pindar states the purpose of this poem, to honour the city of Opous and her son. He turns aside for a moment in epode 1 to express a favourite theme found in many other Odes that the good qualities of men are always endowed by 'divine power'—natural or inborn gifts. To illustrate this he quotes stories of Heracles, who as a son of Zeus was semi-divine. Heracles when attacking the city of Pylos fought with Poseidon, who with other gods was defending the city. On another occasion he stole from Delphi the tripod on which the priestess of the oracle sat, and as a result Apollo fought with him: when he carried off the dog Cerberus from the Underworld, Hades fought him. Pindar none the less then expresses, as in the first Olympian Ode, his condemnation of the idea that the gods can be held guilty of criminal acts or violence.

The myth which begins in antistrophe 2 is then devoted to the legend of Deucalion and Pyrrha, the Greek equivalent of the story of Noah and the Flood. Like Noah, Deucalion and Pyrrha built an ark, which came to rest, when the waters subsided, on Mount Parnassus, which lies to the south of the district of Locris. Descending from Parnassus, they founded the city which was later called Opous, and on the orders of Zeus created a new human race out of stones. From this race, Pindar claims, came the ancestors of the people of Locris and of Epharmostus. Strophe 3 tells the further story of the adoption by the childless Locrus, an early king of Locris, of Opous the son of Zeus, who gave his name to the city. In antistrophe 3 we are told how Opous gathered followers from other famous places in Greece, including Menoetius, the father of the famous Patroclus, a native of Locris. The friendship of Patroclus and Achilles, and the death of Patroclus in the Trojan war, form one of the main features of the story told in Homer's *Iliad.*

In epode 2 and onwards the poem returns to the many honours won by Epharmostus. Towards the end Pindar introduces once again the favourite theme, already touched upon earlier in the Ode, of the superiority of natural over acquired gifts, emphasizing that nothing praiseworthy can be achieved without the help of heaven. His praise of Epharmostus ends on this note.

str. 1 Voices that chanted at Olympia
The melody of Archilochus, ringing
With its threefold refrain the victor's praise,
Gave a fit lead to the triumphant march
Of Epharmostus and his loyal friends
Beside the hill of Cronos.
But now with a far-ranging flight
Of arrows from the Muses' bow,
Let us enfold Zeus, lord of the red lightning,
And with a like aim shower
The headland of revered Elis,
Which Lydian hero Pelops long ago
Chose for Hippodamia, a splendid dower.

str. 1 *The melody of Archilochus:* see foreword.

Lydian hero Pelops: Pelops and his father Tantalus came from Lydia in Asia Minor.

Hippodamia: the bride of Pelops, whom he won by defeating her father Oenomaus in a chariot-race in which Oenomaus died. Pelops succeeded him on the throne of Elis, which thus became Hippodamia's 'splendid dower'.

ant. 1 And let an arrow wing its joyful way
To Pytho too. No word of ours shall fall
Spiritless to the ground, while the lyre's notes
Throb through the air to enrich a wrestler's glory,
A man from famous Opous, and to honour
The city and her son.
For Themis and her noble daughter,
Eunomia the preserver, hold
This city a bright jewel in their crown.
Castalia knows well
Her flowers of valour, and Alpheus' stream,
Whose crowns, most prized of all, raise to high fame
This tree-clad city, mother of Locrian men.

ep. 1 Now with the glowing fires of song
Shall I exalt the name of this dear city;
And swifter than a well-bred steed,
Or a ship's wingéd sails,
My message shall go speeding far and wide,
If Fate's decree grants that my hand may till
The precious beauty of the Graces' garden.
For of their gift is every joy,
And from a divine power
Are noble and wise hearts endowed to man.

str. 2 How was it else the hands of Heracles
Could wield his club against the Trident's power,
When by the walls of Pylos stood Poseidon
And pressed him hard; and with his silver bow
Phoebus Apollo menaced him close in battle;
And Hades too spared not
To ply him with that sceptred staff,
Which takes our mortal bodies down
Along the buried road to the dead world.
Away, away this story!
Let no such tale fall from my lips!
For to insult the gods is a fool's wisdom,
A craft most damnéd, and unmeasured boasting

ant. 1 *To Pytho too:* a reference to a victory of Epharmostus at the Pythian Games.
Themis: the goddess of Right.
Eunomia: the personified spirit of Lawfulness.
Castalia: the spring at Delphi, i.e. the Pythian Games.
Alpheus' stream: i. e. Olympia.

str. 2 *The Trident:* the traditional weapon of Poseidon, god of the Ocean. For the story told here, see foreword.

ant. 2 Is music for mad minds. Let no voice babble
Such follies: keep far from the immortal gods
All war and battle. Let Protogenia's city
Play on your tongue, where by decree of Zeus,
God of the lightning's quivering flash, there came
Deucalion and Pyrrha,
Down from Parnassus' height, and first
Made them their home, then without wedlock
Founded a people of one origin,
A race made out of stone;
And from a stone they took their name.
For them raise high your chant of song. Old wine
Praise if you will, but for the flowers of song

ep. 2 Fresh blooms are best. Now the tale runs
That earth's dark soil was flooded by the waters,
But by the arts of Zeus, their strength
Suddenly ebbed again.
And of that race were sprung your ancestors,
Bearers of brazen shields, sons of the maids
Of the stock of Iapetus, and from
The sublime sons of great Cronos.
And ever, since those days,
Have they ruled, kings of this their native land.

ant. 2 *Protogenia:* there were two Protogenias. The first was the daughter of Deucalion and Pyrrha. She married a king of Elis and had a son called Opous. His daughter was the second Protogenia who was carried off by Zeus as related in strophe 3, and became the wife of Locrus, king of Locris.

And from a stone they took their name: the Greek word for 'people' is 'laos' and for a stone 'laas'. The connection assumed here between the two words is however etymologically incorrect, since they have not the same derivation.

ep. 2 *Fresh blooms are best:* Pindar indicates that his version of the genealogy of the Locrian race differs from the story commonly accepted in his time. What the exact differences are we cannot now trace. This sentence is said by an ancient commentator to have been Pindar's answer to a criticism of one of his legends made by the poet Simonides, condemning it as new wine, unmatured.

Iapetus: the grandfather of Deucalion.

Sons of great Cronos: descendants of Opous, the son of Zeus and the second Protogenia.

str. 3 Until it fell that the lord of Olympus
From the Epeians' land bore off the daughter
Of Opous, and the glades of Maenalus
Witnessed their happy union. Then he took her
To Locrus, lest his old age leave him childless.
But his bride held within her
The mighty seed, and he rejoiced
To see a son so given, and named him
By the same name his mother's father bore.
And he grew up to manhood,
In beauty and alike in deeds
Beyond all praise. And Locrus gave to him
The city and its people for his rule.

ant. 3 And many a stranger joined him there, from Argos
From Thebes and from Arcadia and from Pisa.
But chief of all newcomers he bestowed
Honour upon Menoetius, the child
Of Aegina and Actor. His son it was
Came with the sons of Atreus
To the broad plain of Teuthras. There
He with Achilles stood his ground
Alone of all, when Telephus cast back
The warrior Danai
Down on their ships. Well might be seen
By a wise eye the brave heart of Patroclus.
Thereafter, midst the fray of murderous battle,

str. 3 *The Epeians:* inhabitants of Elis.

The daughter of Opous: the second Protogenia, whose son by Zeus was named after his grandfather Opous, and adopted by Locrus the childless king of the Locri. This Opous gave his name to the city of Opous and became its king.

The glades of Maenalus: Maenalus is a mountain in Arcadia.

ant. 3 *Menoetius:* see foreword.

His son: Patroclus.

The sons of Atreus: Agamemnon and Menelaus.

Plain of Teuthras: the kingdom of Teuthras is in Mysia in Asia Minor. When the Greek army under Agamemnon and Menelaus sailed from Greece to begin the war against Troy, the fleet missed its way and landed in Mysia. Telephus, the son of Teuthras, resisted their invasion and drove them back to their ships, but Achilles and Patroclus joined the battle, and Telephus fled, being wounded by the spear of Achilles.

The warrior Danai: Danai, or Danaans, was, like 'Achaeans', a general name used by Homer and other poets for the Greeks of early times.

Thereafter, etc.: in the Trojan war Achilles allowed Patroclus to fight only under his own protection, but when the Trojans were on the point of burning the Greek ships, Patroclus joined the battle without Achilles and was killed by Hector.

ep. 3 The son of Thetis bade him never
Take post save by his own all-conquering spear.
Now may invention grant my tongue,
Riding the Muses' car,
Fit words to tell my tale, and a bold mind
Endow me with wide-ranging power to frame
This song of mine. For I am come to pay
Due homage to Lampromachus,
First, for his Proxeny,
Then for the Isthmian crowns that proved his valour,

str. 4 When he and Epharmostus on one day
Both won the victor's place. And twice again
By the sea gates of Corinth, triumph blessed them.
And Epharmostus in Nemea's valley
And at Argos amongst men won glory,
And amongst boys at Athens.
And barely freed from beardless years,
Finely he matched with older men
At Marathon for the silver prize. His swift
And deftly-balanced craft,
Unthrown himself, felled all his rivals.
How mighty a shout hailed the parading victor,
For youth and beauty and fine deeds achieved.

ant. 4 Amongst the people of Parrhasia too
At the feast of Lycaeon Zeus, they marvelled
To see his skill, and at Pellene also
When he bore off the cloak, that warm protection
From the chill breeze. The tomb of Iolaus
Witnessed his glories too,
And the city Eleusis by the sea.

ep. 3 *Lampromachus:* a friend or relative of Epharmostus who was proxenos (a post equivalent to that of a modern consul) at Opous for the Thebans. It was in all probability Lampromachus who commissioned this Ode from Pindar on behalf of Epharmostus. It appears from these lines that Lampromachus had himself won victories at the Isthmian Games.

str. 4 *Beardless years:* there were three classes of competitors in the Games: grown men, youths (the beardless class) and boys.

ant. 4 *Parrhasia:* a city of Arcadia, whose Games were held near the temple of Zeus which stood near Mount Lycaeon.

Pellene: a city in Achaea in the northern Peloponnese where the prize in their local Games was a woollen cloak.

The tomb of Iolaus: at Thebes; Iolaus was the charioteer of Heracles.

Ever are natural gifts the best,
But many a man struggles to win renown
By skills learnt from a teacher.
But each deed that a man may try
Without heaven's help, is best buried in silence.
Some paths there are may find a further goal

ep. 4 Than may some others, but no single
Study will nurse all men alike to skill.
True art is a steep road to climb.
But treating of this prize
He has now won, be bold with a clear voice
To tell abroad that by the gift of heaven
This man was born strong-handed, nimble-limbed
And in his eyes the light of valour,
And at the feast of Oileus
Has set his victor's crown on Ajax' altar.

ep. 4 *Ajax' altar:* this Ajax, not to be confused with the greater Ajax, the son of Telamon, of the clan of Aeacus, was Ajax the son of Oileus, a legendary hero of Locris. It appears that Epharmostus celebrated his victory at a fête, or banquet, in honour of Oileus, and laid his Olympian crown on the altar of Ajax. Possibly this Ode was performed on that occasion.

OLYMPIAN X (XI)

For

AGESIDAMUS OF EPIZEPHYRIAN LOCRI

Winner of the Boys' Boxing-Match

THIS Ode and Olympian XI which follows were both written for the victory of Agesidamus at the Olympian Games of 476 B.C. This short Ode was written and performed at Olympia immediately after the victory and it contains the promise of a longer Ode to follow, a promise kept after some delay.

Epizephyrian (Western) Locri was a Greek colony on the coast of southern Italy, founded probably by the Locrians of Opous.

Most editions of Pindar's Odes, following the traditional order, place this Ode and the one which follows it in the reverse order of that given to them here. Since lines in both Odes indicate that the present Ode was composed at an earlier date than the one which follows it, it has seemed better, for the sake of clarity, to print them in the order given here.

str. 1 Often man's need is for the wind's breath blowing,
Often he prays from heaven the showering rain,
Child of the cloud. But if success
Wins him the hard-fought crown, then for rich choirs
Of sweet-flown song the debt is entered, prelude
To age-long story for his deeds of valour,
A pledge that will not fail.

ant. 1 Ample this store of praise and gladly given
For Olympia's victors: here my Muse shall tend
Her flock. Yet only of god's giving
In a poet's heart is born the flower of song.
Thus for your boxing skill, Agesidamus,
Son of Archestratus, a poem I pledge you,
Music to herald a rich

ep. 1 Blazon of glory for your crown of olive,
And to bring honour to your race in Locri
Under the western sky.
There join me, Muses, in the songs of triumph;
No grudging hosts I promise shall await you,
But a folk that have dared noble deeds,
Scaling the heights in poetry and in battle.
Well I know
Nor russet fox nor roaring lions can change
Their inborn nature.

OLYMPIAN XI (X)

For

AGESIDAMUS OF EPIZEPHYRIAN LOCRI

Winner of the Boys' Boxing-Match

THIS Ode which Pindar promised in the previous Ode X starts with his apology for the delay in its arrival. The victory of Agesidamus was gained in the Olympian Games of 476 B.C., the same year which saw the victories of Hieron and Theron, celebrated in the first three Olympian Odes, which were written during Pindar's visit to Sicily in that year. It is not surprising that Pindar did not find time for this Ode until later. We do not know how long afterwards it was written and delivered.

After the apology there follows in epode 1 an expression of praise for Locri, and a tribute to Ilas the trainer of Agesidamus. In strophe 2 begins the story, which takes up the greater part of the Ode, of the founding of the Olympian Games by Heracles.

In epode 4 mention of the festal songs which ended this celebration of the first Olympian Games affords a transition to bring us back to Agesidamus and the present Ode. The last triad renews Pindar's apology for the delay in its delivery, comparing it to the late arrival of a long expected son and heir. Then follows some final praise of Locri and of Agesidamus, at whose victory at Olympia Pindar makes it clear that he had himself been an onlooker.

str. 1 Olympian victor, son of Archestratus,
Where on my heart is writ that name?
Read it me now.
For a poem I owed to him, a pleasant song,
And I forgot. Ah Muse, I beg you, and Truth
Daughter of Zeus, with your right hand upraised
Shield me from this reproach of a pledge broken,
And a friend's dues dishonoured.

str. 1 *With your right hand upraised:* the hand of justice, or the hand that crosses off the debt.

ant. 1 For time, eating up the days from long ago,
Has shamed me for my heavy debt;
Yet of this blame
Payment with interest can heal the wound.
Look then, so surely as the surging wave
Sweeps down the rolling pebble, so my song
Honouring you and yours, shall the debt render
And grace the bond of friendship.

ep. 1 For in Locri of the West, Integrity
Has honour. In Music's art
And in brazen War their pride is high. To Cycnus
Yielded the day
Even mighty Heracles. Let Agesidamus,
Victorious in Olympia's boxing contest,
A due tribute
To Ilas render, as of old Patroclus
Gave honour to Achilles.
For he who tempers fine the spirit's blade
In a man to valour born, may with god's help
Bring him to high renown.

str. 2 Few without toil can win the joy that lights
This life for each deed truly done.
The laws prescribed
Of Zeus now bid me sing the matchless contest,
Founded beside the ancient tomb of Pelops

ant. 1 *Payment with interest:* this is perhaps a suggestion that Pindar intends to make this Ode longer than the length commissioned, or in some other way to make it of special value. Some editors take the phrase as evidence that Ode X is the 'interest', and that it was not written and delivered earlier than Ode XI, but at the same time.

ep. 1 *Cycnus:* believed to have been a Locrian freebooter of legendary times who successfully resisted Heracles.

Ilas: the trainer of Agesidamus. The inclusion in an Ode of a tribute to the trainer was sometimes one of the terms of the contract by which the poem was commissioned.

Patroclus: the Locrian s took a special pride in Patroclus, who was a native of Locris in Greece.

str. 2 *The laws prescribed of Zeus:* that is to say the practices of the Olympian Games, laid down in conformity with the requirements of Zeus, their patron god.

Tomb of Pelops: the tomb and sanctuary of Pelops, known as the Pelopion, was a central feature of the precinct of Olympia. Modern archaeology has discovered its remains.

By Heracles, who set six altars there,
After that he had slain Poseidon's son,
The warrior Cteatus,

ant. 2 And Eurytus too he slew, so to exact
From Augeas, that proud despot,
Rewards for service
He would not deign to pay: under Cleonae,
Hiding in ambush on the road, he felled
Those haughty Moliones, and avenged
The day they lay in Elis vale, and ravaged
The host he led from Tiryns.

ep. 2 Nor waited long that lord of the Epeians,
King Augeas, who broke
Faith with his guest, till that he saw his homeland
And all his wealth
In the fell strokes of iron-handed war
Wasted beneath the breath of stubborn flame,
And his own city
Sunk in the pit of doom. Strife with the mighty
Is hard to set aside.
And he in his unwisdom last of all
Fallen into captive chains, could not escape
The headlong sword of death.

str. 3 Then gathering all the host and his rich spoils,
The valiant son of Zeus in Pisa
Measured and founded
In his great father's name a holy precinct,

Six altars: the six twin altars, also referred to in Ol. V. ant. 1.

str. 2, ant. 2, ep. 2 — The fifth Labour of Heracles was the cleansing of the stables of Augeas, king of Elis. Augeas agreed to pay Heracles a tithe of cattle for this task, but on its completion refused to keep his side of the bargain. Later Heracles collected an army from Tiryns and marched into Elis to take his revenge. Cteatus and Eurytus, the 'Moliones', sons of Molione by Poseidon, allied themselves with Augeas and inflicted a defeat on the army of Heracles in Elis, while he was sick. Later Heracles ambushed these two brothers and killed them while they were travelling through Cleonae, a town near Nemea. Heracles raised another army, invaded Elis, sacked the capital city and threw Augeas into prison where he died.

ep. 2 *The Epeians:* a name frequently given to the inhabitants of Elis.

str. 3 *The valiant son of Zeus:* Heracles.

And fenced and marked out on clear ground the Altis,
And the encircling plain he ruled should be
For rest and feasting, to honour Alpheus' river
With the twelve kings divine.

ant. 3 And he named the Hill of Cronos, for long years
While Oenomaus ruled, a hill
Nameless and showered
With winter's snow. Now in that birthday hour
The Fates stood by, this new-established rite
To consecrate, and Time, whose proof at last
Stands the sole judge of Truth that shall abide.
And now the rolling years

ep. 3 Make plain the tale, how from the gifts of war
He set aside the first-fruits,
And after sacrifice founded a feast
For each fourth year,
The first Olympiad and its victors' honours.
Say then, who won the new-appointed crown
For strength of arm,
For speed of foot, or in the chariot's course,
His prayer for victory's glory
Burning within his soul, and thence the crown
Won by his body's act? In the foot-race,
The stadium's straight course,

str. 4 Licymnius' son Oeonus won the day,
Who from Midea led his host.

The Altis: the name given to the enclosure which surrounds the precinct of Olympia.

With the twelve kings divine: the gods to whom the six twin altars (str. 2) were set up. One of these was in honour of Artemis and Alpheus.

ant. 3 *The Hill of Cronos:* the hill beside Olympia.

Oenomaus: the former king of Elis, killed and succeeded by Pelops.

Winter's snow: perhaps an echo of a tradition of a colder climate in far earlier times.

str. 4, ant. 4 *Licymnius:* of the six winners mentioned in this passage nothing is known of three of them, Doryclus, Phrastor and Niceus. The father of *Oeonus, Licymnius,* was the brother of Alcmene, mother of Heracles. His death, perhaps accidental, at the hands of Tlepolemus the son of Heracles which led to the exile of Tlepolemus and his colonization of the island of Rhodes, is told in the seventh Olympian Ode.

In the wrestlers' match
Echemus brought glory to Tegea.
Next Doryclus who dwelt in Tiryns city
Carried the boxer's prize, and in the race
Of four-horsed chariots, Halirothius' son
Samos of Mantinea.

ant. 4 Then Phrastor with the javelin hit the mark,
And Niceus with his circling arm
Won the long throw,
Past all his rivals hurling the disc of stone.
Then from the warrior company flashed forth
A cheer of thundering praise, while to the hour
Of evening's beauty the unclouded moon
Distilled her lovely light;

ep. 4 And all the precinct rang with festal song
In triumph's mode of revel.
Now in this ancient pattern shall my songs,
To grace the name
Of victory's proud spirit, sound the praise
Of thunder and the fire-wrought bolt of Zeus,
Lord of the tumult,
And the almighty symbol of his power,
The lightning's burning stroke.
Then shall the graceful melodies of song
With the flute's note enchant the air, those strains
Promised so long ago

Echemus: king of Tegea, a city to the north of Sparta. At a later date he became famous, according to the legend, by accepting the challenge to single combat of Hyllus the son of Heracles, who was leading an invasion of the Peloponnese from the north. The condition made by Hyllus was that if successful he should be given the throne of Mycenae, but if defeated the invaders would postpone any further attack for 50 years. Hyllus was killed by Echemus and the invasion postponed. This legend derives from the historical Dorian invasions.

Halirothius: the father of Samos, was a son of Poseidon, and so a hereditary charioteer.

ant. 4 *The disc of stone:* by Pindar's time the discs used for 'hurling the discus' were made of copper. In earlier times stones were used, as recorded in Homer.

ep. 4 *The fire-wrought bolt:* the thunderbolt was represented on the coins of Epizephyrian Locri, and also on coins of Elis.

str. 5 From famous Dirke. As when a man, whose years
Have past the surging tides of youth,
Receives with joy
The dear son of his marriage, and his heart
Warms with a father's love—for if the wealth
Of his own house must fall to foreign hands
And strangers' tillage, spells thence a bitter thought,
Bane to his death-bed hour—

ant. 5 Or if a man takes down to Hades' gate
Brave deeds unheralded in song,
Then all in vain
His labour's breath, and brief his span of joy.
But you, Agesidamus, the lyre's rich notes
And the sweet pipe shower with their joyful honour,
And the Pierides, the maids of Zeus,
Make widespread your renown.

ep. 5 With these are linked my songs eager to spread
Their wings o'er Locri's fame,
And on her glorious manhood shed a grace
Sweeter than honey.
Praise have I given to Archestratus' son,
That comely youth, whose strength of arm I saw
That far-off day,
Victorious beside Olympia's altar.
Lovely his body's grace,
That spring-tide hour of beauty, which long since
Freed Ganymede—so willed the Cyprian queen—
From death's relentless power.

str. 5 *Dirke:* the well-known stream near Pindar's Theban home.

ant. 5 *The Pierides:* daughters of Zeus, another name for the Muses.

ep. 5 *Ganymede:* the beautiful youth who was appointed by Zeus to be cup-bearer to the gods.

So willed the Cyprian queen: Aphrodite, goddess of love, had her home at Paphos in Cyprus. This phrase is the poet's way of saying that it was because of his love for Ganymede that Zeus made him immortal.

OLYMPIAN XII

For
ERGOTELES OF HIMERA
Winner of the Long Foot-Race

ERGOTELES was a native of Knossos in Crete. Driven from there by political faction he migrated to Himera in Sicily in or about the year 476, soon after Theron the ruler of Acragas had taken forcible possession of that city, and as part of his reorganization called for new immigrants from Greece. The troubles of Himera were not to cease for some years. Theron gave command of Himera to his son Thrasydaeus whose government was inefficient and tyrannical. The people of Himera rebelled and turned for help to Hieron of Syracuse, who was on the point of becoming involved in open war with Theron, the position which finds its echo in the second Olympian Ode. Hieron gave no help to the people of Himera, but denounced them to Theron, who punished them severely. Theron died in 472 B.C. and was succeeded by Thrasydaeus. War broke out between him and Hieron, who defeated and exiled him and became the ruler of Himera, whose people he treated leniently, giving them their so-called liberty. The invocation in the opening lines of this Ode, addressed to Fortune, the daughter of Zeus, giver of Freedom, reflects this position. The remainder of the strophe and antistrophe reflect equally clearly the unhappy and constantly changing fortunes of Himera in these years, and the consequent vicissitudes of its people, in which Ergoteles no doubt had his own share.

Ergoteles was an athlete of the first rank. It is recorded that he won a second Olympian victory after the one here celebrated, of which the date is 472 B.C., as well as the two Pythian victories and the Isthmian victory mentioned towards the end of this Ode. According to the historian Pausanias he won eight victories altogether at one or other of the national Games. Since we know that the second of his Pythian victories was won in 470, the present Ode must have been written not less than two years after the Olympian victory of 472 which it celebrates.

As Pindar implies in the first half of epode 1 the Cretans rarely, if ever, took part in the Greek national Games. They had however, Games of their own, and were noted for producing good runners. The long foot-race, in which Ergoteles gained this victory, was almost certainly over a course of twenty-four 'stades', or three miles.

str. 1 Daughter of Zeus, who holds the gift of Freedom,
Fortune our saviour goddess,
I pray your guardian care for Himera,
And prosper her city's strength. For your hand steers
The ships of ocean on their flying course,
And rules on land the march of savage wars,
And the assemblies of wise counsellors.
And yet the hopes of man
Now ride on high, now are sunk low,
Cleaving their way through seas of false illusion.

ant. 1 For no man born of earth has ever yet
Found a trustworthy sign
From heaven above, what future days may bring.
Blind are the eyes of our imagination
Of times to come. How often is man's thought
Thwarted by the event, now disappointing
Expected joy, now when a man has met
The surge of sorrow's pain,
In a brief hour of time changing
His bitter grief to profound happiness.

ep. 1 For you, son of Philanor,
Well may we see that like a fighting cock,
Whose skill only his homely hearth may know,
The glory of your racing feet
Had fallen like the fleeting leaves of autumn
Unhonoured to the ground,
Had not revolt, man against man, denied you
Knossos, your own homeland. Now, as it falls,
Winning Olympia's crown, Ergoteles,
Twice victor, too, at Pytho and the Isthmus,
You have brought glory to the Nymphs' warm springs,
Here in this land which is your new-found home.

str. 1 *Savage wars:* the strife and bloodshed from which Himera had been suffering.

ep. 1 *Son of Philanor:* Ergoteles.

A fighting cock: cock-fighting was popular in Greece. Coins of Himera carried the engraving of a cock.

The Nymphs' warm springs: at Himera there were springs of warm water, which are still in existence under the modern name of Termini.

OLYMPIAN XIII

For

XENOPHON OF CORINTH

Winner of the Short Foot-Race and the Pentathlon

THE date of this double Olympian victory of Xenophon was 464 B.C. This Ode, in addition to celebrating Xenophon's unusual feat, is in fact a panegyric in praise of the innumerable athletic victories won by members of Xenophon's clan, the Oligaethidae, and does not omit also to include the praises of the city of Corinth. The structure of the Ode is simple. The first triad sings the glories of Corinth; the second those of Xenophon for his present successes at Olympia, and for his previous victories at the Isthmian and Nemean Games, and commemorates victories won by his father and other near relatives. The third triad turns again to Corinth, and tells of her notable legendary figures, Sisyphus and Medea, and of Glaucus, the leader of the Corinthians of Lycia in Asia Minor, who had settled there in earlier years.

The mention of Glaucus affords the opportunity for the introduction, in epode 3, of the story of his grandfather Bellerophon and the winged horse Pegasus. Bellerophon of Corinth, because of murders he had committed, fled as a suppliant to Proetus king of Tiryns. Proetus' wife Anteia accused him falsely of trying to seduce her. Proetus, enraged, but not willing to commit the sacrilege of killing a suppliant, sent Bellerophon to his wife's father Iobates, king of Lycia, with a secret note asking him to destroy Bellerophon for having tried to violate Anteia. Iobates, unwilling to put to death a guest of royal blood, asked Bellerophon to do him the service of destroying the Chimera, the fire-breathing dragon. Bellerophon consulted the seer Polyeidus on how he should achieve this, and was advised to catch the winged horse Pegasus. How he achieved this, with the help of Pallas Athene, near the Corinthian fountain of Peirene, is described in this Ode (ep. 3–ep. 4). Bellerophon killed the Chimera by flying above her and riddling her with arrows. Iobates then asked Bellerophon to undertake the further task of defeating his enemies the Solymi and their allies the Amazons, the race of feminine warriors. This Bellerophon again achieved by adopting the same tactics. Eventually Iobates was persuaded of Bellerophon's innocence of the offence against Anteia, gave him his daughter in marriage and made him heir to the Lycian throne. Bellerophon at the height of his good fortune was presumptuous enough to try to fly up to heaven on Pegasus. Zeus however sent a gad-fly to sting Pegasus, so that he threw off Bellerophon, who fell to earth. Pegasus continued his flight to heaven, where Zeus kept him, using him as a carrier of thunderbolts. Bellerophon fell into a thorn-bush, and lame, blind, lonely and accursed wandered over the earth until death overtook him.

The fifth triad returns to the athletic feats of other members of the Oligaethid clan, and the Ode ends with a short prayer to Zeus for the family's continued good fortune.

str. 1 Three times victorious at Olympia
Is the house that I praise; the trusted friend
Of fellow-citizens, and to her guests
  A generous host. Herein is mirrored
Corinth the happy city, the proud portal
Of Isthmian Poseidon, and the nurse
    Of glorious youth. Here dwells
Eunomia and that unsullied fountain
Justice, her sister, sure support of cities;
And Peace of the same kin, who are the stewards
    Of wealth for all mankind—
Three glorious daughters of wise-counselled Themis.

ant. 1 Far from their path they hold proud Insolence,
Fierce-hearted mother of full-fed Disdain.
Fair words have I to say, and a bold heart
  Calls to my tongue to speak them frankly;
No man can hide what nature breeds within him.
But to you, sons of Aletes, how often
    The Hours, decked in their wreaths,
Have given the glory of the victor's triumph
For supreme valour in the sacred Games,
All rivals far surpassing, and how often
    For men of your own kin,
Have they implanted in their hearts the skills

str. 1 *Three times:* the two victories of Xenophon won on the same day, which this Ode celebrates, and one gained forty years previously by Xenophon's father Thessalus, in 504 B.C., referred to in ant. 2.
Eunomia: the personified spirit of Lawfulness.
Themis: the goddess of Right.

ant. 1 *Aletes:* an early king of Corinth.

ep. 1 Of ancient times? The inventor's craft
Makes every work of man.
Whence came the graceful dithyramb
Of Dionysus with its prize of oxen?
Who first with harness tamed the horse's power?
Or on the temples of the gods
First set the double image of the eagle?
The sweet breath of the Muse adorns your city,
And your young warriors with their dreaded spears
To Ares pay full honour.

str. 2 O sovereign lord, who rules Olympia,
Grant, father Zeus, your blessing for all time
Upon my songs, and let no mischief touch
This people; and for Xenophon
Grant to his lot the fair breeze of good fortune.
And pray accept for him this chant of triumph
For the crowns that he brings
From Pisa's plain, where first he won the prize
In the Pentathlon contest, then again
Crowned victor in the foot-race of the stade.
Never before this day
Has one man thus achieved this double glory.

ep. 1 *Dithyramb:* the invention or development of the dithyramb is attributed to Arion of Corinth in the seventh century B.C., although elsewhere Pindar attributes its invention to the island of Naxos or to Thebes. It was a form of poetry and music associated especially with festive occasions, and with the god Dionysus.

Prize of oxen: the meaning of this phrase is uncertain. It may refer to the prize given to the victor in a dithyramb competition, or possibly it relates to the symbolical identification of Dionysus with a bull.

First with harness: this does not refer to the invention of the bit, the story of which is told later in this Ode, but to the improved methods of controlling horses which Pindar attributes to the Corinthians.

The double image of the eagle: this seems to mean that the Corinthians were the first to place two eagles as 'finials' on their temples, one on each gable.

Ares: the god of war.

str. 2 *Pisa's plain:* Olympia.

The Pentathlon: a contest made up of five events, the foot-race, the long-jump, hurling the discus, hurling the javelin, and the wrestling match.

The stade: the single stade was a race of about 200 yards, the short foot-race: the double stade one of twice that length.

ant. 2 Twice too the wreath of parsley on his brow
Declared him victor at the Isthmian Games,
Nor can Nemea tell a different story.
And by the banks of Alpheus' river,
The lightning speed of foot of Thessalus,
His father, is inscribed in glory's roll.
In the foot-race at Pytho,
Both for the single and the double stade,
In one brief day he took the prize of honour;
And the same month in Athens rock-built city
A day of sparkling feet
Set on his locks three times the crown of splendour.

ep. 2 Seven crowns Hellotia's feast presented;
And where Poseidon guards
Between two seas the rules of contest,
Too long 'twould be to sing of Ptoiodorus,
His grandfather, or tell of Terpsias
And Eritimus. And your triumphs
On Delphi's field, or on the Lion's plain,
I would defy a host of men to match;
As easy would it be for me to number
The pebbles of the ocean.

str. 3 But for all things there is a measure set:
To know the due time, therein lies true skill.
Now I, one man charged with a common purpose,
Whether I sing the ancient wisdom,
Or of the wars and the heroic valour
Of Corinth and her ancestors, no falsehood
Shall dwell upon my tongue—

ep. 2 *Hellotia' :feast:* a festival held at Corinth in honour of the goddess Athene.

Between two seas: the Isthmian Games, sacred to Poseidon.

Terpsias, Eritimus: members of Xenophon's family, whose exact relationship to him we do not know, probably uncles or near relatives.

Your triumphs: victories won by members of his clan.

Delphi's field: the Pythian Games.

The Lion's plain: the Nemean Games. The killing of the Nemean Lion was one of Heracles' well-known exploits.

str.3 *To know the due time:* Pindar frequently points to the importance of the right timing of deeds or words, particularly in reference to poetic composition. Here he seems to imply that although he could continue at still greater length the enumeration of the many victories of Xenophon's relatives, this would not be consistent with the proper planning of this Ode.

Sisyphus, with a craftsman's hand of genius
Like to a god: Medea who defied
Her father's word, and took of her own will
The husband of her choice,
And saved the Argo and her warrior crew:

ant. 3 Or again in the heroic strife of old
Beneath the walls of Troy, your valiant sons
Were deemed to sway the battle on either side,
Some faithful to the sons of Atreus,
Striving to rescue Helen, others resisting
With all their warrior might. For when there came
Glaucus from Lycia,
The Danaans' hearts were chill with deadly fear,
Hearing him boast that in Peirene's city
His own forbear once held the sovereign power,
And the great heritage
Of kingly palace and wide patrimony:

ep. 3 That grandsire who once strove in vain
Beside Peirene's spring,
And suffered much, seeking to yoke
The snake-head Gorgon's offspring, Pegasus.

Sisyphus: the legendary founder of Corinth. For his various misdeeds, he was condemned by Zeus to eternal punishment—to roll a gigantic stone up to the brow of a hill and topple it down the farther slope. But just as he reaches the summit the stone falls back again to the bottom.

Medea: some traditions, which Pindar follows here, allow Medea, the famous sorceress, to have had her origins in Corinth. The usual story makes her the daughter of Aeëtes, king of Colchis, on the Black Sea coast. Medea fell in love with Jason, the leader of the Argonauts, and helped him by her magic to obtain the Golden Fleece, in spite of the fierce obstructions of Aeëtes. When the Argonauts made their escape, Medea accompanied them as Jason's bride.

ant. 3 *On either side:* the Lycians of Asia Minor were descendants of emigrants from Corinth. In the Trojan war they were allies of Troy, while the Corinthian forces fought with the Greeks under Agamemnon.

Glaucus: the Lycian leader whose meeting on the battlefield with Diomede, the famous Greek warrior, is told in the sixth book of Homer's *Iliad.*

Peirene's city: Corinth. Peirene was the name of a fountain on Acrocorinthus, the high rock citadel of Corinth.

His own forbear: Bellerophon, the grandfather of Glaucus.

ep. 3 *Pegasus:* the winged horse, the offspring of Poseidon and Medusa before she was turned into the snake-headed Gorgon.

Till Pallas, goddess maid, brought him the bridle
  And golden headband, and behold
A dream was truth. 'Sleep not, Aeolid king,
Said she, 'but take this charm of steeds, and offer
The Horse-Tamer, your sire, a snow-white bull,
    And show to him this bridle.'

str. 4 Such words, as he lay slumbering in the dark,
It seemed the maiden of the shadowy aegis
Spoke unto him, and he leapt to his feet
  And seized the magic bit, that lay
Beside him on the ground; and went with joy
To find the prophet of his country's people
    The son of Koiranus.
And he made known to him the whole issue
Of this strange matter—how that he had lain
The whole night through upon the goddess' altar,
    As the seer had foretold him,
And how the child of Zeus, whose sword is lightning,

ant. 4 In her own hands brought him the golden charm
That tames the savage spirit. And the prophet
Bade him obey at once the magic vision,
  And to Poseidon, the earth-holder,
To sacrifice the strong-limbed bull. Then too
That he should build an altar with all speed
    To Athene, queen of steeds.
Yet the gods' power can lightly bring to pass
Such things as will deny both the sworn word
And all the hopes of men. Thus with all zeal
    Mighty Bellerophon
Seized the winged steed, setting between his jaws

Aeolid king: Bellerophon was descended from Aeolus, god of the winds.

The Horse-Tamer, your sire: 'sire' means ancestor. The Horse-Tamer is Poseidon, who was the reputed father of Aeolus.

str. 4 *The shadowy aegis:* the traditional shield carried by Pallas Athene. The origin of the name was a goat-skin, worn as a protection; hence its stock epithet 'dark' or 'shadowy'.

The son of Koiranus: Polyeidus of Corinth, a noted seer.

ant. 4 *Queen of steeds:* the goddess Athene was often associated with horses

ep. 4 The soothing charm, and mounting him,
In his bronze panoply
Played him in sport, to try his pace.
And once, with him, he smote the Amazons,
From the chill bosom of the lonely air,
That archered host of women-kind;
And felled Chimera breathing fire, and slew
The Solymi. His fate—'twere best unspoken.
But Pegasus dwells in the ancient stalls
Of Zeus upon Olympus.

str. 5 But for my words, like whirring javelins
Sped on their course, let not my eager strength
Launch such a shower of darts wide of the mark.
For I come with intent to honour
The Muses on their glorious thrones, and pay
Like service to the Oligaethidae.
No more than a brief word
Must tell their thronging triumphs at the Isthmus,
And at Nemea; but the trusty herald,
Chanting his welcome cry at either contest
Attests with me the truth
Of sixty victories won by this clan.

ant. 5 And of their prizes at Olympia
My song has told already. If more shall come,
Then should I ring their praises loud and clear.
Now I must hope; yet will the issue
Lie in the hands of heaven. But if the genius
Of their inheritance plays its true part,
Then shall we trust in this
To Zeus and Ares for the accomplishment.
Six crowns they won beneath Parnassus' brow,
More at Argos and Thebes; in Arcady,
There will the sovereign altar
Of Zeus Lycaeus testify their deeds.

ep. 4 *The Amazons, etc.:* see foreword for the incidents mentioned in this epode.

str. 5 *The Oligaethidae:* the clan to which Xenophon belonged.

ant. 5 *Parnassus' brow:* i.e. at the Pythian Games. Mount Parnassus overlooks Delphi.

Zeus Lycaeus: Parrhasia, city of Arcadia, held its Games near the temple of Zeus which stood near Mount Lycaeon.

ep. 5 Pellene too, and Sicyon
And Megara saw them victors,
And the Aeacid strong-built precinct;
Eleusis too and Marathon's fair plain,
And the rich cities by the soaring height
Of Aetna; from Euboea and all
Hellas, a search would find more than the eye
Could see. Now on light feet, we say farewell.
Zeus, who brings all to pass, pray grant them honour,
And fortune's dearest joys.

ep. 5 *The Aeacid precinct:* the island of Aegina. Aeacus was the first legendary king of Aegina.

On light feet: in compliment to the racing feet of Xenophon.

OLYMPIAN XIV

For

ASOPICHUS OF ORCHOMENUS

Winner of the Boys' Foot-Race

ORCHOMENUS was an ancient city of Boeotia, the home of the Minyan race in Mycenaean times. The city maintained the old cult of the three Graces, and the present Ode is as much a eulogy of the Graces as of the boy Asopichus for whose Olympian victory it was written. The date of the victory and of this Ode is uncertain but was probably 488 B.C., when Pindar was thirty years old. If so, it is the earliest of Pindar's Olympian Odes.

str. 1 Whose haunts are by Kephissus' river,
You queens beloved of poets' song,
Ruling Orchomenus, that sunlit city
And land of lovely steeds,
Watch and ward of the ancient Minyan race,
Hear now my prayer, you Graces three.
For in your gift are all our mortal joys,
And every sweet thing, be it wisdom, beauty
Or glory, that makes rich the soul of man.
Nor even can the immortal gods
Order at their behest the dance and festals,
Lacking the Graces' aid;

str. 1 *Kephissus' river:* a river near Orchomenus in Boeotia.
Minyan race: the Minyans were a people of early origin who inhabited Eastern Thessaly and Boeotia. They were the Vikings of Greek legend.
The Graces: a cult of the three Graces was prominent at Orchomenus. Their names are variously given in different ancient writers. Pindar follows the pattern of names given in the second strophe, associated with the qualities mentioned in the first strophe: Euphrosyne, wisdom or talent, particularly poetic talent; Thalia, beauty; Aglaia, glory.

Who are the stewards of all rites of heaven,
Whose thrones are set at Pytho
Beside Apollo of the golden bow,
And who with everlasting honour
Worship the Father, lord of great Olympus.

str. 2 Euphrosyne, lover of song,
And Aglaia revered, daughters
Of Zeus the all-highest, hearken, and with Thalia,
Darling of harmony,
Look on our songs of revel, on light feet
Stepping to grace this happy hour.
For in this Lydian measure, harvested
From the rich fruits of mind, I come to praise
Asopichus, whose Minyan house, Thalia,
Now of your favour wears the pride
Of the Olympian victor. Then let Echo
Speed to Persephone's
Dark-walled dwelling, to his father Cleodemus
Bearing the glorious tidings,
That his young son, matched in the famous games
Of Pisa's far-renownéd vale,
Has set the wingéd garland on his brow.

Beside Apollo: the Graces had, like the Muses, a natural affinity with Apollo, the god of prophecy, music and the arts.

str. 2 *Lydian measure:* the Lydian 'mode', to which the music for this Ode was set, appears to have been especially suitable for poetry of a light and graceful type.

Persephone: the wife of Hades, and queen of the Underworld. Cleodemus, the father of Asopichus, was no longer alive.

'*Wingéd garland*': literally 'has crowned his brow with wings'. The use of the term 'wings' for the victor's wreath occurs in one other passage in Pindar (Pythian Ode IX. ep. 5). This may be merely a picturesque phrase, or it may have some connection with the idea expressed in many monuments of antiquity, picturing a Winged Victory proffering a wreath to the victor.

PYTHIAN I

For

HIERON OF AETNA

Winner of the Chariot-Race

This Ode was written for a victory won by Hieron in the chariot-race at the Pythian Games of 470 B.C. By this date Hieron had reached the summit of his power, and Pindar makes of this poem not merely an epinician Ode but a panegyric in praise of Hieron's successes and virtues, almost a portrait of the ideal sovereign.

The victory over the Carthaginians at Himera in 480 B.C., in which Hieron took part—his elder brother Gelon was in command of the Greek forces—and the naval victory of the Syracusan fleet over the Etruscans in 474 off Cumae in southern Italy had staved off if not finally removed these external threats to the Greek cities of the west. Hieron succeeded to the rule of Syracuse in 478 B.C. and had been steadily building up his power. In 472 B.C. Theron, the powerful ruler of Acragas, died and was succeeded by his son Thrasydaeus who was foolish enough to quarrel with Hieron. He was completely defeated and fled overseas. The city of Acragas was leniently treated, and under a new government was unlikely to cause Hieron further trouble. Such, in brief, was the political situation when this Ode was written, and it makes reference to the various events, though only indirectly in the case of the recent trouble with Thrasydaeus.

Not long after 480 B.C. Hieron had turned out the inhabitants of Catana and Naxos on the east coast of Sicily, who seem to have been potential sources of opposition to him, and founded in their place a new city of Aetna. He peopled it with 5,000 immigrants from the Peloponnese and 5,000 from Syracuse, and established in it a 'Dorian', that is to say aristocratic or oligarchic, adminstration, the type of government for which Pindar frequently, as in the present Ode, expresses his approbation. It is clear that Hieron took great interest and pride in the city of Aetna, not only because it gave him the prestige which in Greek eyes attended the founder of a new city, but because he intended it to be the future home of his family. The rule of Syracuse, which he had inherited from his elder brother Gelon, was due to pass on his death to his younger brother Polyzelus. Deinomenes, Hieron's young son, was therefore designated as the ruler of Aetna, as this Ode makes clear. An indication of Hieron's pride in his new city is that he caused the Pythian victory here celebrated to be proclaimed as that of 'Hieron of Aetna', a point to which the Ode does not fail to draw attention.

Except for the short passage on Philoctetes, there is no myth in this Ode, and the section where it would normally occur is devoted to the praises of Hieron. The poem opens with a tribute to the power of music, then embarks on a vivid description of Mount Aetna in eruption, of which Pindar must at some time have been an eyewitness, no doubt during his visit to Sicily in 476–75 B.C. There is no evidence to show that he visited Sicily when he wrote this Ode, though it is clear that it was written for performance at the city of Aetna.

Pindar's reference to Philoctetes in the third triad derives from the fact that for a good many years before his death in 467 B.C. Hieron was suffering from an illness, and is said to have been carried to his campaigns on a litter. The legend of Philoctetes tells that he was left on the island of Lemnos by the Greek army while on their way to the Trojan war, because he was suffering from a poisoned wound. Ten years later, when Troy was still untaken, an oracle declared that the city could not be captured without the help of the arrows of Heracles, which had been given by him, when he died, to Philoctetes. The Greeks therefore sent two of their chief leaders, Odysseus and Diomede, to Lemnos to persuade Philoctetes to come to their aid. Though still crippled by his wound, he was brought to Troy, killed the Trojan prince, Paris, with his arrows, and the city was captured soon afterwards. Pindar emphasizes the parallel with Hieron in the third antistrophe, 'Proud hearts have fawned on him . . .'. This may be a general reference to the growth of Hieron's power and prestige, or may point to a particular event, possibly the submission of the rulers of Acragas after the defeat of Thrasydaeus referred to above.

In the fourth antistrophe and epode Pindar makes reference to the famous battles of Salamis, 480 B.C., and Plataea, 479 B.C., the victories by which the Greeks of the mainland dispelled the menace of Persian conquest. In the same passage he refers to the battle of Himera in Sicily, 480 B.C.—in which Hieron took part—which dispelled the simultaneous and equally grave threat to the Greeks of Sicily and South Italy of the power of Carthage. Also mentioned in this passage is the later naval victory of 474 B.C. of the Syracusans under Hieron off Cumae, a town of South Italy, which put an end to the threat of the Etruscans, at that time the strongest military power in Italy. Pindar's reference to Himera and Cumae in the same breath with his mention of Salamis and Plataea has the implication, as he no doubt intended, that Hieron can take his place as one of the great saviours of civilization. To an audience keenly conscious of the importance of these comparatively recent events—the date of this Ode was 470 B.C.—this passage would appear a most effective climax to Pindar's praises of Hieron.

From words of praise, Pindar proceeds in the fifth triad to words of advice—one of the many passages in the Odes from which it can be judged that he regarded it as part of the poet's function to preach as well as to praise. It seems that in addressing a ruler of such eminence as Hieron, Pindar felt drawn to exercise this function even more freely than usual. This triad is prefaced in strophe 5 by lines expressing the need for good writing to be brief and to the point, advice found in more than one other Ode. The lines also suggest that though the praises of Hieron could be continued still further, Pindar must not allow them to run on too long. Before the end of the poem the familiar theme finds expression that enduring fame can only be secured by the work of writers and poets.

str. 1 O glorious lyre, joint treasure of Apollo,
And of the Muses violet-tressed,
Your notes the dancers' step obeys, leading
The festal's joyous glory;
And the singers heed your bidding,
When on the vibrant air your prelude strikes,
To guide the harmonies of choral song.
Your power subdues the lightning's sword
Of everlasting flame. On the sceptre
Of Zeus, his swift wings folded on his side,
The eagle sleeps, the king of birds,

ant. 1 When o'er his arching head your melodies
Have thrown a mist of shadowy dark,
A gentle seal upon his eyes. And he slumbers,
His smooth and supple back
Rising and falling, held
By your flowing tones in thrall. And strong-armed Ares
Lays far aside his harshly-pointed spears
And soothes his soul in mellow dream;

And on the immortals' hearts your shafts instil
A charméd spell—by grace of Leto's son
 And the low-girdled Muses' skill.

ep. 1 All things that Zeus loves not fall riven down
Before the voice of the Pierides,
Whether on land or on the restless sea;
He too, that enemy of the gods, who lies
 In fearsome Tartarus,
Typhon the hundred-headed, who long since
Was bred in the far-famed Cilician cave.
Today the cliffs that bar the sea o'er Cumae
 And Sicily's isle, press heavy on
His shaggy breast, and that tall pillar rising
To the height of heaven, contains him close—Aetna
 The white-clad summit,
Nursing through all the year her frozen snows.

str. 2 From the dark depths below she flings aloft
 Fountains of purest fire, that no
Foot can approach. In the broad light of day
 Rivers of glowing smoke
 Pour forth a lurid stream,

ant. 1 *Leto's son:* Apollo.
Low-girdled: this is the stock epithet applied to the Muses, and sometimes also to the Graces and to other women or goddesses. In the sculpture of ancient Greece, statues of women, other than some figures of nymphs or goddesses, are commonly attired in flowing robes with folds falling over a low girdle. To the Greek mind this epithet when applied to the Muses no doubt served mainly to suggest fertility of ideas and generosity in giving inspiration.

ep. 1 *The Pierides:* another name for the Muses.
Typhon: this mythical monster, the largest ever born, was the son of Mother Earth and Tartarus. As well as having a hundred heads, he consisted from the legs down of coils of serpents and instead of hands had innumerable serpent heads. He attacked Zeus and the other gods and almost overcame them, but was eventually overcome by the thunderbolts of Zeus, who hurled Mount Aetna on top of him. This legend probably derives partly from early struggles between the Hellenes, who worshipped Zeus and the patriarchal gods of Olympus, with non-Hellenic tribes whose religion was based on the earlier worship of the great Earth Mother.
Cilician cave: Typhon's birthplace in Asia Minor.
Cumae: on the west coast of southern Italy. Pindar pictures Typhon as lying underneath all the volcanic area of Sicily and south Italy.

And in the dark a red and rolling flood
Tumbles down boulders to the deep sea's plain
In riotous clatter. These dread flames
That creeping monster sends aloft, a marvel
To look on, and a wondrous tale even
To hear, from those whose eyes have seen it.

ant. 2 Such is the being bound between the peaks
Of Aetna in her blackened leaves
And the flat plain, while all his back is torn
And scarred by the rough couch
On which he lies outstretched.
O Zeus, grant us thy grace, lord of this mountain
Fronting a fruitful land, the peak whose name
Her famous founder has bestowed
To be the glory of its neighbour city:
Whose name the herald spoke at Pytho's games,
Proclaiming in the chariot-race

ep. 2 Hieron the victor. Men who sail the sea
Ask first the blessing of a kindly breeze
To set their voyage forth: better then their hope
For prosperous return to mark its end.
So let us reckon now
From this success, hereafter shall this city
Win glorious honour for her victors' crowns
And racing steeds, and in the banquet-songs
Win wide renown. O Lycian Phoebus,
Ruler of Delos, lover of the fountain
Castalia by Parnassus, may this prayer
Live in your heart,
And make this land a mother of brave men.

str. 2 *That creeping monster:* Typhon with his serpents.

ant. 2 *This mountain:* Mount Aetna.

ep. 2 *Lycian Phoebus:* the epithet 'Lycian' seems to have derived from an early legend which located the birth-place of Apollo in Lycia in Asia Minor. A line in Homer refers to him as 'born in Lycia'. The island of Delos however came to be his generally-accepted place of birth.

Castalia: the spring close to Delphi, beneath Mount Parnassus.

str. 3 For from the gods comes every skilled endeavour
Of mortal quality, be it
Wisdom, or strength of arm, or eloquence.
So when the praise I purpose
Of this great man, let not
My song fall like a bronze-tipped javelin
Flung from the hand astray outside the line,
But may a lengthy throw outstrip
Its every rival. May future days, as now,
Keep safe his wealth and great possessions, and grant him
Forgetfulness of times of toil.

ant. 3 Well might he call to mind the wars and battles
Which he endured with steadfast soul,
When there was won, under god's hand, such honour
As no man in all Hellas
Has reaped e'er now, a proud
And lordly crown of wealth. Like Philoctetes
Has he today taken the path of war:
And when their bitter need constrained them
Proud hearts have fawned on him to win his friendship.
To Lemnos once, they tell, there came those heroes
Of godlike fame, to bear away

ep. 3 The archer son of Poias, who lay wasted
With lingering wounds; who destroyed Priam's city,
To end the long toils of the Danai.
Feeble his step and sick his body's form,
But thus had Fate ordained.
So too may a god's hand be near to guide
Hieron's path through all the years to come,
And grant fufilment of his heart's desires.
For Deinomenes too, sing, Muse
This praise of the four-horsed car. His father's crown
Can be no alien joy to him. Come then,
For Aetna's king
Let us unfold a song to charm his soul.

str. 3 *Bronze-tipped javelin, etc.:* in the javelin contest there was no target, but the prize went to the longest throw. If a badly-aimed throw crossed the side-lines it was disqualified.

ant. 3 *Philoctetes:* see foreword.

ep. 3 *Son of Poias:* Philoctetes.
Deinomenes: Hieron's young son.
Aetna's king: Deinomenes.

str. 4 For him has Hieron founded this fair city
In freedom built of heaven's will,
Within the pattern of the laws of Hyllus;
For sons of Pamphylus,
Yes, of great Heracles,
Who dwell beneath Taygetus' height, love ever
To abide under Aigimius' laws of Doris.
Coming from Pindus' distant mount
They held Amyclae's city in wealth and fame,
Neighbours of the white-horsed Tyndaridae:
And great the glory of their spears.

ant. 4 Zeus, who brings all to pass, grant to this city
Beside the banks of Amenas,
That such fair fortune men's report may ever,
In words of truth, assign
To her citizens alike,
And to her kings. With thy aid may her prince,
Charging likewise his son, honour her people
And bring them harmony and peace.
I pray thee, Cronos' son, let no Phoenician
Or Tuscan war-cry stir from home, who saw
Their pride of ships wrecked before Cumae—

str. 4 *Hyllus:* a son of Heracles, the reputed leader of an early and unsuccessful invasion of the Peloponnese by the Dorians.

Pamphylus: another Dorian leader.

The sons . . . of Heracles: the descendants of Heracles, regarded as important leaders of the Dorian invaders; many Peloponnesians claimed descent from them.

Taygetus: the highest mountain of the Peloponnese, not far from Sparta.

Aegimius: an early king of one of the invading peoples.

Pindus . . . Amyclae: Mount Pindus in N. West Greece, and Amyclae, a city south of Sparta, represent approximately the north to south progress of the Dorian invasion. Described here in a single sentence, it was in fact a gradual process extending over a long period of time.

Tyndaridae: the Spartans—sons of Tyndareus, king of Sparta.

ant. 4 *Amenas:* a stream near the city of Aetna.

Phoenician: Carthage, on the north coast of Africa, was a colony of the Phoenicians, whose country, with the cities of Tyre and Sidon, lay on the Mediterranean coast of Syria.

Cumae: for this reference to the naval battle of Cumae, 474 B.C., and to the battles of Salamis, Plataea and Himera in the following epode, see the foreword.

ep. 4 That ruin laid upon them by the leader
Of Syracusan warriors, who hurled
Their flower of youth from their swift ships of war
Down to the ocean wave, and saved Hellas
From grievous slavery.
From Salamis, in thanks from men of Athens,
I shall seek my reward; in Sparta's city
Tell of Kithaeron's battle, where disaster
Came to the Medes with curving bows.
But by the fertile shores of Himera
The sons of Deinomenes fill the song,
Which for their valour
They won amidst the downfall of their foes.

str. 5 To tell a timely tale, weaving a pattern
Of many threads in brief compass,
Wins less reproach of men; for dull surfeit
Blunts eager expectation,
And to recount the praise
Of other men burdens a citizen's heart
With hidden anger. Yet since envious eyes
Hurt less than looks of pity, renounce
No good design. With justice at the helm
Govern your people's course, and on the anvil
Of truth let all your words be forged;

ant. 5 Should but a trivial spark flash from your tongue,
From you 'twill seem a light inspired;
You are the steward of many, and many can bear
True witness to your deeds,
Be they or this or that.

ep. 4 *From Salamis:* in this rather ambiguously worded sentence Pindar means that the best way for him to earn the gratitude of the Athenians is by praising the glorious part they played at the battle of Salamis. This praise is implied in the present passage, but this is probably also a reference to the famous dithyramb which he wrote in 474 B.C.—a poem of which his audience would be well aware—extolling Athens as the 'bulwark of Hellas' against the Persian invaders (Dithyramb 76). The next sentence pays a similar tribute to the Spartans for the victory of Plataea, in which their forces played a major part. The final lines of the epode praise '*the sons of Deinomenes*' i.e. Gelon and his brother Hieron for their part in the battle of Himera.

Kithaeron's battle: Plataea lies close to Mount Kithaeron in Boeotia.
The Medes: an alternative name for the Persians.

str. 5 See foreword on this passage.

Guard well the fair flower of your spirits' temper;
Would you have sweet praise ever in your ear.
  Let not your purse-strings tire of spending,
But like a pilot spread to the winds your sail;
Nor be deceived, my friend, by tempting gains.
  Only in chronicle and song

ep. 5 Is known beyond the grave the sounding glory
Of how they fared in life who are no more.
The generous heart of Croesus cannot die;
But for his burnings in the brazen bull,
    Phalaris' ruthless soul
Earns hate and infamy from all mankind;
Not for him sounds the blended harmony,
Under the roof-trees echoing to the lyre,
  Of children's lips in soft refrain.
First in life's contest is to win good fortune,
Next is to hold an honourable name;
      He who can find
And grasp both these, has gained the highest crown.

ep. 5 *Croesus:* the sixth century B.C. ruler of Lydia in Asia Minor, whose enormous wealth was, and has remained, a by-word. Pindar's use of this stock example of great riches, in a Pythian Ode, was perhaps because of the generous gifts that Croesus made to the temple of Delphi.

Phalaris: an early tyrant of the Sicilian city of Acragas who burnt his enemies in a brazen bull.

PYTHIAN II

For

HIERON OF SYRACUSE

Winner of the Chariot-Race

THIS Ode, placed since early times amongst the Pythian Odes, was certainly not written to celebrate a victory at the Pythian or any other Panhellenic festival. If it had been, the Ode would have mentioned this. It was probably written for a victory won at some minor games, of whose locality and date we have no knowledge. The chariot victory is in fact given only one brief mention in the opening stages of the Ode.

The poem is of special interest in that it has the character and tone of a private and intimate letter written by Pindar on matters of serious concern to him, rather than that of an epinician ode. It is in fact a plea to Hieron, expressed in the strongest terms, that he should not allow the friendship and trust which he had previously accorded to Pindar to be undermined by the intrigues and misrepresentations of Pindar's enemies. The main theme of the Ode is the importance of gratitude for favours received—'A friendly deed will ever stir the grace of reverent praise' (ep. 1)—and *per contra*, the punishment that attends the lack of such gratitude. This is illustrated by the myth of Ixion, who was punished for his treacherous ingratitude to Zeus by being tied eternally to a revolving wheel—not the happiest story for an epinician ode, but appropriate to Pindar's theme, and vividly told. In later sections of the Ode Pindar praises Hieron in the highest terms, and in denouncing slanderers and mischief-makers makes it clear that such methods are no part of his own equipment, but that his praises of Hieron are those of an honest man, speaking truths well deserving of Hieron's belief.

The points that this Ode makes are clear enough. What is more difficult, in the absence of clear dating, is to know what were the circumstances which provoked this poem and its emotional outburst. Its intimate tone would obviously not have been possible before Pindar had become personally known to Hieron during his visit to Sicily in 476–75 B.C., and that it was written after Pindar's return to Greece is clear from lines which state that Pindar is sending the Ode to Hieron across the sea. In his second Olympian

Ode, written while he was in Sicily, Pindar makes caustic comments against rival poets—'a pair of ravens' (Ol. II. str. 5)—almost certainly directed against the poets Simonides and his nephew Bacchylides. Simonides is believed to have been in Sicily at this time. Pindar may well have had reason to suspect the two poets of intrigues against him during these years at the court of Hieron, and have written the present Ode as a counter to their designs. If so it is likely that the poem was written in or not long after the year 475 B.C.

Another view is that this Ode was written in 468 B.C., after Hieron had won his chariot victory in the Olympian Games of that year. Eight years previously, in his first Olympian Ode celebrating Hieron's victory in the horse-race, Pindar had expressed the hope that he would before long be able to write in honour of a victory by Hieron in the Olympian chariot-race, the event which was held in the highest prestige, and for which Pindar says that his Muse 'nurses her strongest dart of all' (Ol. I. ep. 4). When this success at last came to Hieron, he did not commission an Ode to celebrate it from Pindar, but from Bacchylides, who wrote his third Ode for the occasion. It is thought that the present Ode may have been the result of Pindar's angry disappointment at being thus overlooked in favour of his hated rival. It is not easy however to reconcile this view with the superlative praises of Hieron which this Ode expresses. These, including a remarkable line (ep. 3) in which Pindar calls upon Hieron to be the man that he is, seem more appropriate to an appeal to Hieron to avoid an act of ingratitude to Pindar than to an expression of anger and disappointment that such an act had already been committed. The reference to Zephyrian Locri (ep. 1) also points to an earlier rather than a later date, since the event referred to (the saving of the city by Hieron from the hostile designs of Anaxilas of Rhegium) occurred in 478 B.C. Pindar closely contrasts the gratitude of this city with the ingratitude of Ixion. It seems more likely that he would have used this event in this way if it had occurred only three or four years before, than if he was writing in 468, ten years later.

str. 1 Great city of Syracuse, precinct of Ares
The god of surging war, you divine nurse
Of men and horses in their armoured pride,
Now in your honour am I come
From sunlit Thebes,
Bringing this music to proclaim
The four-horsed team, striding the trembling earth
Which has given victory to Hieron,
Lord of the chariot's speed.
With wreaths of shining glory has he crowned
Ortygia, seat of the river-goddess
Artemis, by whose aid
The light touch of a gentle hand
Restrained those fillies with their spangled reins.

ant. 1 For the goddess, archer maid, lends of both hands
With Hermes, god of contests, to set ready
His gleaming harness, when to the polished car
And wheels tense to the bridle's bidding,
He firmly yokes
His horses' strength, and breathes a prayer
To the great god of might, the trident-wielder.
Various men in various ways can fashion,
Each for his lord and king,
A sounding harmony of song, his tribute
To deeds of valour. How often does the voice
Of Cypriot men resound
With praise of Kinyras, who won
The happy love of golden-haired Apollo,

str. 1 *Am I come:* i.e. this poem is coming. Pindar did not go to Syracuse himself at this time.

Ortygia: the small island, part of the city of Syracuse and joined to it by a causeway. It is believed that Hieron had his racing-stables on Ortygia. There was a special cult of the goddess Artemis on the island.

Fillies: races with mares were not introduced into the Panhellenic Games until a later date. This is further evidence that this victory was won at one of the minor local games.

ant. 1 *Archer maid:* Artemis was traditionally associated with hunting and archery.

Hermes: traditionally associated with athletic contests.

The trident-wielder: Poseidon, traditionally associated with horses and chariot-driving.

Kinyras: a mythical king of Cyprus, renowned for his prosperity and generosity, who was also a priest of Aphrodite and a favourite of Apollo. Pindar's choice of his name to exemplify his theme here is perhaps because Hieron also held a hereditary priesthood, that of Demeter.

ep. 1 And was the cherished priest
Of Aphrodite; a friendly deed
Will ever stir the grace of reverent praise.
Thus for you, son of Deinomenes,
Locris Zephyria, the maiden city,
Saved by your power
From her despairing toils with enemy hands,
Sings at her door and lifts her eyes to freedom.
But by the gods' command, so the tale runs, Ixion
Rolling full circle on his wingéd wheel
Speaks thus to mortals:—
'See that your onward path fails not to pay
Your benefactor fair return of kindness.'

str. 2 Well had he learnt. For given a life of joy
By goodwill of the sons of Heaven, such bliss
He could not compass, but in frenzied madness
His passion sought the bed of Hera
Whose wedded joys
Are for the right of Zeus alone.
But pride and insolence drove him to this
Outrageous folly, nor was he slow to suffer,
As such a man well might,
Anguish unutterable. Two sins were his
That brought him to his pain; one that this warrior
Had been the first who brought
Into the world of men the shedding
Of kinsman's blood, and that with treachery;

ant. 2 Then, that in the profound and secret depths
Of her own bridal chamber, he assailed
The wife of Zeus. Well is it for a man
To take the measure of each deed
By his own stature.

ep. 1 *A friendly deed . . . reverent praise:* here, and in the last two lines of this epode, Pindar announces the main theme of this Ode.

Son of Deinomenes: Hieron.

Locris Zephyria: the city of Locri-in-the-West, was an independent Greek colony on the coast of southern Italy. In 478 B.C. Hieron prevented its annexation by the tyrant Anaxilas of Rhegium.

Ixion: was a proverbial example, with Tantalus and Sisyphus, of the dire punishment inflicted by the immortals for sacrilege committed against themselves. Ixion had treacherously murdered his father-in-law, but Zeus pardoned him for this and gave him a place in heaven. He nevertheless attempted his further crime against Hera. His punishment was to be tied everlastingly to a revolving wheel.

Unto the full deep tides of woe
Loves which transgress the law cast a man down,
Who sets foot there. For with a cloud he lay,
Pursuing a sweet falsehood,
That man of folly. In semblance like the all-high
Sovereign daughter of Cronos son of Heaven,
This phantom came, this guile
Proffered him by the hands of Zeus,
A beauteous bane. Thus on the four-spoked wheel

ep. 2 He gave his limbs to bondage,
His own destruction. Fallen in chains
From whence is no escape, he heard the message
That he must spread to all the world.
Far were the Graces when the mother bore—
Ne'er such a mother,
Never such son—her babe of monstrous breed,
Who had no honour amongst men nor in
The laws of Heaven. She reared him up and named him Centaur,
And the Magnetian mares knew him as mate
By Pelion's ridges;
And that strange race was born, like to both parents,
Their mother's form below, above their sire's.

str. 3 God achieves all his purpose and fulfills
His every hope, god who can overtake
The wingéd eagle, or upon the sea
Outstrip the dolphin; and he bends
The arrogant heart
Of many a man, but gives to others
Eternal glory that will never fade.

ep. 2 *The mother:* the cloud, or phantom, made in the likeness of Hera.
Magnetian: the district near Mount Pelion on the east coast of Thessaly was in early times inhabited by a people known as the Magnetes.
That strange race: the wild and savage Centaurs. They were unrelated to the immortal and kindly disposed Centaur, Chiron, who was the son of the god Cronos and the mortal Philyra.

str. 3 The connection of thought here with what has preceded is that the power of the Almighty is unlimited in any direction, whether in inflicting punishment or in giving rewards. Pindar seems glad at this point to provide a happier contrast to the savage story just concluded. His main purpose however in turning thus abruptly from the story of Ixion was no doubt to emphasize the sincerity and seriousness of the praises of Hieron that follow, and his claim that his own motives have nothing in common with slander and flattery.

Now for me is it needful that I shun
The fierce and biting tooth
Of slanderous words. For from old have I seen
Sharp-tongued Archilochus in want and struggling,
Grown fat on the harsh words
Of hate. The best that fate can bring
Is wealth joined with the happy gift of wisdom.

ant. 3 This gift is yours and with a liberal heart
You clearly show it, you prince and lord of many
A battlemented street and host of men.
If there be anyone to say
That in all Hellas
A man was born e'er now more blessed
In great possessions and in glory's honour,
His vain wit struggles with a fruitless aim.
Decked with fair flowers shall be
The ship that brings my song, to speak the praise
Of your brave spirit. The brunt of savage wars
In your young heart bred courage;
From whence also shall I affirm
That you have found an infinite renown,

ep. 3 Wielding your sword now 'midst
The horsemen's ranks, now upon foot.
In elder years the wisdom of your counsel
Allows me, free from any fear,
To spread your praises to the furthest height
That tongue can tell.
Farewell. Like to Phoenician merchandise
This song is sent across the foaming seas;
But for the song of Castor in Aeolian strains,

Archilochus: a lyric poet writing some 200 years before Pindar, noted for his keenly satirical work.

ep. 3 *The song of Castor in Aeolian strains:* this appears to refer to another poem which Pindar intends to send to Hieron. This may have been a 'hyporchema' or dance-song addressed to Hieron, of which only a fragment has come down to us.

In the last two lines of this epode there begins what seems almost like a postscript. Pindar has said his farewell, and what follows appears to be designed as a last word to impress Hieron again with the earnestness of this intimate communication.

Pray you, in honour of the seven-stringed lyre
Greet it with favour.
Be what you are, the man whose worth you have heard.
In the eyes of a child an ape is lovely,

str. 4 Always lovely. But the best blessing came
To Rhadamanthus, who was given the fruit
Of mind that knows no wrong, who takes no pleasure
Within his heart in false deceits,
Such words as ever
Are partners to the deeds of men
Who whisper in the ear. Secret purveyors
Of slander are an evil without cure,
Alike to those who speak it
And those who hear—like a fox is its temper.
Yet, as for gain, where does it prove of profit?
For I, while all the nets
And gear ply deep below the sea,
Float, like the cork, undrenched upon the water.

ant. 4 No man of guile can utter from his lips
A word compelling to a good man's ear;
Yet fawning upon all he weaves around them
His fateful ills. No share have I
In his bold craft:
Let it be mine to love my friend,
But as a foeman to my foes, like to a wolf
Shall I pursue them stealthily, now here
Now there setting my tracks
In winding ways. But he whose tongue speaks truth,

An ape is lovely: Pindar appears in this surprisingly sudden ejaculation to be making the point that in children's eyes a monkey may appear a beautiful creature, but will not appear so in the eyes of a man of mature judgment such as Hieron, who by the implication of the sentence which follows is compared to the most impartial judge of all, *Rhadamanthus*, the judge of departed souls.

Pindar means that the falsehood of the intrigues and slanders made against him at the court of Hieron, emphasized in the following triad, will be clearly recognized by Hieron, while Pindar's character, and what he is saying in this Ode, will be understood by him at its true worth.

str. 4 *The nets and gear:* this sudden change of metaphor gives added force to Pindar's claim that the efforts of intriguers are of no avail against honest men. Corks are of course used as floats attached to the upper edge of the fishing-net.

ant. 4 *But as a foeman . . . winding ways:* it may seem surprising to a modern reader that Pindar should advocate behaviour not very different from

Comes to the fore, whosoe'er makes the law,
Be it a tyrant, be it
The milling crowd, be it wise men
Who rule the state. But must we never strive

ep. 4 Against god, who upholds
Today the power of these, tomorrow
To others gives high glory. But the souls
Of envious men not even this thought
Can soothe; but like a man who drags too far
His measuring line,
They pierce their own hearts with a grievous wound,
Ere they can win that which their dreams devise.
Lightly to bear upon our neck the yoke that we
Have taken up, is wisdom's way. To kick
Against the pricks
Leads to the path of doom. May it be mine
To dwell amongst good men and earn their praise.

that which he has just been condemning. It must be remembered that to a Greek of Pindar's day to take vigorous action against his enemies was a duty which his self-respect demanded no less strongly, perhaps even more strongly, than that of giving help to a friend.

ep. 4 *His measuring line:* the measuring line is pictured as fitted with an earth pin at its end. If the greedy man tries to stretch it too far the pin will jump out and fly back to strike him.

PYTHIAN III

For

HIERON OF SYRACUSE

ALTHOUGH written in the form of an epinician ode, this poem was not in fact written in celebration of a Pythian victory, but has as its main theme the illness from which Hieron suffered for many years before his death in 467 B.C. There is mention in the fourth strophe of victories won for Hieron at the Pythian Games 'in times past', or 'long since', by his racehorse Pherenikus, and it is no doubt for this reason that early editors assigned to it a place amongst the Pythian Odes.

The subject-matter of the Ode is largely self-explanatory and its structure is not complex. The Ode launches at once into the expression of Pindar's wish that he could bring back to earth again the mythical Centaur, Chiron, and his pupil the healer Asclepius. The story of the birth and death of Asclepius takes us to the third antistrophe, when Pindar points briefly to the moral of the story, that to attempt to obtain good things beyond the normal lot of humankind is to court disaster. In the third epode and fourth strophe Pindar explains the purpose of his narration of the Chiron-Asclepius story, coupled with expressions of praise for Hieron, and his reference, mentioned above, to Hieron's victories at the Pythian Games. In the fourth antistrophe Pindar expresses a prayer to the 'great Mother', presumably for Hieron's recovery, and words of advice to Hieron give an easy transition to the theme of the changeability of human fortune. This theme, illustrated by the stories of Peleus and of Cadmus, takes us to the fifth epode, where obedience to the will of heaven is again emphasized. The final lines of the Ode turn to the theme so often expressed by Pindar, that it is through poetry that men must look for immortality.

The date of this Ode cannot be fixed with any certainty. The Pythian victories to which it refers were won in the years 482 and 478 B.C. but we do not know how long afterwards this Ode was written. Its intimate tone makes it virtually certain that it was not composed before Pindar's visit to Hieron's court in 476–75 B.C., and since the Ode makes it clear that Pindar is sending it to Hieron from across the sea, it must have been written after Pindar's return to Greece. It makes no mention however of Hieron's victory at the Pythian Games of 470 B.C., celebrated in Pythian Ode I, and may therefore be presumed to have been written before that date. The tone and temper of this Ode, with its expression of Pindar's sympathy for Hieron in his illness, are in strong contrast to the violently emotional language which is so marked a feature of Pindar's pleas to Hieron in Pythian Ode II. If that Ode was written, as seems probable, not long after Pindar's return from Sicily, that is in 475 or 474 B.C., it seems a possible assumption, judging from the content of the two Odes, that the angry one was the earlier, and the present sympathetic one the later of the two.

str. 1 Would that Chiron, the son of Philyra—
If so be that my lips the prayer must utter
That lives in every heart—
Would that he might regain the life he left long since,
That man of widespread power, the son of Cronos son of Heaven,
And that wild creature of the woods,
That lover of mankind,
Were lord of Pelion's valleys still;
Such as he was when long ago he nursed
Gentle Asclepius, that craftsman of new health
For weary limbs and banisher of pain,
The godlike healer of all mortal sickness.

ant. 1 His mother, daughter of Phlegyas the horseman,
Ere with the help of Eleithuia, the nurse
Of childbirth, she could bring
Her babe to the light of day, was in her chamber stricken

str. 1 *Chiron:* was famous in Greek mythology as the Centaur who lived on Mount Pelion in Eastern Thessaly, where he gave appropriate training to many heroes of Greek legend including Jason and Achilles, and as described in the present Ode, to Asclepius, the legendary founder of medical science.

Cronos: the father of Chiron by Philyra; he was the son of Ouranos (Heaven), husband of the goddess Rhea, and the father of Zeus.

ant. 1 *His mother:* Coronis by name.

Eleithuia: the goddess of childbirth.

By the golden shafts of Artemis, and to the hall of Death
Went down. For so Apollo willed.
Not lightly falls the wrath
Of the children of Zeus. For she
In the madness of her heart had spurned the god,
And unknown to her father took another lover,
Even though her maiden bed she had already
Shared with Apollo of the flowing hair,

ep. 1 And bore within her the god's holy seed.
She waited not to see the marriage feast,
Nor stayed to hear
The sound of swelling bridal hymns,
Such notes as maiden friends of a like age are wont
To spread in soothing songs upon the evening air.
But no! her heart
Longed for things far off, things unknown, as many another
Has longed ere now. For in the race of men
There is a throng whose minds are utmost vanity, who
Disdaining that which lies to hand, peer ever forward,
Hunting for folly's phantom, feeding on hopes
Never to be fulfilled.

str. 2 Such the all-powerful, ill-fated madness
That held the proud heart of fair-robed Coronis;
For with a stranger, come
From Arcady, she lay in love's embrace. Yet failed not
A watching eye to see; for at Pytho, amidst the lambs
Of sacrifice, the temple's king
Loxias stood; yet saw;
Seeking advice from none, save that
Most true consultant, his all-knowing mind.
For all things that are false he touches not, nor can
A god, nor can a man deceive him, whether
In aught they do or aught the will may purpose.

Shafts of Artemis: the origin of illnesses, especially infectious illnesses, was attributed in legend to arrows shot from the bow of Artemis, the goddess of hunting. She and Apollo were the twin children of Zeus and Leto. There is some reason for thinking that in the case of female victims this function was attributed to the arrows of Artemis, but in the case of males to the arrows of Apollo.

str. 2 *Loxias:* another name for Apollo, god of the temple and oracle of Pytho (Delphi).

ant. 2 Thus now, he saw that son of Eilatus,
Ischys, the stranger, share her bed of love,
That impious treachery;
And sent his sister storming in resistless anger
To Lakereia, where by the high banks of Boibias
The maiden had her home. And fate
Of a far other kind
Turned to her ruin and smote her down:
And many a neighbour, too, suffered alike
And was destroyed beside her; as when on the mountain
From one small spark a raging fire leaps up,
And lays in ruin all the widespread forest.

ep. 2 But when upon the high wood pyre her kinsmen
Had set the maid, and the flames of Hephaestus
Shot their bright tongues
Around her, then cried out Apollo:
'No longer shall my soul endure that my own son
Here with his mother in her death most pitiable
Should perish thus,
In sorry grief.' So spoke he and in one stride was there,
And seized the babe from the dead maid; and round him
The blazing flames opened a pathway. Then he took
The child to the Magnetian Centaur, that he teach him
To be a healer for mankind of all
Their maladies and ills.

str. 3 All then who came to him, some plagued with sores
Of festering growths, some wounded by the strokes
Of weapons of bright bronze,
Or by the slinger's shot of stone, others with limbs
Ravaged by summer's fiery heat or by the winter's cold,
To each for every various ill
He made the remedy,
And gave deliverance from pain,
Some with the gentle songs of incantation
Others he cured with soothing draughts of medicines,
Or wrapped their limbs around with doctored salves,
And some he made whole with the surgeon's knife.

ant. 2 *His sister:* Artemis.
Boibias: a large lake, still called by this name, in Eastern Thessaly near Mount Pelion.

ep. 2 *Hephaestus:* god of the forge, and of fire in general.
Magnetian: this epithet derives from the Magnetes, a tribe of Eastern Thessaly.

ant 3 And yet to profit even the skills of wisdom
Yield themselves captive. For a lordly bribe,
Gold flashing in the hand,
Even this man was tempted to bring back to life
One whom the jaws of death had seized already. With fierce hands
Swiftly the son of Cronos loosed
His anger on these two;
His blazing bolt stripped from them both
Their breath of life, and hurled them to their fate.
A man must seek from heaven only that which is fitting
For mortal minds, perceiving well the path
Before his feet, the lot that is our portion.

ep. 3 Pray for no life immortal, soul of mine,
But draw in full depth on the skills of which
You can be master.
Now if Chiron the wise dwelt still
Within his cave, and if some spell to charm his soul
Lay in the honeyed sweetness of my songs, then might I
Surely persuade him
For men of noble mind to grant them a physician
Of feverish ills, some son born of Apollo,
Or even the son of Zeus himself. Then might my ships,
Cleaving the waves of the Ionian sea, have brought me
To Arethusa's fountain and the home
Of my good host of Aetna,

ant. 3 *On these two:* both Asclepius and the man whom he resuscitated suffered this punishment. The name of this man is uncertain.

ep. 3 *Some son born of Apollo:* i.e. a man skilled in medicine as was Asclepius. Apollo was the god of prophecy and the arts, which included that of medicine.

The son of Zeus: i.e. Apollo himself.

Arethusa's fountain: this well-known fountain was on Ortygia, the small island which was joined to Syracuse by a causeway. Hieron kept his stables on Ortygia and possibly had a palace there as well.

Host of Aetna: Hieron is here referred to as 'of Aetna' because he had re-peopled and re-founded the town of Catana on the east coast of Sicily under the new name of Aetna. He took pride in being the founder of a new city, and looked forward to its becoming the home of his family after his death, when the rule of Syracuse was to pass to his younger brother. Pythian Ode I, written in 470 B.C., is addressed to 'Hieron of Aetna'.

str. 4 The king of Syracuse, who rules his people
With a mild hand, jealous of no good man,
And to his guests a friend
Most fatherly. Had I then touched upon his shores
Bringing a double blessing, first the gift of golden health,
Then this triumphant song, to throw
Its bright ray on the crowns
That graced him at the Games of Pytho,
When Pherenikus led the field long since
At Kirrha—then my sail had seemed for him, I doubt not,
Crossing the deep seas, a more glorious
And radiant light than any star of heaven.

ant. 4 But now is it my wish to voice a prayer
To the great Mother, the revered goddess
To whom, and to great Pan
Young maids before my door at nightfall often sing
Their praise. But if, Hieron, your mind perceives the deeper truth
Of spoken words, then have you learnt
From men of old this teaching:
'For every good bestowed to man
The immortals give two evils.' To receive
Such truth, however, with an ordered temper, fools
Cannot endure, but only noble minds
Turning the good side outwards to the eye.

str. 4 *King of Syracuse:* Pindar gives the title of 'king' to Hieron only here and in a passage of Olympian Ode I. That a Greek ruler, at this period in the development of the Greek city-state, should assume this title, which to the Greeks of those times was associated with the evil of despotic tyranny, is indicative of the unusual power and wealth of Hieron's autocratic rule.

Pherenikus: the racehorse with which, as noted in the foreword, Hieron had won two victories at the Pythian Games of 482 and 478 B.C. and also at Olympia in 476, as recorded in Pindar's Olympian Ode I.

Kirrha: also known as Krisa, was a town near the coast below Delphi, where the racing events of the Pythian Games were held until the year 450 B.C., when they were moved, except for the horse-races, to the new stadium above Delphi. The people of Kirrha had in early times established a local musical festival at Delphi. In 582 B.C. it was enlarged to become the Panhellenic festival of the Pythian Games. The name of Kirrha or Krisa is used frequently in Pindar's Odes to denote the Pythian Games.

ant. 4 *The great Mother:* the goddess Rhea, the wife of Cronos and mother of Zeus. It is recorded by Pausanias and other ancient writers that Pindar had built next to his house a 'temple of the mother of the gods and of Pan'.

Turning the good side outwards to the eye: a proverbial saying, roughly equivalent to the English phrase 'Looking on the bright side'.

ep. 4 Yours is a destiny of happy fortune;
In you, if any man, all-powerful fate
Beholds a leader
And sovereign monarch of a people.
Yet a life free from care came neither to Peleus,
Aeacus' son, nor to Cadmus that godlike king;
Though they of all men
Won, so men say, the highest bliss, who heard the Muses
In golden diadems chanting their songs
Upon the mountain and within the seven gates
Of Thebes, when one took for his bride Harmonia,
The dark-eyed maid, the other glorious Thetis,
Daughter of wise Nereus.

str. 5 And the gods shared with both their marriage feasts,
And seated upon golden thrones beside them
They saw the royal children
Of Cronos, and received from them their wedding-gifts:
And by the grace of Zeus were from their former toils uplifted,
And peace was in their hearts established.
Yet at another time
One of them by the bitter woes
Of his three daughters saw himself stripped bare
Of all his happiness, what though to one, Thyone
The white-armed maiden, Zeus the almighty father
Came down to her to share her lovely bed.

ep. 4 *Peleus:* the son of Aeacus, the first legendary king of Aegina, was a noted hero of Greek mythology, and his exploits are told in several of Pindar's Odes. By the commands of Zeus he was awarded the immortal sea-nymph Thetis as his bride. The wedding-feast was arranged by Chiron on Mount Pelion, and attended by all the gods. The son of Peleus and Thetis was Achilles, of Trojan war fame.

Cadmus: another noted mythological hero, was the first king of Thebes. Especially favoured by the goddess Athene, he was awarded as his bride Harmonia, the daughter of Ares and Aphrodite. His marriage feast in Thebes was also attended by all the gods.

Nereus: the immortal marine deity, the equivalent of our 'Old Man of the Sea'. He was the father of the fifty sea-nymphs, the Nereids, of whom Thetis was one.

str. 5 *Children of Cronos:* these were Hestia, Demeter, Hera, Hades, Poseidon and Zeus.

One of them: Cadmus. The tragic stories of the daughters of Cadmus were well-known legends. Semele, here referred to by her other name Thyone, became the mother of Dionysus by Zeus, but through the devices of the jealous Hera was destroyed by a thunderbolt. Dionysus later brought her up from Hades to live with the immortals. Her sister

ant. 5 And Peleus' son, that one son whom the immortal
Thetis in Phthia bore, gave up his life
In the fore-front of war,
To the sharp arrow's point, and o'er him as his body
Burnt on the funeral pyre, the Danai raised up on high
Their grievous cry of woe. And yet
If any mortal man
Holds in his heart the way of truth,
Then must he seek only from heaven to find
Good fortune's gifts. Now here, now there blow the high-flung
Winds of the sky. Man's wealth lasts not for long,
When it comes in full richness of good measure.

ep. 5 Humble 'midst humble men, great 'midst the great
Shall be the path I tread. But the will of heaven
That each new day
Endows my spirit, this shall I practise
And serve with all my skill. But though a god shall bring me
The joys of wealth, it is my hope to win high fame
Through the days to come.
Nestor and Lycian Sarpedon, those heroes
Of far renown, we know them from old story
In the rich harmonies built by the poets' craft.
In glorious songs brave spirits and brave deeds can live
Long down the years, but only to the few
Is this achievement easy.

Ino, after various tragic adventures, was driven mad and jumped into the sea with her infant son, but became an immortal sea-nymph living with the fifty Nereids. A third daughter, Agave, was responsible for the death of her son and her second husband.

ant. 5 *That one son:* Achilles, killed in the Trojan war by an arrow which pierced his heel, his only vulnerable point.

ep. 5 *Nestor:* king of Pylos in the south-west Peloponnese. He was the oldest of the Greek leaders in the Trojan war.

Sarpedon: leader of the Lycians, allies of the Trojans. He was killed by Patroclus in the fight which led to the latter's death at the hands of Hector.

PYTHIAN IV

For

ARCESILAS OF CYRENE

Winner of the Chariot-Race

ARCESILAS was the ruler—addressed as 'king' by Pindar—of Cyrene, the wealthy Greek colony on the coast of North Africa in Libya. The victory here celebrated was won by him in the chariot-race at the Pythian Games of 462 B.C. Arcesilas was the descendant—in the eighth generation according to a line in this Ode—of the Greek leader Battus, of the Aegean island of Thera (the modern Santorin). Battus was known to fame as having been the leader, about the year 530 B.C., of the Greek colonists from Thera who established themselves in Libya and made Cyrene their capital city. Their expedition was prompted, according to the story, by the oracle of Delphi. Battus is said to have suffered from a stutter, and to have gone to consult the priests of Apollo at Delphi with a view to a cure. The answer given by the oracle was to proclaim that Battus was destined to lead the expedition from Thera and establish the Greek colony in Libya. This he did, and established the line of Greek rulers to which Arcesilas belonged. Battus was the reputed descendant of Euphemus, one of the legendary band of 'Argonauts' who under the leadership of Jason sailed to Colchis, the kingdom of Aietes on the coast of the Black Sea, to bring back the Golden Fleece. The story of the young Jason's quarrel with the usurper Pelias and the subsequent expedition to Colchis occupies the greater part of this quite exceptionally lengthy Ode.

After the conventional compliments, briefly paid in the first strophe, to the name of the victor and to the deities of Pytho, and a reference to Battus and his achievement, Pindar turns at once in the first antistrophe to his mythical theme. He anticipates the main story of Jason and the Argonauts by portraying an episode which occurred on their return journey from Colchis, when they had reached the island of Thera. Here Medea proclaims to the Argonauts her prophecy of the future founding by Battus of the colony of Cyrene and explains why this was destined to be done from Thera by descendants of Euphemus and not directly, at an earlier date, from the Peloponnesus where Euphemus had his home. Medea, the daughter of Aietes of Colchis, was the famous prophetess and sorceress who helped Jason to obtain the Golden Fleece against the designs of Aietes, and when the Fleece was secured fled from Colchis with Jason and his companions.

The speech of Medea continues until the third antistrophe, after which Pindar announces to Arcesilas his intention of telling the story of the quest for the Golden Fleece. This story then proceeds, giving in fact a great deal of its length to the quarrel between Jason and Pelias, the usurper of the throne of Jason's father and ancestors in Iolcus, and dealing more cursorily with the events in Colchis which led to the seizure of the Fleece. As Pindar says in a comment to Arcesilas in the eleventh epode, this is a well-known story, and as 'a leader in the poet's craft' he feels entitled to cut it short. In the twelfth strophe Pindar re-emphasizes the descent of Arcesilas and the Greeks of Cyrene from Euphemus and the Argonauts, derived from their union with the women of the island of Lemnos before their return to their Peloponnesian homes. The normal tradition places the visit of the Argonauts to Lemnos on their outward voyage to Colchis. Pindar's version appears to picture it on their return journey.

In the twelfth antistrophe Pindar turns to an entirely different subject which is to occupy the remainder of the Ode, namely an appeal to Arcesilas to grant a pardon to a nobleman of Cyrene named Demophilus, who had been involved in some aristocratic dissensions against Arcesilas and had been sent into exile. It is clear that he spent some time at Thebes and was known to Pindar. Arcesilas did not himself come to Delphi to attend the Pythian Games on this occasion, but as we shall see from the next following Ode (Pythian V) which celebrates this same victory, he sent as his representative his brother-in-law Carrhotus, who also acted as charioteer in the race. There can be little doubt that it was Carrhotus who commissioned these two Odes from Pindar, of which the present Ode was written for performance, as the opening lines indicate, at the palace of Arcesilas, no doubt at a banquet, while Pythian V, as that Ode makes clear, was to be performed to celebrate the return of the charioteer and his team to Cyrene. In his conversations with Carrhotus Pindar no doubt pressed the claims of Demophilus, and whether as a result of this, or more probably for other reasons as well, it seems likely that Carrhotus took a favourable view of the case, and that a pardon for Demophilus and permission for his return to Cyrene were very likely to be granted if not already a foregone conclusion. If it had not been at least a strong probability it would have been less than discreet for Pindar to make the representations with which he concludes this Ode. We may judge from the length and manner of the Ode that Pindar was concerned to construct a rich and telling framework into which his concluding representations on behalf of Demophilus could be suitably fitted. It was of course his common practice in his Odes to recount the glories of the victors' ancestors. The story of the Argonauts gave him an opportunity to do this with notable emphasis and at exceptional length. It seems likely that in his lengthy description of the interview between Jason and Pelias he was concerned to emphasize the desirability of agreements reached by peaceful discussion rather than by force, and of the value to this end of mutual concessions.

As readers will note, Pindar approaches the subject of Demophilus somewhat gingerly. He begins in antistrophe 12 with the implied compliment of comparing the wisdom of Arcesilas with that of Oedipus, who solved the riddle of the Sphinx, and the riddle he sets before Arcesilas is the allegory of the lopped branches of the oak-tree. It can be guessed without much difficulty that the oak-tree and its lopped branches represent those people, including Demophilus, who had been punished for their differences with Arcesilas. Pindar implies that their inherent goodness still exists. Epode 12 needs no explanation. In strophe 13 the quotation from Homer implies that a message which is delivered in the fine form of the present Ode would not be sent in support of an undeserving cause. The name of Demophilus is then introduced, with praise of his good qualities. In antistrophe 13 his punishment is compared to that of Atlas who was condemned, for taking part with his brother Titans in their battles against Zeus, to the endless task of carrying the sky on his shoulders. But, Pindar points out, Zeus showed mercy to the other Titans, and changing circumstances allow changes of policy. The final epode contains an appeal, feelingly expressed, for Demophilus to be allowed to return to his own home and people, and the last lines of the Ode imply that Pindar found Demophilus, while he was in Thebes, to be a man well deserving of any help that Pindar's poetic talent could afford him, and that now he is only too happy to be sending this poem on his behalf.

str. 1 Come Muse, today I bid you stand beside
A man well-loved, Cyrene's king, that city
Of noble steeds, and in his hour of triumph
Honour Arcesilas,
Raising on high a gale of song,
Hymns due to Leto's children and to Pytho.
There long ago the priestess on her throne
Beside the birds of Zeus, the golden eagles,
Foretold—nor was Apollo far away—
That in the fruitful land of Libya,
Leaving his holy isle in days to come,
Battus should found
A city famous for her chariots
On a white-breasted hill:

ant. 1 And thus Medea's word, spoken in Thera,
In the seventeenth generation he should fulfil:
That word which long since the princess of Colchis,
The inspired child of Aietes,
Breathed forth upon her deathless tongue;
When to those demi-gods, the sailor comrades
Of warrior Jason, thus she spoke: 'Hearken,
Ye sons of dauntless mortals and of gods,
This I proclaim, that from this sea-girt isle
There shall be born in days to come a root
That shall in Epaphus' daughter's land engender
Cities far-famed
To mortal hearing, founded in the soil
Sacred to Zeus of Ammon.

str. 1 *City of noble steeds:* this phrase, and similar expressions such as 'riders of white steeds' or 'a horseman folk' are frequently found in Pindar to describe a city or people not lacking in wealthy and aristocratic members.

Leto's children: Apollo and Artemis.

His holy isle: the Aegean island of Thera, the modern Santorin.

A city famous: Cyrene.

ant. 1 *Epaphus' daughter's land:* Epaphus, son of Zeus and the Greek maiden Io, was a legendary king of Egypt. His daughter Libya gave her name to Libya of North Africa.

Zeus of Ammon: the temple of Zeus Ammon lay to the east of Libya. His 'soil' is used here as a general term for North Africa.

ep. 1 No more the short-finned dolphins shall escort them,
But racing steeds shall carry them;
Reins they shall ply instead of oars, and drive
Chariots swift as wind. A sign there was
To tell that Thera
Shall prove the mother of great cities,
When, leaping from the prow where Lake Tritonis
Pours to the sea, Euphemus took the gift,
Token of a host's friendship, from a god
In mortal guise who gave a clod of earth;
And from aloft, to mark the sign,
A peal of thunder
Sounded from Zeus the father, son of Cronos.

str. 2 This so befell, as on our ship we hung
The bronze-fluked anchor, the bridle of our swift Argo,
When for twelve days we had carried from the Ocean
Over earth's desert backs
Our good ship's hull, when we had beached
And drawn her to the shore by my designs.
Then came to us this deity, all alone,
Clad in the noble semblance of a man
Of reverent bearing, and with friendly speech
Made to address us with a kindly greeting—
Such words with which a man of good intent
Speaks to invite
The strangers newly come to share his table,
And bids them a first welcome.

ep. 1 *Thera:* the modern Santorin, one of the most southerly islands of the Aegean.

Lake Tritonis: the exact position in mythical geography of Lake Tritonis in North Africa need not concern us, but it is clear that Pindar pictures it as having an outlet to the Mediterranean.

Euphemus: one of Jason's company of Argonauts.

A clod of earth: this gift was an invitation to the Argonauts, or as it proved in this case, a prophecy, that they or their descendants should make their homes in that territory.

str. 2 *The Ocean:* there were many differing legends of the route followed by the Argonauts on their return journey from Colchis. Pindar appears to follow the version which gave them a route from the Black Sea via the river Phasis to the Caspian; thence to the Indian Ocean (part of the 'Ocean' which was believed to surround the whole of the known earth); thence to the Red Sea, then overland carrying their ship across the African desert to Lake Tritonis and the Mediterranean coast. From there they sailed to Thera and, according to Pindar, to the island of Lemnos before finally returning to the Greek mainland. The usual legend however places their visit to Lemnos on their outward journey before they reached Colchis.

ant. 2 Yet did the dear plea of our homeward voyage
Call to us and forbade our stay. His name
He gave, Eurypylus, saying he was
The son of the immortal
Holder of Earth, Ennosides;
He saw our haste to be away, and straightway
He stopped and seized a clod beside his foot
And in his right hand proffered the gift of friendship.
And, for he felt no misbelief, Euphemus
Lept to the shore and grasped his outstretched hand,
And took the earth, that sign of heaven's will.
But now I learn
That it is lost, washed down as evening fell
From the ship's deck, to wander

ep. 2 On ocean's dark smooth tide, with the sea spray.
Many a time, indeed, did I
Charge to the serving-men who ease our toil
To watch it well; but they forgot. Thus now
The deathless seed
Of Libya's far-spreading plains
Is spilt upon this isle, e'er the due time.
For had that prince, son of the horseman's god
Poseidon—whom Europa, Tityus' daughter
Bore by Kephissus' banks—had he, Euphemus
Come home to holy Taenarus
And cast that seed
Where cleft earth opens to the mouth of hell,

ant. 2 *Ennosides:* another name for Poseidon. The traditional story was that it was the deity Triton who made this appearance and offered the clod of earth, pretending to be Eurypylus, the first mythical king of Libya.

ep. 2 *This isle:* Thera.

Taenarus: a city on the central promontory in the south of the Peloponnese, the modern Cape Matapan. This was the home of Euphemus, though he was born, as these lines indicate, near the river Kephissus in Boeotia.

Cleft earth: there was a large cave near Taenarus, reputed to be an entrance to the underworld.

str. 3 Then had his sons in the fourth generation
Seized with the Danai this broad mainland.
For then from mighty Sparta and Argos' gulf
And from Mycenae the peoples
Shall rise and move from their abode.
But now Euphemus, taking from a breed
Of foreign women one to be his bride,
Shall found a chosen race. And they shall come,
Paying due honour to the gods, unto
This island, where they shall beget a man
Born to be lord of those dark-misted plains.
And on a day
In time to come, this man shall tread the path
Down to the shrine of Pytho,

ant. 3 And Phoebus from his golden-treasured hall
Shall speak to him his oracle, proclaiming
That he shall bring a mighty host in ships
To the rich land of Nile
The precinct of the son of Cronos,'
So rang Medea's rhythmic utterance.
Bowed down in silent wonder, motionless
The godlike heroes heard her potent wisdom.
O son of Polymnestus, richly blessed,
Your path it was the prophecy made plain,
The inspired prediction of the Delphic Bee;
For thrice she named you
Fortune's predestined king, who shall raise high
The glory of Cyrene,

str. 3 *The fourth generation:* Pindar puts into the mouth of Medea this forecast of the large movement of peoples which in fact occurred after the Dorian invasions in the twelfth and eleventh centuries B.C. and the overthrow of the Mycenaean civilization.

This broad mainland: i.e. North Africa.

His bride: the name of his Lemnian bride, not given here, was Malache.

They shall come . . . unto this island: the descendants of Euphemus will come from the Peloponnese to Thera.

Shall beget a man: i.e. Battus.

Dark-misted plains: Libya.

ant. 3 *Son of Polymnestus:* Battus.

The Delphic Bee: a term applied to the priestess of Apollo at Delphi.

ep. 3 When you rode down to ask of heaven's will
Some remedy for your laboured speech.
Yes, verily now, even in these after-days,
As in the prime of purple-flowering spring,
Arcesilas
Born of this stock, eighth in descent,
Prospers no less. Apollo and Pytho's field
Granted him fame amidst the neighbouring peoples
For his racing steeds; and I the Muses' gift
Shall dower him, of the golden fleece recounting
The tale. For when the Minyae
Sailed on that quest,
Glory from heaven was planted in their race.

str. 4 What then begot their sea-borne journey forth?
What peril bound their spirits to the task
With adamantine bonds? It was foretold
That Pelias should die
Or by the hands or by the untiring
Designs of the proud sons of Aeolus;
And in its icy grip a prophecy
Held the depths of his soul, that word spoken
From tree-clad mother-earth's deep navel-stone;
That above all he should keep watch and ward,
If one should come wearing a single sandal,
From a high home
On mountain steeps, unto the sunlit land
Of glorious Iolcus,

ep. 3 *Your laboured speech:* Battus suffered from a stutter. See foreword.
Apollo and Pytho's field: i. e.the Pythian Games.
The Minyae: Minyas was an early king of Orchomenus in Boeotia. The name Minyae or Minyans is usually applied to the people of Boeotia; Pindar uses it here to cover the people of Iolcus as well.

str. 4 *Pelias:* was Jason's second cousin. He had usurped the throne of Iolcus from Jason's father Aeson.
Sons of Aeolus: Aeolus was the great-grandfather of both Jason and Pelias. For the family tree see note to antistrophe 6.
Deep navel-stone: the oracle of Delphi.
A high home: Jason was brought up by Chiron the Centaur, who lived on Mount Pelion near Iolcus.

ant. 4 Whether he be stranger or citizen.
And lo, after due time there came a man
Of wondrous strength. Two spears he carried
And wore a twofold vesture,
A garment of the countrymen
Of the Magnetes' race covering close
His splendid limbs, and slung upon his shoulder
A leopard-skin to shield the hissing rain.
And locks of glorious hair fell rippling down
In gleaming streams unshorn upon his back.
And swiftly coming, as if in trial to prove
His dauntless spirit,
He took his station in the market-place
Amidst the surging crowd.

ep. 4 They knew him not; and looked on him in wonder;
And one amongst them spoke, and said:
'This man is not Apollo, surely, nor
The god of the bronze chariot, the lord
Of Aphrodite?
Iphimedeia's sons, they say,
In gleaming Naxos died, Otus and you
King Ephialtes the daring. And indeed
Tityus by Artemis was hunted down
With darts from her unconquerable quiver
Suddenly sped, so that a man
May learn to touch
Only those loves that are within his power.'

str. 5 Thus were the folk their idle tales exchanging
One to another's ear, when suddenly,
Driving his team of mules in headlong haste,
Pelias came riding by
Mounted upon his polished car.

ant. 4 *Magnetes:* the name of a tribe who lived near Mount Pelion.

ep. 4 *God of the bronze chariot:* Ares, the god of war.
Otus and Ephialtes: giant sons of Poseidon and Iphimedeia. They put Ares into chains and were destroyed by Apollo.
Tityus: a giant who attempted to violate Leto, the mother of Apollo and Artemis. He was killed by their arrows and condemned to eternal punishment in the underworld.

And terror seized him when his glancing eye
Fell on the clear sign of the single sandal
On the man's right foot. But he concealed the fear
Within his heart, and spoke to him; 'What country,
Tell me, stranger, you boast your own? What woman
Of earth-born mortals bore you from a belly
        Hoary with age?
Tell me your birth and see you sully it
      With no unlovely lies.'

ant. 5 But he, with a bold heart and gentle words
Answered him thus: 'Chiron my teacher was,
This shall I prove. From Chariclo, I say,
      And Philyra's cave I come,
   Where the chaste daughters of the Centaur
Nursed my young days. Through all my twenty years
I gave them no rough word or hasty deed;
And now I tread my homeward path, to claim
The ancient honours of my father. Here
A kingship is installed, not by the right
Derived of heaven, which the hand of Zeus
        Long since assigned
To chieftain Aeolus and to his children,
      To hold a throne of honour;

ep. 5 But, so I learn, yielding in godless trust
   To the cold thoughts of envy's evil,
Pelias by force has stolen the dominion
My parents held of old. For they, when first
      I saw the light,
   Fearing that leader's overweening
And cruel pride, laid forth within the house
Dark robes of mourning, as though their babe were dead;
And amidst wailing women sent me forth
Secretly, wrapped in purple swaddling clothes,
   That only the dark of night might know
      My path, and gave me
To Chiron, Cronos' son, to be my guardian.

str. 5 *Hoary with age:* the meaning of this epithet is not clear and has been variously interpreted. One suggestion is that Pelias, seeing Jason's handsome appearance and long hair, meant to imply that he was an effeminate and spoilt child of elderly parents. It is clear at any rate that the remark implies contempt.

ant. 5 *Chariclo* was the wife, and *Philyra* the mother, of Chiron the Centaur.

str. 6 But of this story the main part you know.
But show me clear, grave citizens, the house
Of my forefathers, riders of white steeds.
For I, the son of Aeson
Born of this soil, let me not come
To find my home a foreign land of strangers.
My name that godlike creature gave to me
And called me Jason.' So he spoke, and coming
Into his house, his father's eyes failed not
Straightway to know him, and his ageing lids
Poured forth a flood of tears, for he rejoiced
Through all his soul
To see his son a man most excellent,
Fairest of all mankind.

ant. 6 And both his brothers came and stood before them,
Hearing the famed report of his arrival,
First Pheres from his nearby home beside
The spring of Hypereis,
And Amythaon from Messene;
And quickly came Admetus and Melampus
To give him kindly greetings. And a banquet
Was spread for all, and Jason welcomed them
With gracious words. And he made ready for them
The due gifts of a hospitable house,
And served them all the joys of mirth and gladness,
And for five nights
And five long days they culled the blessed fruit
And flower of happy living.

str. 6 *That godlike creature:* Chiron.

ant. 6 The genealogy of Jason's family is as follows:

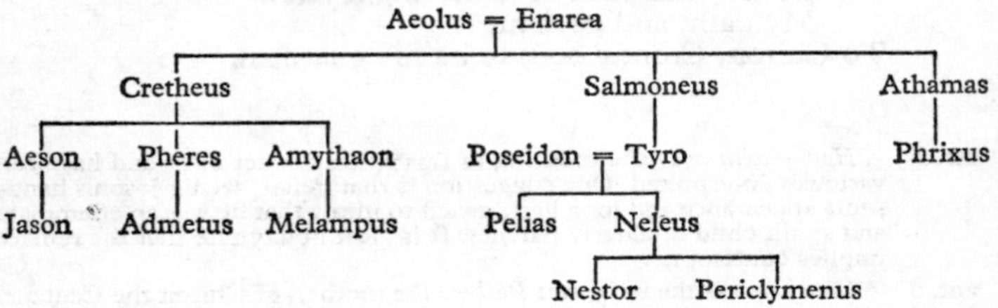

ep. 6 But the sixth day Jason in grave discourse
Told to his kinsmen all the story
From its first hour. And all were of one mind
To follow him. And he rose from his seat
Straightway, and they
Likewise; and to the palace doors
Of Pelias they flocked with surging steps
And took their stance within. And he, that son
Of Tyro, maiden of the lovely hair,
Heard, and himself came forth to meet them there.
But Jason with soft-flowing speech
And gentle voice,
A sure foundation laid of words of wisdom,

str. 7 Saying: 'Son of Poseidon of the Rock,
Too prone are mortal minds, against all right,
To choose a treacherous gain, howe'er it be
Their footsteps onward roll
To a disastrous reckoning.
But you and I must with a sacred pledge
Contain our wrath, and for the future weave
A happier fortune. This, which you know, I tell:
One mother's womb bore Cretheus and bold-hearted
Salmoneus; and we now, their grandsons bred,
Look on the golden sun's broad ray. But if
Enmity breeds
Twixt men of the same race, to hide the shame
Even the Fates veil their eyes.

ant. 7 It ill befits us two with bronze-edged swords
Or javelins to quarrel the division
Of our fathers' great honours. No, for I
Give you the flocks of sheep
And herds of tawny cattle, and all
The fields whence, though you robbed them of my parents,
You tend their culture and make fat your living.

str. 7 *Poseidon of the Rock:* this title of Poseidon was current amongst the people of Thessaly, because of the tradition according to which he had opened up the valley of the river Tempe between Mount Olympus and Mount Ossa.

Nor do I take amiss that these furnish
Your house with wealth beyond all measure. But
Both for the royal sceptre and the throne
On which long since the son of Cretheus sat
Dispensing justice
To his horsemen folk, these with no wrath between us
Release to me again,

ep. 7 Lest out of these some further ill should rear
Its ugly head.' So did he speak.
And Pelias answered softly: 'As you have willed
So shall I be. But now the elder portion
Of a man's years
Holds me already in its toils;
But for you the full flower of blossoming youth
Burgeons apace. You have it in your strength
To undo the vengeful anger of the powers
Of earth below. To bring his spirit again
Phrixus commands us journey to
Aietes' hall,
And fetch from thence the thick fleece of the ram,

str. 8 Which saved him from the ocean long ago,
And from the impious darts of his step-mother.
This bidding a wondrous dream declared to me;
And I sent to consult
Castalia's oracle, if any
Quest should be made. They bade me with all speed
Make ready a sea-borne mission. Now, do you
With good-will take this challenge and complete it,

ant. 7 *The son of Cretheus:* Aeson, Jason's father.

ep. 7 *Phrixus:* the son of Athamas king of Boeotia. Owing to the machinations of his step-mother Ino, he was about to be sacrificed by his father Athamas. He was saved by the intervention of the gods who sent down from Olympus a winged golden ram, on which Phrixus fled accompanied by his sister Helle. Helle fell off over the straits since known as the Hellespont. Phrixus was brought to Colchis where he sacrificed the ram in gratitude to Zeus. Its golden fleece was hung in a sacred grove, guarded day and night by a dragon. When Phrixus died in Colchis, he was denied proper burial. The Delphic Oracle declared that the land of Iolcus where many of his relatives were settled would never prosper until the soul of Phrixus was brought back together with the Golden Fleece.

Aietes: the king of Colchis.

str. 8 *Castalia's oracle:* the Delphic oracle.

And I, I swear to grant to you the crown
And kingdom for your rule. To this great oath
May he who is our common ancestor,
    Zeus, be the witness.'
And on these terms they were agreed, and parted.
    Jason, losing no moment,

ant. 8 Himself sent heralds far and wide, proclaiming
The voyage now to be. And the three sons,
Tireless in battle, of Zeus the son of Cronos,
    Came with all haste, the child
  Born of the dancing-eyed Alcmene,
And Leda's twin sons; and that pair of heroes
Of the high-crested locks, sons of Poseidon
The earth-shaker, those men of no less honour
Than of valour, from Pylos and the steeps
Of Taenarus; wide fame they won, Euphemus
And Periclymenus that man of strength;
    And from Apollo,
That master of the lyre of happy fame,
    Orpheus, father of song.

ep. 8 And Hermes of the golden wand sent forth
  His two sons to the stubborn toil,
Eurytus and Echion, happy souls
Of joyful youth; and swift came two who dwelt
    Beneath the strong
  Foundations of Pangaeon's height;
For gladly with a joyful heart their father
Boreas, sovereign of the winds, commanded
Zetes and Calais to the task, those heroes
Whose backs on either side bear fluttering wings
  Of purple. In these demi-gods
    The goddess Hera
Kindled the all-persuading sweet desire

ant. 8 *Three sons of Zeus:* Heracles, son of Alcmene, and Castor and Pollux, the twin sons of Leda.

Sons of Poseidon: Euphemus from Taenarus, Periclymenus from Pylos.

Pindar gives only a few names of the company of Argonauts. Various lists were compiled by writers of antiquity, usually amounting to some fifty names.

ep. 8 *Pangaeon's height:* Mount Pangaeon is in eastern Thrace.

str. 9 For the ship Argo, that not one should stay
Left at his mother's side to nurse a lifetime
Free from danger, but each, even at the risk
Of death, amidst companions
Of a like age should win that fair
And potent spell that should redound his valour.
And when this flower of sailor-men had come
To Iolcus city, Jason mustered them
And gave thanks to them all. And at his side
Mopsus, the seer, studied the will of heaven
By flight of birds and drawing of sacred lots,
And right gladly
He gave the signal for the host to embark.
When they had raised the anchor

ant. 9 And slung it high upon the ship's bowsprit,
Then their commander, standing on the stern,
Took in his hands a golden cup and called
To Zeus whose spear is lightning,
The father of the sons of heaven,
To the swift-running tides of wave and wind,
To the nights and to the highways of the ocean,
To days propitious and the friendly hand
Of Fate that grants return. Then from the clouds
Answered the fateful thunder's voice, and far-flung
Broke the bright flashes of the lightning's ray.
And the heroes
Took breath of courage, trusting in these signs
From heaven. Then the seer

ep. 9 Rang out his bidding to lay on the oars
And spoke them words of cheerful hope,
And on they sped with swiftly-swinging blades
In tireless rhythm. The South wind's breezes blew
To send them onwards,
And when they came before the mouth
Of the inhospitable sea, they founded

ant. 9 *Called to Zeus, etc.:* the observance of these traditional rites at the start of a sea voyage appears to have been continued down to Classical times. Thucydides writes of a ceremony of this kind in his account of the departure of the Athenian fleet for the Sicilian expedition in the year 416 B.C.

ep. 9 *The inhospitable sea:* the Euxine, or Black Sea.

A holy place, a precinct of Poseidon
God of the Ocean, where was a red herd
Of Thracian bulls, and an altar new built
Of hollowed stone. Then driving onwards
Into deep peril,
They offered prayer to the great Lord of Ships

str. 10 That of the Clashing Rocks they might escape
The devastating onset—two pillars
Alive, that rolled with hurtling speed more swiftly
Than the embattled ranks
Of the loud-roaring gales. But now
That voyage of the heroes ended their mischief.
They came then to the Phasis, where they joined
In bitter conflict with the swarthy-faced
Men of the land of Colchis, in the kingdom
Of Aietes himself. Then from Olympus
The queen of swift arrows, the Cyprian goddess,
Sent down the wry-neck,
Its dappled feathers spread and firmly tied
To the four spokes of a wheel,

ant. 10 That bird of passion's frenzy, never before
Seen amongst men. And the goddess made plain
To Aeson's son the lore of prayers, and spells
Of magic incantation,
That he might rob Medea's heart
Of reverence for her parents, and a dear
Desire for Hellas light in her mind a flame,
Driving her with Persuasion's lash. And soon

str. 10 *The Clashing Rocks:* these Clashing or Wandering Rocks, the Symplegades, are pictured by Homer as in Sicilian waters. Here they have been transferred to the Bosphorus.

Ended their mischief: after failing to crush the Argo between them, the Rocks, according to a prophecy, remained rooted in their place, one on each side of the straits.

The Phasis: a river, now known as the Rion, which runs down to the eastern coast of the Black Sea.

The Cyprian goddess: Aphrodite.

The wryneck: this bird, sometimes referred to as 'the cuckoo's mate', was used as a love-charm, tied to the spokes of a wheel, with suitable incantations.

She showed him all the tests he should accomplish
Set by her father's hand. And she distilled
Medicines with olive oil, and gave to him
Ointments to allay
The pains of burning; and they vowed to join
In sweet wedlock together.

ep. 10 But when Aietes set within their midst
The ploughshare hard as adamant,
And oxen breathing flames of burning fire
From nostrils tawny-red battered the ground
With brazen hooves,
Pawing the soil this side and that,
Single-handed Aietes brought them in
And threw the yoke upon them. And he marked out
And ploughed straight furrows, cutting the earth's loam
Two cubits depth; and said 'O king,
Whoe'er you be,
Who rules this ship, this task complete for me,

str. 11 Then take the imperishable coverlet,
The fleece with fringe of gleaming gold.' He spoke,
And Jason threw aside his saffron cloak,
And putting his trust in heaven
Set to the task. Nor could the flames
Give pause to his brave spirit, thanks to the counsels
Of the stranger maid, mistress of pharmacy.
And he dragged forth the plough, and on the oxen
Thrust the compelling yoke to bind their necks,
And in their strong-ribbed frames unceasingly
Plunging the goad, this man of might toiled through
The allotted measure.
Aietes, speechless, groaned aloud in woe,
Aghast to see his strength.

ant. 10 *All the tests:* the main test imposed by Aietes was, as this Ode goes on to describe, that Jason should plough the 'Field of Ares' with a pair of fire-breathing oxen. Pindar omits the further condition, that he should sow the field with dragon's teeth (some of the teeth left over from a similar sowing made by Cadmus of Thebes). From these teeth armed warriors sprang up overnight. Jason induced them to fight with one another instead of against himself, and was thus able to kill the wounded survivors.

ant. 11 But his comrades stretched out their hands to greet
Their mighty leader, crowned him with green garlands
And welcomed him with words of dear rejoicing.
Straightway Aietes spoke,
That wondrous son of Helios,
And told where Phrixus' knife had laid outstretched
The shining fleece; yet in his heart he hoped
That Jason might even so this further labour
Fail to accomplish. For the fleece was laid
In a deep thicket, held within the fierce
Jaws of a ravenous dragon, far surpassing
In length and breadth
A ship of fifty oars, welded and built
By many a hammer's blow.

ep. 11 Long were my path upon the beaten high-road,
And time presses apace. I know
A shorter way; to many another man
Can I be leader in the poet's craft.
With cunning hands—
Well known the tale, Arcesilas—
He slew that dragon of the glaring eyes
And speckled back, and with her own aid stole
Medea, who brought death to Pelias.
Then to the Ocean main and the Red Sea,
And to the race of Lemnian women
Who slew their menfolk,
Where for a garment's prize they showed their prowess

ep. 11 *Long were my path:* as in several other Odes, Pindar makes his excuses here for not allowing the story to run on too long. He omits all details of the final events of the Argonaut story, pausing only in the next strophe to emphasize again the lineal descent of Arcesilas from the Argonaut Euphemus.

With her own aid: Medea was of course only too willing to accompany Jason when he left Colchis. She had made it a condition of her help that she should do so. It was largely by means of her magic that Jason was able to kill the dragon, seize the golden fleece and make good the escape of the Argonauts from the hostile designs of Aietes.

Brought death to Pelias: When Jason finally returned to Iolcus, he found that Pelias had put to death Aeson and other supporters of Jason, and was quite unwilling to hand over the kingdom. It was Medea's craft, again, that devised a means of killing Pelias and securing Iolcus for Jason.

Lemnian women: before the arrival of the Argonauts, the women of Lemnos, according to the legend, had massacred their husbands. (This suggests that the matriarchal system was still in existence on the island.)

str. 12 In contests of strong limbs; and with those women
They mated. Yes, there in a foreign soil
Some fated day, maybe, or the night watches
Witnessed that seed implanted,
From which should spring the glorious light
Of your high fortune. There Euphemus' line
Was bred, to last forever; then, mingling
With men of Lacedaemon blood and custom,
They brought their home in due time to the land
Once named the Fairest Isle; thence to your race
The son of Leto granted Libya's plain,
To make it rich
Under god's honour, and give government
To the divine city

ant. 12 Of golden-throned Cyrene, there devising
The rule of wisdom and of righteous counsel.
Now let your thought, I pray, rival the wisdom
Of Oedipus. For if
With his sharp-bladed axe a man
Strips off the branches from a mighty oak,
And brings to shame its lovely form, yet still
Though reft of its fair fruit it may give witness
Of its true being, whether it comes at last
To feed the fires of winter, or bear the load
On rising columns of its master's palace,
Serving a drear
And lonely task, and amidst alien walls
Knows its own place no more.

str. 12 *In contests:* Games, in which the Argonauts competed, were organized by Hypsipylia, the queen of Lemnos.

Of your high fortune: i.e. of Arcesilas.

Euphemus' line: the son of Euphemus by a Lemnian woman, Malache, was Leucophanes, who became the ancestor of the Battus-Arcesilas line.

The Fairest Isle: the ancient name, Calliste, of Thera.

The son of Leto: Apollo. The story of his abduction of the maiden Cyrene to Libya, where she gave her name to the city of Cyrene, is told in Pindar's ninth Pythian Ode.

ant. 12 On the allegory of the oak tree and its lopped branches, see the foreword.

ep. 12 You are a doctor prompt to the moment's hour;
Paean pays honour to your name;
To heal a festering wound there needs the touch
Of gentle hands. To cast a city in ruins
Easy enough
Even for men of meanly stature;
Once more to raise it to its high estate
Is hard indeed, sobeit no deity
Comes suddenly to take the helm, and steer
The rulers' course. For you the heavens are weaving
Of such blest gifts a lasting pattern.
Be bold to seek
With all your spirit Cyrene's happy fortune.

str. 13 Take too, and ponder in your heart, the word
That Homer spoke: 'By a good messenger
Is brought' said he 'to every matter spoken
The highest honour.' So too
The Muse by a true-made report
Wins the more praise. Well has Cyrene's city
And Battus' hall, that palace of renown,
Seen in Demophilus a man of just
And righteous mind. Bred here, a boy midst boys,
His counsel drawn as from a hundred years
Of elder wisdom's fruit, he brings to naught
The far-flung boasting
Of evil tongues, knowing well to hate the man
Whose deeds are insolence.

ant. 13 He quarrels with no good men, nor brooks delay
To end a task. For fit occasion grants
But a brief hour to men. This he knows well,
And waits on the due moment
As a good servant and no slave.
Of all pains this, they say, cuts the most sore,
If one who knows good fortune finds his footstep

ep. 12 *Paean:* the god of healing. In Homer the name is applied to the physician of the Olympian gods. It was later associated with the healer Asclepius, and more particularly with the god Apollo as the patron god of all the arts, including that of medicine. The name Paean was also transferred from Apollo to songs chanted to him to avert an evil, or before a battle.

str. 13 *A true-made report:* i.e. this Ode.
Demophilus: see foreword.

Shut from the door by harsh constraint. Does not
Even now great Atlas struggle to bear up
The weight of heaven, far from his fathers' land
And his possessions? But almighty Zeus
Set free the Titans.
For as time passes and the breeze abates,
The sails are set anew.

ep. 13 But now it is his prayer, when this drear cup
Of grievous ill is drained at last,
To see his home, and by Apollo's fountain
Joining the banquet's throng, to spend his soul
Oft and again
In youthful joys, 'midst citizens
Lovers of skill, playing his rich-wrought lyre,
And to find peace, bringing harm to no man,
And from his townsfolk suffering naught himself;
And to you would he tell, Arcesilas,
How that he found a glorious spring
Of heavenly songs,
When of late times he was a guest at Thebes.

ant. 13 *Atlas:* was the leader of his brother Titans in their struggle against Zeus and the other Olympian gods. When defeated he was condemned to the eternal punishment of carrying the sky on his shoulders.

ep. 13 *Apollo's fountain:* a well-known fountain in the city of Cyrene.
A glorious spring of heavenly songs: i.e. Pindar himself.

PYTHIAN V

For

ARCESILAS OF CYRENE

Winner of the Chariot-Race

THIS Ode celebrates, as does the preceding Ode IV, the victory won by Arcesilas in the chariot-race at the Pythian Games of 462 B.C. While Ode IV was written for performance at the palace of King Arcesilas, the present Ode was clearly intended to celebrate the return of the winning team to Cyrene after their success at Delphi. It seems very possible, from the mention in antistrophe 3 of the Carneian feast, that the performance of this Ode coincided with the celebration of the religious festival in honour of Carneian Apollo—an important ceremony observed at Sparta and amongst other peoples of Dorian stock. Readers of Pindar's Pythian IX will see that he tells in that Ode the story of the abduction of the Greek maiden Cyrene by Apollo, who set her up as queen of a city in Libya to which she gave her name. Thus it is not surprising that the name of Apollo receives considerable emphasis throughout this Ode.

Pindar gives prominence, in a passage extending from epode 1 to the end of antistrophe 2, to a tribute to Carrhotus, who was the brother-in-law of Arcesilas and had been the charioteer of the winning chariot. If, as suggested in the foreword to Ode IV, it was Carrhotus who commissioned that Ode, and if Pindar thought, as is very probable, that Carrhotus would be largely instrumental in securing the pardon for Demophilus for which Pindar makes a strong appeal in Ode IV, it is easy to understand the reason for the inclusion here of this passage in praise of Carrhotus. It may be that Pindar's reason for writing this second Ode in honour of the same victory, containing as it does unusually lengthy and strongly expressed praises of Arcesilas, was to give further support to his appeal on behalf of Demophilus. These praises occupy most of the first triad and the whole of the last. After his tribute to Carrhotus, Pindar turns in epode 2 to Battus, who was the ancestor of Arcesilas, and who, as described in Ode IV, was proclaimed by the Delphic oracle as the man who was due to lead a company of Greeks from the island of Thera to colonize Libya and make Cyrene their capital city. The usual story of how Battus was freed from his stutter (in some versions he is pictured as being actually dumb), was that after arriving in Libya he met a lion, and was so startled that the shock gave him back his full powers of speech. In Pindar's more interesting version the shock to the lions seems to have been greater than that to Battus. Ode IV tells that Battus went to Delphi to ask for a cure for his stutter, but does not record that the oracle which promised him the kingship of Libya made any mention of a cure for his speech. Here the last lines of epode 2 seem to imply that the promise of a cure was either directly or indirectly included in the answer.

Strophe 3 turns to the praise of Apollo and goes on to imply that the settlement in the Peloponnese of the 'sons of Heracles and of Aegimius', that is to say the Dorian invaders, was due to Apollo or to his 'secret shrine', the Delphic oracle. There is more than one story connecting utterances of the Delphic oracle with events of the Dorian invasions. Pindar then refers to a matter in which he took pride, that he was himself a member of the Aegeid clan, a well-known family of ancient aristocratic stock who claimed descent from Aegeus, a legendary king of Athens and the father of Theseus. There were members of this clan at Sparta and in Spartan colonies including Cyrene, and a branch of the clan, to which Pindar belonged, at Thebes. Here in linking Battus and his followers, and their descendants Arcesilas and the Greeks of Cyrene, with this distinguished ancestry, Pindar was paying what was to his mind—and no doubt to the ears of his audience—a high compliment. It implies too that the government and administration of Cyrene were of the aristocratic type found in Sparta and other 'Dorian' cities, which from Pindar's conservative point of view was again a mark of merit.

In epode 3 mention is made of the 'straight-cut' and 'stone-paved' road built by Battus 'for processions'. Modern archaeology has confirmed the existence of this road. It seems probable that the return of Carrhotus was celebrated by a triumphant procession along the road, and that the performance of this Ode was linked with this. Pindar's knowledge of the stone-paved road, and of the position of the tombs of Battus and of other former kings, is sometimes taken as evidence that Pindar visited Cyrene, presumably to direct the performance of this Ode. There is no other evidence however to show that he did so, and it seems more probable that he derived this knowledge from Demophilus while in exile in Thebes, or from Carrhotus.

The Ode ends with a prayer that Zeus may allow Arcesilas to win the chariot-race at the Olympian Games, the event which was held in the highest prestige of all. Arcesilas in fact achieved this success two years later.

str. 1 Wide is the power of wealth,
Whenever a mortal man brings home,
Linked with untarnished honour, this gift of destiny,
A follower that shall win him many a friend.
Arcesilas, favoured of heaven, this to achieve,
Joined with fair fame,
Has been your journey's goal, since first your footsteps mounted
The firm foundation of your life's renown,
By the kind grace of Castor of the golden chariot,
Who after wintry storms sheds on your happy homestead
Serene and sunlit days.

ant. 1 Wise men can better bear
The power bestowed on them by heaven;
And for you, as you travel on your road of justice,
Abundant is the fortune that enfolds you.
Firstly, for that you are a king of mighty cities,
The genius bred
Of your inheritance sees this majestic honour
Here allied to the wisdom of your mind.
Next that now too, upon the famous field of Pytho,
You have won glory with your steeds, and this triumphant
Chorus of manly voices,

ep. 1 Wherein Apollo takes delight. Therefore forget not,
While at Cyrene in Aphrodite's pleasant garden
Your praise is sung, to ascribe
This glory to none other but the hand of god.
Nor fail to welcome first of your companions
Carrhotus in true friendship,

str. 1 *Castor:* there is said to have been a temple of Castor at Cyrene, one of the finest buildings in the city, sited beside the stone-paved road mentioned later in this Ode. Castor was a patron of charioteers, and also, with his brother Pollux, a protector of sailors and giver of fair weather.

After wintry storms: an allusion to the internal struggles which had troubled Cyrene in previous years.

ep. 1 *Aphrodite's pleasant garden:* this phrase may be Pindar's way of referring to the fertile region surrounding Cyrene, or there may have been a garden of this name in Cyrene of which Pindar had heard.

Carrhotus: see foreword. He was the brother of the wife of Arcesilas.

Who to the palace of the sons of Battus,
Who rule by right divine, has not returned
To bring with him Excuse
Daughter of late-contriving Afterthought;
But as a guest beside Castalia's fountain
Has set upon your brow
The crown of honour of his racing chariot.

str. 2 For with unbroken reins
He drove his flying-footed team
The twelve laps of the sacred course. Of his strong chariot
He broke no single piece of gear, but all
That skilful workmanship of craftsmen's hands he brought
Past Krisa's hill
To the god's deep valley; there it hangs now, consecrated
Within the shrine of cypress wood, hard by
That statue shaped from one tree's native growth, which once
The Cretan bowmen dedicated in their chapel
Beneath Parnassus' height.

ant. 2 Forth then, to welcome him
With true goodwill, who served us well.
Alexibiades, your name shines with the glory
Lit by the Graces of the lovely hair.
Blest is your lot indeed, who after mighty toil
Win for your name
A lasting monument of noble words. For you

Castalia's fountain: the well known spring at Delphi.

str. 2 *That skilful workmanship:* the Cyreneans were noted for the excellence of their chariots.

Past Krisa's hill: Krisa, also known as Kirrha, lay some miles down the valley from Delphi, and until the year 450 B.C. the events of the Pythian Games were held at Krisa. (See note to Pyth. III. str. 4). After his victory, Carrhotus drove his chariot from Krisa up to Delphi and consecrated it there. Pausanias, writing in the second century A.D., records that there were two chariots dedicated at Delphi by the Greeks of Cyrene, one of which contained a statue of Battus.

Hard by that statue: the Cretans had apparently dedicated at Delphi a statue formed of the trunk of a tree, which resembled a human figure. The Cyrenean chariot was probably placed near the Cretan statue because of an old connection between Crete and Cyrene.

ant. 2 *Alexibiades:* Carrhotus.

When forty drivers fell, with dauntless courage
Brought through your chariot unscathed, and now are come
Back from the glorious Games to Libya's plain, and to
The city of your fathers.

ep. 2 No man is spared his lot of ill, nor ever shall be.
Yet does the happy fortune given of old to Battus
Still ride its course, faring
Or high or low—a towering fortress for the city,
Shedding a radiant light to every stranger.
Battus it was, from whom
The roaring lions fled away in terror,
When spoken words fell from his tongue, made free
By powers across the sea.
For Apollo, founder and leader of his venture,
Struck the fierce creatures with that deadly fear,
That for Cyrene's master
His oracle might not be found to fail.

str. 3 To Apollo, too, we owe
The cures he gives to man and woman
For sore disease. He it was bestowed the lyre, and grants
The Poet's gift to those for whom he wills it.
He sets within man's heart the love of lawful living
And peaceful concord,
And rules the secret shrine where breed his oracles;
Whence for the valiant sons of Heracles
And of Aegimius he made their home in Sparta,
In Argos and holy Pylos. Mine to sing the lovely
Glory that came from Sparta,

Forty drivers fell: this seems a heavy casualty list and indicates a large number of competitors. No doubt the race was run in heats, but these were probably full enough to make collisions likely, particularly at the turns.

ep. 2 *Or high or low:* the history of Cyrene had not been without its ups and downs.

The roaring lions: see foreword.

By powers across the sea: i.e. Apollo through his oracle at Delphi.

str. 3 *Whence for the valiant sons, etc.:* as noted in the foreword Pindar is here implying that it was Apollo who through his Delphic oracle brought the Dorian invaders to cities of the Peloponnese—always regarded by Pindar as a beneficent event.

Aegimius: an early king of a people who joined the Dorian invaders.

ant. 3 For thence were bred the sons
Of Aegeus seed, my ancestors,
Who came to Thera, not without the gods' goodwill,
But destiny decreed their path. Thence came
Our heritage of the banquet, rich in sacrifice,
Where we pay honour
In the Carneian festal to your name Apollo,
And to the fair-built city of Cyrene,
Where once the bronze-armed Trojans dwelt, sons of Antenor,
Who came with Helen, when they saw their home in ashes,
Burnt in the flames of war.

ep. 3 And that proud horsemen's race receives a gracious greeting,
Since with rich gifts and sacrifice those warriors met them,
Whom in their ships of war
Aristoteles led, driving an open pathway
Through the deep seas. And honouring the gods
He founded greater precincts,
And for processions in Apollo's worship,
Sureties of mortal safety, he ordained
That there be made a road
To run straight-cut across the level plain,
Stone-paved, resounding to the horses' tread.
There in his grave, where ends
The market-place, he lies apart in death.

str. 4 Blest was his life 'mongst men.
Thereafter have his people worshipped
His hero's grave. And other sacred kings who trod
The road of death are laid before the palace

ant. 3 *Aegeus:* see foreword.
The Carneian festal: see foreword.
The bronze-armed Trojans: refugees from Troy, after its destruction by the Greeks, were supposed to have settled on the site which afterwards became Cyrene. According to one version of the story Helen, the famous cause of the Trojan war, fled to Africa before she was eventually restored to her husband Menelaus, king of Sparta.

ep. 3 *A gracious greeting:* Battus and his followers, on arriving at Cyrene, are said to have honoured the memory of these Trojans as tutelary heroes of the city, and Pindar's words imply that this ceremony in their honour was still maintained.
Aristoteles: another name for Battus.
A road . . . stone-paved: see foreword.
The market-place: as in several other cities of Greece, the tomb of the founder was set in the market-place.

In tombs apart. Maybe to souls below the earth
Great deeds are known,
Sparkling in the soft dew of flowing songs of triumph,
A wealth of joy for them and glorious honour
Shared with their son, Arcesilas—his due tribute.
With young men's voices must he now give praise to Phoebus,
God of the golden sword,

ant. 4 For he has won from Pytho,
Due reward for his rich endeavour,
The gracious song that hails the victor. Such a man
Wins the praise of the wise. On all men's tongues
These words I hear: that in the wisdom of his mind
And of his speech
He far surpasses all men of his age: in courage
A broad-winged eagle amongst birds; in combat
A tower of strength: to share the Muses' gift, he soared
Even from his mother's arms aloft: in racing chariots
His skill is now revealed.

ep. 4 All roads that lead to fame in his own countryside
He has been bold to tread. Now does the hand of heaven
Gladly ensure his power;
Grant him in times to come, oh blessed sons of Cronos,
A like success in action and in counsel.
And may no cruel breath
Of wintry winds that waste the fruits of autumn,
Strike to make havoc of his years hereafter.
The mighty mind of Zeus,
As all know well, governs the destiny
Of men he loves. I pray him now to grant
That at Olympia
A like renown falls to the race of Battus.

str. 4 *Young men's voices:* the choir performing this Ode.

ep. 4 *Olympia:* this request of Pindar was granted two years later in 460 B.C., when Arcesilas was victor in the chariot-race at the Olympian Games.

The hopes expressed by Pindar in the immediately preceding lines were not however fulfilled, since at some date between 460 and 450 B.C. Arcesilas lost his throne and his life in a revolt against his rule.

PYTHIAN VI

For

XENOCRATES OF ACRAGAS

Winner of the Chariot-Race

THIS poem was written in the year 490 B.C. Xenocrates, who was the nominal entrant for this chariot-race, was the brother of Theron of Acragas, who succeeded to the rule of that Sicilian city in 488 B.C. and became with Hieron of Syracuse one of the two most powerful rulers in the Greek cities of Sicily. Pindar was to write his second and third Olympian Odes in Theron's honour in the year 476.

While this Ode is addressed to Xenocrates, it is in fact written largely in honour of his son, Thrasybulus, who was probably the charioteer on this occasion. It appears that he was a charming young man and that Pindar, now 28 years old, was present as an onlooker at these Pythian Games and struck up a warm friendship with Thrasybulus, which is reflected in the language and tone of this Ode. The official epinician Ode for this victory is believed to have been commissioned from the poet Simonides, who was now sixty-six years old and more widely known at this date than the young Pindar. If this is so Pindar no doubt felt justified in making this Ode a tribute of a less formal kind to his new young friend. This friendship proved a lasting one, as we know from the second Isthmian Ode, which again celebrated a victory of Xenocrates gained in 477 B.C., though the Ode was not written until after the year 472. That Ode again marks Pindar's warm friendship for Thrasybulus and his family.

The construction of the present Ode follows the normal pattern. In the opening lines, after an invocation to Aphrodite and the Graces, appropriate in a poem which is a tribute to the poet's friendship, the Ode, or the chorus which is to perform it, is pictured as taking its way to the temple of Apollo, showing that the Ode was composed before the close of the festival and performed as an accompaniment to the triumphal march to the temple in honour of the victor. The metrical form of the Ode—a succession of strophes—was suited to this type of performance. The description of the Ode in the first strophe as a 'treasure-house of song' is an appropriate metaphor for an Ode performed at Delphi, where a feature of the sacred precincts was a number of 'treasuries', chapels stored with precious offerings, built by several city-states of Greece in honour of Apollo and the Delphic Oracle. Their remains can still be seen, and one of the best known, the Treasury of the Athenians, has in modern times been restored to its original shape.

After praises addressed to Xenocrates and to Thrasybulus the Ode proceeds in strophe 3 to the story of Antilochus, a hero of the Trojan war, who saved his father Nestor at the cost of his own life—a story chosen as an example of fidelity of a son to his father. At its close in strophe 5, Pindar points briefly to the parallel filial services of Thrasybulus in winning this victory for his father and in bringing glory to him and his uncle, Theron. The parallel is stretched rather far, but other Odes of Pindar are not without similar instances, and in a poem composed by a young man of twenty-eight years one need not grumble at a little exaggeration of this kind. The Ode ends with some charming phrases in further praise of Thrasybulus.

str. 1 Listen, I plough the meadow
Of Aphrodite of the glancing eyes, or of the Graces,
While to the shrine and centre-stone of sounding earth
We take our way. For here,
For the blest fortune of the Emmenidae,
For Acragas by her river, and for Xenocrates,
To grace the crown he won at Pytho,
A treasure-house of song is built and ready
In Apollo's golden-gifted vale.

str. 1 *The centre-stone of sounding earth:* the large stone in the hollow of a rock in the temple precinct of Delphi, on which the priestess of Apollo sat when issuing the oracle. It is often referred to in Greek literature, sometimes under the name of the 'navel of the earth'. The epithet 'sounding' is appropriate in an area liable to earthquakes.

The Emmenidae: the family name of Xenocrates and his brother Theron.

Golden-gifted: the temple of Apollo at Delphi was enriched with many precious gifts from individuals or states, including the 'treasuries' as noted in the foreword.

str. 2 This neither winter's rain,
The harsh invading host, born of the thunder-cloud,
Nor down to the deep sea-bed, flung with the rolling shingle
Shall the gales bear away;
But in unclouded light its front shall stand,
And for your father's honour, Thrasybulus, shared
By all his race, it shall proclaim
Your chariot victory in Krisa's dell
Glorious on the tongues of men.

str. 3 On your right hand you set him,
And thus fulfil the charge, given of old they say,
By Chiron on his hill to Achilles, far from home,
The strong-armed son of Peleus:—
'To Cronos' son, first of all gods, I bid you
To deep-voiced Zeus, lord of the lightnings and the thunder,
Your worship in full measure pay;
Then to your parents while their life shall last,
Like honour never fail to render.'

str. 4 In years of old this bidding
Mighty Antilochus obeyed full well, giving
His life to save his father. Firm he stood awaiting
The Ethiop captain's might,
Death-dealing Memnon, when the darts of Paris
Stayed Nestor's horse and chariot, and in hot pursuit
On old Messene's king bore down
Memnon's great spear. Shaken in terror's grip
Then loudly he cried to his son.

str. 2 *Krisa's dell:* i.e. the Pythian Games. See note on Pyth. III. str. 4.

str. 3 *On your right hand you set him:* i.e. you keep constantly in mind the duty you owe to your father.

Chiron: Achilles was sent as a boy (as were many other mythical heroes) to be educated by Chiron the Centaur, who lived on Mount Pelion.

str. 4 *Antilochus:* see foreword.

Ethiop captain: Memnon, the leader of the Ethiopians, who were allies of the Trojans in the Trojan war.

Paris: son of Priam, king of Troy. His abduction of Helen from Sparta was the cause of the Trojan war.

Messene's king: Nestor, the most elderly warrior of the Greeks, was king of Pylos in Messenia in the south-west Peloponnese.

str. 5 Nor to the empty air
Called he in vain. There stood, godlike, heroic courage,
And bought with his own death his father's life. This deed
Young men of old deemed glorious,
In pride of place for valour's debt to parents.
Those days are gone. Now Thrasybulus follows still
This rule of a father's due, and kindles,
Matching his uncle's honour, a flame of glory.
Wisely he rules his wealth, and reaps

str. 6 The rich fruit of his youth
In due justice, nor with rough pride's intemperate ardour;
And in the Muses' vale his skill is known. On thee
Poseidon, great earth-shaker,
Proud monarch of the chariot's racing steeds,
He now attends with loyal gifts, well pleasing to you.
Sweet is the temper of his heart,
In friendship and friends' company more sweet
Than the bees' storeyed honeycomb.

str. 5 *His uncle:* Theron.

str. 6 *The Muses' vale:* i.e. Thrasybulus is a poet or musician.
Poseidon: god of the sea and of sub-terranean powers. He was also closely associated with horses and credited with their creation. It is thus appropriate that Thrasybulus should be pictured as rendering thanks to this god.

PYTHIAN VII

For

MEGACLES OF ATHENS

Winner of the Chariot-Race

MEGACLES was a member of the Alcmaeonid clan which had for several generations been one of the most powerful and wealthy families of Athens. After the introduction of democratic government the family fell into disfavour, and according to Herodotus were suspected of favouring the Persians at the time of their invasion of Greece. Megacles gained this victory at the Pythian Games of 486 B.C., four years after the defeat of the first Persian invasion at the battle of Marathon. A few months before his Pythian victory Megacles had been banished from Athens.

The antistrophe recalls that the Alcmaeonid family had in the previous century charged themselves with the responsibility for rebuilding the temple of Apollo at Delphi, which was destroyed by fire in 548 B.C. They secured subscriptions from many parts of the Mediterranean world including Amasis, king of Egypt, and Croesus, king of Lydia, and the temple was rebuilt. It was damaged again by an earthquake in 373 B.C. and again rebuilt during the fourth century.

str. 1 Prelude most fair is Athens, the great city,
For a monument of song, founded to honour
The swift steeds of the sons
Of Alcmaeon, that race of widespread power.
For what land or what household could you boast,
Whose name can be proclaimed more glorious,
Through all Hellas?

ant. 1 For in all cities runs on every tongue
The story of Erechtheus' citizens,
Who made your house, Apollo,
At divine Pytho, glorious to behold.
Five wreaths at the Isthmus prompt my song, and one
Most famed, before Zeus at Olympia,
And two at Kirrha

ep. 1 Won by you, Megacles, and your forebears.
Now for your new success
My heart rejoices, but I grieve
That noble deeds find for their recompense
The wounds of envy. Yet so runs the saying,
If a man holds the flower of happy fortune
For many a day,
Then will it bring both good and ill.

ant. 1 *Erechtheus' citizens:* the Athenians. Erechtheus was an early mythical king of Athens.

Olympia: this Olympian victory was won by Alcmaeon, the great-grandfather of Megacles. Pindar does not mention how many of the other seven victories were won by Megacles, how many by his ancestors.

Kirrha: the Pythian Games. (See note to Pythian III. str. 4).

ep. 1 *Your new success:* this Pythian victory.

The wounds of envy: i.e. Megacles' banishment, which was decided upon by the method known as 'ostracism', a vote of the citizens of Athens.

PYTHIAN VIII

For

ARISTOMENES OF AEGINA

Winner of the Boys' Wrestling Contest

THIS Ode is written throughout in an exceptionally serious tone. It begins with an invocation to Peace, and its concluding lines are a prayer that the island of Aegina may enjoy freedom in the days to come. There is too in the final epode a remarkable passage on the ephemeral nature of human life and happiness, and their dependence on the will of heaven. This seems an unusual poem with which to celebrate the victory of a boy in an athletic contest. For an explanation one must look at the historical circumstances of the island of Aegina at the time when this Ode was written, and remember too the long-standing affection which Pindar had for Aegina and her people.

Though some editors have suggested an earlier date, the balance of evidence seems to point to 446 B.C. as the year of Aristomenes' Pythian victory and the composition of this Ode. In 456 B.C. the long-standing hostility between Athens and Aegina had culminated in the subjugation of the island, after a two-year siege, by the superior power of Athens. Forced to accept a government chosen by the Athenians and to become a tribute-paying member of the Athenian empire, it seemed that the days of Aegina's independence were over. In 447 B.C. however Athens suffered a severe defeat at the hands of Thebes at the battle of Coronea, and the strength of her position seemed in many directions by no means so secure. Early commentators on this Ode have noted that at the time of Aristomenes' Pythian victory, internal dissensions had arisen in Aegina. These may well have been the result of efforts on the part of the islanders to throw off the yoke imposed by Athens, efforts which enabled her to regain at least some small measure of her independence.

It is thus not surprising that in this Ode, written at a time when the final result of this movement in Aegina could not be known, Pindar includes his opening lines on Peace and his final prayer for Aegina's freedom. It is also thought very probable that in his references in the first triad to the overthrow of the giants Porphyrion and Typhon, Pindar is pointing a finger at the power of

Athens and her recent defeat at Coronea. It was a far cry now, some thirty years, to the days when Pindar had eulogized Athens as the 'bulwark of Hellas', and in the intervening years her growing power and imperialist policies had brought many of her former voluntary allies against the Persian menace to regard her not as the defender but as the enemy of the freedom of other city-states. Nor is it surprising if Pindar, now seventy-two years of age, with a keen recollection of the misfortunes of his Aeginetan friends during the last ten years and more, and with better hopes for their future by no means certain as yet, should allow this Ode to a young Aiginetan to reflect a more than usually contemplative and even sorrowful note.

The second triad is occupied with praise of Aegina and of Aristomenes, before turning in epode 2 and the third triad to the well-known legend of the second expedition against Thebes. In epode 3, apparently in order to show a connection between the present Ode and Alcman, the son of the prophet Amphiaraus, one of the heroes of that legend, Pindar uses phrases which appear to show that there was a shrine of Alcman not far from his home, and that while on his way to Delphi Pindar had had a dream or vision in which Alcman made a prophecy, perhaps of this victory of Aristomenes at the Pythian Games.

The fourth strophe and antistrophe express thanks to Apollo for granting Aristomenes his present victory and other successes, and offer a prayer for his continued goodwill. Then follows a note of warning that success can only be achieved through the favour of heaven, lines expressed as if in anticipation of the more deeply-felt phrase of the concluding epode. Praise of the victor is continued through strophe 5 and ends in antistrophe 5 with a vivid picture of the exultant, almost limitless joy which can attend a young man in the flush of his success. Then in marked contrast Pindar returns us to thoughts of the brevity and frailty of human happiness and its dependence on the divine will, and concludes with his prayer for Aegina.

str. 1 Peace, goddess of friendly intent,
Daughter of Justice, you who make cities great,
Holding the supreme keys of counsel and of wars—
For Aristomenes I beg your welcome,
For the honour of his victory at Pytho.
You understand well both to give and to receive
Gifts from a gentle hand in due season.

ant. 1 But when a man breeds in his heart
Pitiless wrath, then does your spirit fiercely
Rise up to face the enemies' power, and to throw down
Insolence to the depths. Porphyrion
Even he knew not your strength when he provoked you
Beyond all measure. Dearest of all good things to win
Is from the house of one who gives it freely.

ep. 1 But violence brings to ruin even
The boastful hard-heart soon or late.
Cilician Typhon of the hundred heads
Could not escape his fate, nor could
Even the great king of the Giants,
But by the thunderbolt
They were laid low, and by Apollo's shafts;
Who now has graciously welcomed Xenarkes' son
From Kirrha, with the green wreath of Parnassus
Crowning him, and the Dorian song of triumph.

str. 2 Near to their heart the Graces hold
This island, queen of Justice, who knew well
The glorious valour of the sons of Aeacus;
From the beginning perfect was her fame.
In many a song her praise is told, the nurse
Of heroes of supreme renown, victors proclaimed
On the athletes' field and in the surge of battle.

ant. 1 *Porphyrion:* one of the Giants who took part in their struggle against Zeus and the other Olympian deities. It is to him that Pindar refers as 'king of the Giants' in the epode that follows.

Dearest of all good things, etc.: this sentence presumably means to emphasize the greater value of gifts given freely than of possessions taken by force.

ep. 1 *Typhon:* another of the Giants, whose birthplace according to legend was in Cilicia in Asia Minor. In Pythian I Pindar pictures him as confined beneath Mount Aetna.

The thunderbolt: the weapon of Zeus, who overthrew Typhon, while Porphyrion was killed by the arrows of Apollo.

Xenarkes' son: Aristomenes.

Kirrha: i.e. the Pythian Games (see note to Pyth. III. str. 4).

Dorian song: this Ode was written for music in the 'Dorian' mode.

str. 2 *The Graces hold this island:* in other passages in the Odes Pindar speaks of the people of Aegina as lovers of music and poetry. (e.g. Nem. VII. ant. 1).

This island, queen of Justice: Aegina had a long record of successful maritime trading, and a high reputation for fair-dealing with the many merchants who did business with her.

ant. 2 Glorious too, her breed of men.
Time passes and allows me not to offer
To the lyre and softly-singing voices all the legend
Of her renown—lest surfeit breed resentment.
But for the task in hand, let me now pay
The debt to you, son, for this latest deed of glory,
And by my art raise it on spreading wings.

ep. 2 For in the wrestler's ring your skill
Put not to shame your mother's brothers,
Theognatus victor at Olympia,
And hardy-limbed Cleitomachus,
Matching his Isthmian victory.
But raising high the glory
Of the Meidylid clan you bring to proof
That word of sooth which Oikleus' son long since foretold,
When within seven-gated Thebes he saw
Those sons stand firm in the sharp thrust of battle;

str. 3 When the Epigoni from Argos
Marched on their second journey. Thus he spoke
As the battle raged: 'By nature's gift, father to son,

ant. 2 *To you, son:* to Aristomenes.

ep. 2 Of these two uncles of Aristomenes, nothing further is known to us of Cleitomachus, but Theognatus is probably the man whose statue is said by the historian Pausanias to have been on view at Olympia, in token of his victory in a boy's wrestling contest.

The Meidylid clan: the family to which Aristomenes belonged.

That word of sooth: see note to strophe 3.

Oikleus' son: the legendary Amphiaraus who took part in the disastrous expedition of the 'Seven against Thebes' under the leadership of Adrastus king of Argos. Amphiaraus was a famous prophet as well as a warrior. He lost his life in this expedition, as did all the other leaders except Adrastus. His prophecy, or vision, here recounted by Pindar, refers to the second successful expedition against Thebes, made a generation later, led by Alcmaeon, or Alcman, the son of Amphiaraus, and accompanied by Adrastus and his son Aegialeus. It is not clear from the legend, as told here, how or when the dead Amphiaraus made known to living ears his vision of the success which would attend this second expedition.

Those sons: i.e. Alcman, Aegialeus, and others of the same second generation.

str. 3 *The Epigoni:* the 'Successors', the usual name given to the leaders of the second expedition.

By nature's gift, etc.: this opening sentence is the '*word of sooth*', mentioned in the preceding epode. One of Pindar's favourite themes is the superiority of inherited talent, and by expressing it here, he in this way provides a link between the successes of Aristomenes and the legend of Amphiaraus and his son Alcman.

Do noble souls excel. Clear is the vision
My eyes behold—Alcman, a speckled dragon
Brandished upon his gleaming shield, foremost of all
Sets foot within the gates of Cadmus' city.

ant. 3 'But he who in that first essay
Suffered disastrous loss, hero Adrastus,
Is now upheld by tidings of a better omen:
But for his house far otherwise shall it be,
For he alone of all the Danaan host
Shall gather up his son's dead bones, before he comes
By the gods' fortune with his folk unscathed

ep. 3 To the broad streets of Abas.' Thus
Amphiaraus' voice proclaimed.
But I too with my own hands gladly set
Garlands on Alcman's grave, and shower
The dewdrops of my song upon him.
For he is neighbour to me,
And is the guardian of my possessions,
And when to the centre-stone of earth, that home of song,
I made my way, he met me and proved the skills
Of prophecy that all his race inherit.

Cadmus' city: Thebes. Cadmus was the city's founder and first king.

ant. 3 *That first essay:* the previous expedition of the 'Seven against Thebes'.

Far otherwise: although the second expedition was easily successful, Aegialeus, the son of Adrastus, was killed.

ep. 3 *The broad streets of Abas:* the city of Argos. Abas was a former legendary king of the city. This account varies from the usual version of the story, which tells that on hearing of his son's death Adrastus immediately died of grief, and so did not return to Argos.

For he is neighbour to me: it seems likely that there was a shrine of Alcman not far from Pindar's house in Thebes, and that in naming him '*the guardian of my possessions*' Pindar means that he regarded him as the protector of his home. Possibly the phrase means that Pindar had deposited valuables in the shrine, using it as a treasury, as was frequently done in Greece in those times.

He met me and proved the skills, etc.: presumably Pindar means that while he was on his way to Delphi, Alcman appeared to him in a dream or vision and prophesied an event which proved true. Since this is mentioned in this Ode, it is possible that the prophecy foretold the victory of Aristomenes.

str. 4 But thou, god of the far-shot arrows,
Ruling the glorious temple in the glens
Of Pytho, where all find a welcome, thou hast given
Aristomenes this greatest of all joys;
And once in his own land you gave to him
The treasured prize of the Pentathlon, at the feast
Of Leto's children. O king, now I pray thee

ant. 4 Look down with kind intent to hear
My harmonies, where and for whomsoever
My music brings its varied notes. Those mellow voices
In songs of triumph have Justice at their side.
For the fortunes of your house I beg, Xenarkes,
The gods' unfailing favour. Many a man may think
That he who wins success with no long labour

ep. 4 Is a wise man 'midst fools, arming
His life with skills of prudent counsel.
But success lies not in the power of men;
It is a deity bestows it,
Exalting one man now, another
Crushing beneath strong hands.
Forward then, but with measured step. Megara
And Marathon's plain gave you their prize; and your own country
At Hera's contest, Aristomenes,
Saw you indeed prevailing, thrice a victor.

str. 4 *God of the far-shot arrows:* Apollo.
The feast of Leto's children: a festival held in Aegina in honour of Apollo and Artemis, at which were held competitive athletic events.

ant. 4 *Have Justice at their side:* i.e. the victory of Aristomenes and the consequent honour of the performance of this Ode by the chorus was well deserved by him.
Xenarkes: the father of Aristomenes.

ep. 4 *Megara and Marathon's plain:* local games in which Aristomenes had been successful.
At Hera's contest: apparently another festival held in Aegina in honour of Hera.

str. 5 Now from on high on four young bodies
You hurled your strength with fierce intent. For them
No happy homecoming from Pytho was decreed,
As that of yours, nor at their mother's side
Could pleasant laughter ring a joyful greeting
For their return. But shunning hostile eyes, they creep
By quiet paths, o'erwhelmed by their ill-fortune.

ant. 5 But he to whom is given new glory
In the rich sweetness of his youth, flies up
Aloft, high hope fulfilled, on wings of soaring valour,
In realms that brook no dullard cares of wealth.
But man's delight flowers but for a brief moment,
And no less swiftly falls to the ground again, shattered
By destined will that may not be gainsaid.

ep. 5 Creatures of a day! What is a man?
What is he not? A dream of a shadow
Is our mortal being. But when there comes to men
A gleam of splendour given of Heaven,
Then rests on them a light of glory
And blessèd are their days.
Aegina, mother beloved, grant that in freedom
This city's onward path be set, by the goodwill
Of Zeus and great king Aeacus, of Peleus
And noble Telamon and of Achilles.

str. 5 *On four young bodies:* the wrestling contest won by Aristomenes was clearly an event arranged on the 'knock-out' system, requiring him to win four ties in order to be proclaimed victor.

ep. 5 *Aegina, mother beloved:* Pindar addresses his prayer to the personified spirit and protectress of the island.

In freedom: see foreword.

Aeacus: the first legendary king of Aegina. Peleus and Telamon were his sons, Achilles his grandson. As in all the Odes written by Pindar for Aeginetan victors, he does not fail to pay honour to one or more members of the clan of Aeacus.

PYTHIAN IX

For

TELESICRATES OF CYRENE

Winner of the Race in Armour

This Ode celebrates a victory won at the Pythian Games of 474 B.C. The city of Cyrene, to which the victor Telesicrates belonged, was a prosperous Greek colony in Libya in North Africa. After a brief line of invocation to the Graces, and an equally brief mention of Telesicrates, the Ode embarks upon the story of the maid Cyrene, who gave her name to the African colony when abducted there by the god Apollo. This myth affords a happy example of Pindar's ability to tell in lyric verse a story of gaiety and vivid characterization. At the end of this myth, which takes us to epode 3, it would have been normal for a passage to follow expressing further praise of the victor. There is however only the briefest mention of Telesicrates—'Carneades' son'—and the Ode turns abruptly at the beginning of the fourth strophe to an entirely different theme, occupying almost the whole of the fourth triad. This is prefaced by one of those intrguing generalizations often found in the Odes. The more abruptly, as here, that such an aside is introduced and the more noticeable the pithiness of its thought and language, the more likely is it to be an indication that Pindar wishes to draw special attention to what follows. Here there follows a tribute to the ancient heroes of Thebes and a statement by Pindar in the last lines of antistrophe 4, that at Aegina and Megara (Nisus' hill) he has three times 'sung this city's glory'.

In this context there can be little doubt that in this phrase Pindar is here referring to Thebes, although some editors have adduced reasons, not very convincingly, to show that the reference is to the city of Cyrene. As has been stated in the Introduction to this volume, there were special reasons, at the time this Ode was written, why Pindar was anxious to demonstrate his loyalty to Thebes, and there can be little doubt that this passage, which has little reference to Telesicrates of Cyrene, was intended as a compliment to Thebes. We cannot know to which of his poems Pindar is referring in mentioning the three poems written at Aegina and Megara. It is possible that two of them are the third and fourth Nemean Odes, written in honour of citizens of Aegina probably soon after Pindar's return from Sicily, in which he goes out of his way to pay a tribute to Heracles, who was of course a Theban hero. These references here, together with the opening sentences of epode 4 seem likely, as suggested in the Introduction, to be Pindar's way of emphasizing that his loyalty to Thebes was never far from his mind, and to be his answer to possible criticisms that owing to his absence from Thebes he had done little for the city by way of acts 'well done for the good of all', during the painful times which Thebes suffered in these years after the defeat of the Persians in 479 B.C.

In the second half of epode 4 there is a further brief passage in praise of Telesicrates, followed in strophe 5 by a second myth, telling the story of how an ancestor of Telesicrates, Alexidamus by name, won the hand of a Libyan bride, the daughter of Antaeus of Irasa. This story takes us to the end of the Ode. The first, longer, myth has paid honour to the victor's city, Cyrene; the second honours the victor's ancestors. Both myths have to do with the love affairs of man and maid, and it has been suggested by some commentators that Telesicrates was about to celebrate his own marriage either with a bride from Cyrene, or possibly one from Thebes. There is no confirmation however of this conjecture.

str. 1 The Pythian victory let me now proclaim,
With the deep-girdled Graces' aid,
Of Telesicrates, clad in his brazen armour,
And cry aloud his happy name,
Who brings a crown of glory to Cyrene,
Famed for her charioteers:
She it was whom once Apollo of the flowing hair
Seized from the windswept vales of Pelion,
And in his golden car bore off the huntress maid;
And of a land, most richly blessed
With flocks and fruits, made her the enthronéd queen,
To find on this third root of earth's mainland
A smiling and fertile home.

str. 1 *Pelion:* the high mountain near the east coast of Thessaly in north-central Greece. Mount Pelion was the home of Chiron the Centaur, the immortal and kindly character to whom many of the mythical heroes of ancient Greece were sent in their young days to be suitably educated.

A land most richly blessed: Libya in North Africa.

Third root of earth's mainland: North Africa was regarded by the ancients as the third part of the known world, after Europe and Asia.

ant. 1 And Aphrodite of the silver feet
Welcomed this guest from Delos, laying
The touch of her light hand upon his god-built car,
And o'er the sweet bliss of their bridal
She spread love's shy and winsome modesty,
Plighting in joint wedlock
The god and maiden daughter of wide-ruling Hypseus.
He was then king of the proud Lapithae,
A hero of the seed of the great god of Ocean,
Child of the second generation,
Whom in the famous dells of Pindus once
The Nymph, daughter of Earth, Creusa bore,
Sharing the joys of love

ep. 1 With the river-god Peneius. And by Hypseus
Was reared this maid, Cyrene of the lovely arms.
But she loved not the pacing tread
This way and that beside the loom,
Nor the delights of merry feasts
With her companions of the household. But the bronze-tipped
Javelin and the sword called her to combat
And slay the wild beasts of the field;
And in truth many a day she gave
Of peaceful quiet to her father's cattle.
But of sleep, sweet companion of her pillow,
Little she spared to steal upon her eyes
Towards the dawn of day.

ant. 1 *Guest from Delos:* the island of Delos in the Aegean was the birthplace of Apollo. There was a strong cult of Aphrodite in Libya, sometimes spoken of as her home, so that Apollo can here be referred to as her guest.

Hypseus: the father of Cyrene, is spoken of as a grandson of Poseidon, god of the sea, because his father Peneius was a river-god and thus regarded as a son of the ocean.

Lapithae: the Lapithae or Lapiths were reputed to be a race of northern Greece, whose territory included the area near the mouth of the river Peneius on the east coast of Greece just south of Mount Olympus.

Pindus: Mount Pindus is the large mountain range on the western side of the whole of north and central Greece.

str. 2 Once as she battled with a fearsome lion,
Alone, without a spear, Apollo,
Far-shooting god of the broad quiver, came upon her;
And straightway called from out his dwelling
Chiron and thus addressed him: 'Son of Philyra,
Come from your holy cave,
And marvel at a woman's spirit and mighty vigour;
With what undaunted mind she wages battle,
A young maid with a heart that rides o'er every labour,
And a spirit that is never shaken
By the cold storms of fear. What mortal father
Begot this maid? And from what race of men
Has she been reft, to dwell

ant. 2 'Within the dark dells of these clouded mountains?
For her soul breeds a boundless wealth
Of valour. Is it right to lay on her the touch
Of an ennobling hand, or even
To pluck the flower of love, sweeter than honey?'
Then spoke the inspired Centaur,
Gentle laughter gleaming beneath his kindly brows
And of his wisdom made straightway this answer:
'Secret, great Phoebus, are the keys of wise Persuasion
To love's true sanctities; both gods
And men alike, in reverent modesty,
Are loth to taste in the open light of day
The first sweet fruits of love.

ep. 2 'Yet thou, for whom even to savour falsehood
Is sacrilege, art led by thy desire's delight
Thus to dissemble. Dost thou ask,
O king, of what race is the maiden?
Thou who knowest well the fated end
Of all things, whither all roads shall lead, who know'st the number
Of leaves that earth puts forth to meet the spring,
How many grains of sand the surge
Of ocean, or the sweeping gales
Send rolling down beside the river banks;
Thou who see'st clearly what shall be, and whence
It shall betide! Yet if I needs must rival
My wisdom against thine,

str. 2 *Son of Philyra:* Chiron was the son of Philyra by Cronos, the father of Zeus. Surprised in the act of making love to Philyra by his wife Rhea, Cronos turned himself into a stallion, thus causing Philyra's child to be half-man, half-horse.

str. 3 'Thus shall I speak: to this glade didst thou come
To be a husband to this maid,
With the intent to carry her far o'er the ocean,
To a choice garden of great Zeus.
There thou shalt set her to rule o'er a city,
And gather an island folk
To be her people, where a high hill crowns the plain.
And soon shall Libya, queen of spreading meadows,
Gladly welcome to her gold halls thy glorious bride;
And forthwith will she freely give her,
To be her own lawful domain, a portion
Of land yielding all manner of rich fruits,
And beasts for the hunter's chase.

ant. 3 'There shall she bear a son, whom glorious Hermes
Will take from his fond mother's breast,
And carry to the enthronéd Hours and Mother Earth;
And they will gently nurse the babe
Upon their knees, and on his lips distil
Ambrosia and nectar,
And shall ordain him an immortal being, a Zeus
Or holy Apollo, a joy to men who love him.
And he shall ever be at hand to tend their flocks,
Agreus his name to some, to others
Nomius, and some will call him Aristaeus.'
So Chiron spoke and decreed for the god
His bridal's dear fulfilment.

ep. 3 Swift is the act, and short thereto the paths
When gods make speed to achieve an eager end. That day
That very day saw the decision,
And in a chamber of rich gold
In Libya they lay together.
There she is guardian of a city rich in beauty,
And glorious in the Games. For at holy Pytho
With the sweet flower of his success,
Carneades' son has dowered Cyrene,
And by his victory proclaimed her glory.

str. 3 *Garden of great Zeus:* this means Zeus Ammon, whose sanctuary was not far from Cyrenaica.

ant. 3 *Aristaeus:* a deity associated in many parts of the Greek world with various kinds of agricultural work including particularly sheep-keeping, cheese-making, bee-keeping and olive culture. His name was also associated with healing and prophecy, and with hunting. Aristaeus, also known in different areas by the names of Agreus and Nomius, appears to have been a cult-title of Zeus in Arcadia, of Apollo and Hermes in other areas.

ep. 3 *Carneades' son:* Telesicrates.

Gladly will she receive him, as he brings
From Delphi to his country of fair women
The fame all men desire.

str. 4 Brave deeds, high merits are ever rich in story,
But great themes briefly to embroider
Wins the ear of the wise; yet, above all, true timing
Achieves the furthest goal. This precept
Iolaus long ago was seen to honour,
By Thebes of the seven gates.
For when this hero had struck off Eurystheus' head
With his sword's shining blade, the city laid him
To rest beneath the earth within Amphitryon's tomb,
The charioteer, his father's father,
Where that great guest of the Sparti was laid,
Who came to dwell in the Cadmeans' city,
Those riders of white steeds.

ant. 4 Wife to Amphitryon, and bearing, too,
Within her womb the seed of Zeus,
The wise Alcmene, in single pangs of labour, bore
Twin sons invincible in battle.
Dumb is the man whose tongue never made play
With Heracles' great name,

str. 4 *Brave deeds . . ., etc.:* see foreword. The lines constitute Pindar's apology to Telesicrates for giving an unusually small space in the Ode to praises of his victory, which would normally be expressed here, at the conclusion of the myth. Pindar means that the 'brave deeds' of Telesicrates will never lack people to tell of them, and that to men who are 'wise', or of poetic sensibility—either translation is possible—what matters is that the poem should 'embroider', that is, give an attractive and decorative setting to 'great themes', even if they are 'briefly' stated. Pindar may well claim to have given the attractive setting in the myth just concluded. Thirdly, important 'above all', what is written must be well-timed, 'true timing' being as important in a literary context as in any other. Here Pindar uses the precept to supply a link with what follows, his reference to the timely deed of the Theban hero Iolaus.

Iolaus: the son of Iphicles and nephew of Heracles. When news reached him that Eurystheus, king of Mycenae, was planning to kill the children of Heracles, he prayed that he might be restored to his youthful strength in order to prevent this. His prayer was granted, Eurystheus slain, and the children saved by his timely action.

That great guest: Amphitryon's native city was Argos before he came to settle in Thebes.

The Sparti: the 'Sown Men'. Cadmus, the mythical founder of Thebes, was told by Athene to sow the teeth of a serpent in the soil. From these sprang up warriors who became followers of Cadmus and ancestors of the Thebans.

ant. 4 *Twin sons:* Heracles and Iphicles.

And has not ever in remembrance Dirke's stream,
That nourished him and Iphicles. Now would I
To both sing songs of triumph, who served me in good stead,
Answering my prayer; and may I never
Lose the pure light of the sweet-singing Graces,
For thrice at Aegina and by Nisus' hill
Have I sung this city's glory,

ep. 4 And thus escaped the blame of helpless silence.
Wherefore let no man, whether he be friend or foe
Seek to conceal an act well done
For the good of all, thereby contemning
The rule which Nereus once proclaimed,
The Old Man of the Sea: 'Even to an enemy
If he is acting nobly, we should offer
Full-hearted praise and that most justly'.
How many a crown, too, have you won
At the season's feast of Pallas, where young maidens
Watching, each breathed a silent prayer that one
Like Telesicrates might be her well-loved
Husband or dearest son,

str. 5 Whether at the Olympian Games, or at the contests
In the vale of deep-breasted Earth
And all the games of your own land. But while I seek
To slake my thirst for song, a voice
Bids me requite a debt, and for your forbears
Revive their ancient glory,
Telling the tale, how for a Libyan bride they rode
To the city of Irasa, to seek the hand
Of Antaeus' glorious daughter, maid of the lovely hair.

Dirke's stream: a river close to Thebes.

Who served me in good stead: it is not clear what favour Pindar here claims to have been given.

Nisus' hill: Megara. Nisus was an early king of that city.

This city's glory: see foreword.

ep. 4 *The season's feast of Pallas:* this appears to have been a local festival in Cyrene, in honour of Athene.

str. 5 *Olympian Games . . . the contests in the vale of deep-breasted earth:* since no female spectators were allowed entry to the Panhellenic Games, some editors have concluded that this apparent reference to the Olympian and Pythian Games must in fact refer to local games near Cyrene, which were given names borrowed from Olympia and Delphi. Perhaps an easier solution would be that the 'young maidens watching' at the local games, 'the season's feast of Pallas', hoped for a husband or a son who might win the greater honour of an Olympian or Pythian victory as Telesicrates has done.

Antaeus: an ancester of Telesicrates, through his daughter who married Alexidamus, referred to in epode 5.

Many a gallant chief of men
Of her own kin, and many a stranger sought her
To be his bride, for indeed was her beauty
Wonderful to behold.

ant. 5 And much they longed to cull the ripened fruit
Of Youth's fair vision, golden-crowned.
But planning for his child a yet more glorious marriage,
Her father called to mind the story,
How Danaus long ago achieved in Argos
For eight and forty daughters,
Before the noon of day, the speediest of marriage.
For he set all the gathered company
There at the finish of the race-course, and proclaimed
That all the heroes who were come
To be his daughter's suitors, must decide
By trial of their speed of foot, which maid
For each should be his bride.

ep. 5 So too the Libyan king, to a groom thus chosen
Offered his daughter's hand. And at the line he set her,
Adorned in all her fair array
To be the goal and final prize;
And declared to them all: 'That man
Who first, leading the field, shall touch the maiden's robes,
Shall take her for his bride'. Then down the course
Swiftest of all, Alexidamus
Raced to his prize, the noble maid,
And through the ranks of Nomad horsemen led her
By hand, while they flung countless sprays and wreaths
On him who many a time e'er this had worn
The plumes of Victory.

ant. 5 *Danaus:* this passage refers to the well-known story of Danaus king of Argos, twin brother of Aegyptus king of Egypt, with whom he had quarrelled. Aegyptus, intending to overthrow Danaus, sent his fifty sons to Argos with a demand that they should marry the fifty daughters of Danaus. He refused and the fifty sons laid siege to Argos. To save the city, which ran out of water, Danaus agreed to the marriages and arranged for the suitors to race for their brides as here described. But he secretly armed each of his daughters with a sword, telling them to kill their husbands on the marriage night. All did so except Hypermnestra who spared her husband Lynceus and helped him to escape. Another daughter Amymone had been the bride of Poseidon, and Pindar was apparently omitting these two in speaking of 'forty-eight' daughters.

ep. 5 *The Libyan king:* Antaeus.

PYTHIAN X

For

HIPPOCLEAS OF THESSALY

Winner of the Boys' Double-Stade Foot-Race

THIS Ode, written in 498 B.C. when Pindar was twenty years old, is the earliest of his Odes which has come down to us. The boy victor, Hippocleas, was a native of Pelinna, or Pelinnaeon, a city of western Thessaly. The double-stade, the length of the stadium and back again, was a race of something over 400 yards.

The Aleuadae, the 'sons of Aleuas' mentioned in the opening strophe, were an aristocratic Thessalian family who claimed descent from Heracles and had an important place in the government of Thessaly. It was this family who commissioned this Ode on behalf of Hippocleas, who was a relative or a protégé of theirs. The head of the clan at this time was Thorax to whom Pindar expresses his thanks in the fourth antistrophe. His two brothers, mentioned in the final epode, were Eurypylus and Thrasydaeus. It is recorded by Herodotus that in later years all three took sides, as did the city of Thebes, with the invading Persians under Xerxes in 480 B.C.

For the myth in this Ode, Pindar gives a description of the happy life of the Hyperboreans, the 'Men-beyond-the-North-Wind', a legendary people supposed by the Greeks to have lived in the northerly regions round the river Ister, the modern Danube. They were closely associated with Apollo, which is no doubt Pindar's reason for choosing this subject for inclusion in a Pythian Ode. Coupled with the Hyperboreans are references to Perseus, who visited them while on his journey to find and decapitate the Gorgon, Medusa, a story told at greater length in Pythian XII. The link with Perseus is that as an ancestor of Heracles he was also an ancestor of the Aleuadae.

In this early poem Pindar already shows many of the idiosyncrasies of his outlook, methods of expression and style, which recur constantly throughout his Odes. His liking and respect for high birth and aristocratic rule appear in the opening passage of the Ode and again in its closing lines. In the first line of the poem he is paying a compliment to Thessaly in bracketing her name with that of the more powerful state of Sparta, the outstanding example of conservative government. Other typical Pindaric *motifs* are that man's happiest successes are those which have the approval of heaven, and that inherited skills are the best (ant. 1): the changeability of human fortune is suggested, coupled with the claim that victory in the Games is amongst the 'fairest glories' that mortal men can attain (str. 2 and ant. 2). Epode 3 declares Pindar's belief in the omnipotence of the gods, and continues with an example of his not infrequent habit of suddenly addressing a few lines to himself, in this case, as elsewhere, in order to say that it is time for the Ode to return from mythical stories or other interludes to its main subject. Typical too is the quick change of metaphor in this passage, in which the Ode is likened first to a ship and then to a bee 'flitting from flower to flower'.

str. 1 Happy is Sparta; blessed is Thessaly,
For from one ancestor has each its king,
Sprung from great Heracles valiant in battle.
    And is this boast untimely?
No, for Pytho and Pelinnaeon call me
And the sons of Aleuas, bidding me
Bring for the honour of Hippocleas,
This choir of men in glory's song of triumph.

ant. 1 For he is tasting of the contests' joy,
And the vale of Parnassus has declared him,
To all the neighbouring folk, first of the boys
    Who ran the double course.
Be it sped by heaven's will, sweet, O Apollo,
Is a man's success, its end and its beginning;
And this he owes first to your favour, then
To his heritage of skill, bred from his father,

str. 1 *Pytho:* Delphi, that is to say, the Pythian Games.
Pelinnaeon: also known as Pelinna, the native city of Hippocleas, in Western Thessaly.
The sons of Aleuas: the clan of the Aleuadae. See foreword.

ant. 1 *The vale of Parnassus:* Delphi, which lies close to Mount Parnassus.

ep. 1 Who won Olympia's prize
Twice in the race of men armoured for war;
And at the contest in the folded meadow
Beneath the rock of Kirrha, the fleet foot
Of Phrikias once again
Gave him the victor's crown. May a kind fate
Alike in days to come, grant them
Fresh blossoms to adorn their wealthy splendour.

str. 2 Of the dear joys that Hellas gives, they hold
No meagre share, and may they meet from heaven
No envious turning of the ways. Whose heart
Knows naught of sorrow, let him
Be named a god. But happy, and well worthy
Of poets' song, is he whose valiant skill
Of hand or foot wins for his strength and daring
The highest prize of victory in the Games,

ant. 2 Or he who lives to see his youthful son
By fit decree of fate win Pytho's crowns.
Not for his feet the brazen vault of heaven;
Yet of the fairest glories
That mortals may attain, to him is given
To sail to the furthest bound. Yet neither ship
Nor marching feet may find the wondrous way
To the gatherings of the Hyperborean people.

ep. 2 Yet was it with these that Perseus
The warrior chief once feasted, entering
Their homes, and chanced upon their sacrifices
Unto the god, those famous offerings
Of hecatombs of asses;
For in their banquets and rich praise Apollo
Greatly delights, and laughs to see
The rampant lewdness of those brutish beasts.

ep. 1 *The rock of Kirrha:* i.e. the Pythian Games (see note on Pyth. III. str. 4).
Phrikias: the father of Hippocleas.

ant. 2 *The Hyperborean people:* see foreword.

ep. 2 *The god:* Apollo, with whom the Hyperboreans were closely associated in Greek mythology. He is often pictured in Greek literature as visiting the river Ister (the Danube) where the Hyperborean territory was supposed to be located.

str. 3 Nor is the Muse a stranger to their life,
But on all sides the feet of maidens dancing,
The full tones of the lyre and pealing flutes
Are all astir; with leaves
Of gleaming laurel bound upon their hair,
They throng with happy hearts to join the revel.
Illness and wasting old age visit not
This hallowed race, but far from toil and battle

ant. 3 They dwell secure from fate's remorseless vengeance.
There with the breath of courage in his heart,
Unto that gathering of happy men,
By guidance of Athene,
Came long ago the son of Danaë,
Perseus, who slew the Gorgon, and brought her head
Wreathed with its serpent locks to strike stony
Death to the islanders. But no marvel,

ep. 3 Be it wrought by the gods,
Can to me ever seem beyond belief.
Hold now your oar, and quickly from the prow
Cast anchor to the deep sea-bed, to hold
Our ship from the rocky reef.
For like a bee flitting from flower to flower,
The rich strain of my songs of triumph
Lights now on one tale now upon another.

str. 4 But while the men of Ephyra pour forth
My pleasant songs beside Peneius' bank,
I hope that for the crowns he won, my music
May bring Hippocleas
Yet greater glory amongst his own age-fellows
And amongst elder folk, and tender maids
Cherish his image in their hearts. Who knows?
Or here or there the shafts of love may strike.

ant. 3 *Perseus:* the well known story of Perseus and the Gorgon Medusa is told at greater length by Pindar in Pythian Ode XII. Perseus brought the head of Medusa, which turned anyone who looked at it to stone, back to the island of Seriphos, where his mother Danaë was held captive by king Polydectes, and turned the king and his followers into stone.

ep. 3 *Hold now your oar:* in this passage Pindar is addressing himself; see foreword.

str. 4 *The men of Ephyra:* the Thessalians who formed Pindar's chorus. The name Ephyra, usually meaning Corinth, is applied to more than one place in northern Greece, and here it appears to apply to Thessaly.

Peneius: the large river which crosses Thessaly from west to east, and flows into the sea between Mount Olympus and Mount Ossa.

ant. 4 Let every man who strives, and wins his aim,
Grasp and hold firm today's eager desire;
What may betide a twelve-month hence, the mind
Of no man can foresee.
In Thorax is my trust, my generous host,
Who labours for my pleasure, and has yoked
This four-horsed chariot of the Muse, in friendship
Given and returned, leading my willing steps.

ep. 4 As gold shows its true worth
When tried upon the touchstone, so too shines forth
An upright mind. Now shall my praises ring
In honour also of his noble brothers,
For they make prosperous
And glorify the state of Thessaly.
In good men's hands, born of true blood,
The pilotage of cities rests secure.

ant. 4 *Chariot of the Muse*: this Ode, commissioned by Thorax.

PYTHIAN XI

For

THRASYDAEUS OF THEBES

Winner of the Boys' Foot-Race

THIS Ode is addressed to a fellow-citizen of Pindar, and was written in the year 474, soon after Pindar's return from Sicily, for performance, as the Ode makes clear, at a festival to be held in a Theban sanctuary. In this poem Pindar gives another markedly interesting example of *double entendre*, of his way of launching, as he says in another Ode (Ol. II. str. 5) 'arrows speaking to men of wisdom, but for the throng they need interpreters'. The key to the underlying purpose of this Ode, perhaps in Pindar's mind its main purpose, lies in passages in the fourth strophe and antistrophe. A sentence 'May the gods grant me . . . etc.' breaks suddenly into the theme of the fourth strophe with little or no apparent connection with what has gone before, a feature often indicative, as has been pointed out elsewhere, that Pindar wishes to draw particular attention to what follows. Here the passage condemns over-ambition, declares Pindar's belief in the virtues of government by the 'middle stream of men' and 'deplores' the rule of 'tyrants'. In the antistrophe Pindar goes on to praise the virtues of public spirit, of modesty after success, and of a peaceful way of life, and in lines feelingly expressed claims that man's best possession is 'an honourable name'. It seems that Pindar used this Ode, as he used Pythian IX, as a means of declaring his loyal feelings for Thebes at a time when he or his views were subject to hostile comment. It seems very possible, though there is no firm evidence to this effect, that the more representative type of government imposed upon Thebes after the defeat of the Persians in 479 B.C. looked upon Pindar, with his well-known aristocratic leanings, as a man whom they might well suspect of opposition or of intrigues against themselves. If so, his high reputation and the respect he enjoyed might well have made these suspicions more acute. Be that as it may, there can be no doubt that in the passages in this Ode Pindar was at pains to make clear that his outlook was not such as would allow him to take part in such activities.

In the earlier sections of the Ode Pindar tells the story of Agamemnon, Clytemnestra and Orestes. Commentators from the earliest time have expressed surprise at Pindar's choice of this myth, which has no connection with Thebes or the Thebans. Few stories of Greek mythology however were better known to the Greeks, and few can provide more striking examples of the tragic results of immoderate behaviour in high places. It seems highly probable that Pindar's choice of this story was deliberate, in order to throw, by contrast, a stronger light on his later passages in praise of moderation in individual behaviour and in government.

The intention of the third antistrophe which follows the conclusion of the myth is not at first sight clear, and the early commentators interpreted it as an admission by Pindar that his story of Agamemnon was irrelevant in this Ode—'Some gale, is it, has carried me off course'—and as his apology for including it. An easier interpretation seems possible and more probable. This passage is expressed in quite a different and more light-hearted tone of voice, providing a welcome touch of light relief immediately after the grim Agamemnon story. Pindar seems in fact to be suggesting that the terms of his commission required the Ode to cover both the victory of Thrasydaeus and two former victories of his father, a task that might normally be expected to require more than one Ode, and correspondingly higher fees. However his 'Muse', says Pindar, having accepted the commission, will see to it that it is carried out according to the terms agreed, although this may perhaps involve (as in fact it does) a lack of clear distinction between the successes and the praises of one victor and those of the other.

Ancient records show that Thrasydaeus won two Pythian victories, one in 474 B.C. in the boys' single-stade foot-race, and the other in 454 B.C. in the men's double-stade. The balance of evidence makes it virtually certain that this Ode is in celebration of the earlier victory, and includes the fact that Pindar makes only brief mention of Thrasydaeus, and always in association with the name of his father. For a boy's victory this is understandable; for a man of more than thirty years old, as Thrasydaeus would have been by 454, with the victory of 474 and possibly others in the interim to his credit, the present Ode would hardly have been regarded by Thrasydaeus and his family, or by Pindar, as paying sufficient tribute to his honours. The previous victories won by his father were a chariot-race at Olympia and a foot-race at Delphi. These are praised in epode 3 and strophe 4, while in epode 1 Pindar writes that Thrasydaeus has enriched his family with a third victor's crown.

In the first triad, in order no doubt to emphasize that the fortunes of Thebes are to hold a prominent place in the theme of this Ode, Pindar calls on famous Theban heroines of mythology to come and assist at the festival of which the performance of this Ode would be a part, at the Ismenion, a temple named after the mythical Ismenus, who was the son by Apollo of his Theban bride Melia. This shrine, devoted to the worship of Apollo, lay on a small hill a short distance outside one of the gates of Thebes. Pausanias records that this building together with its store of golden tripods mentioned in this Ode was still in evidence in the second century A.D.

The Ode then proceeds to the sections discussed above. In the final epode we are brought easily back again from the present to the legendary past, and the end of the Ode is thus in harmonious balance with the mythical references with which it begins.

str. 1 Daughter of Cadmus, Semele
From your high place amidst the queens of heaven,
And Ino Leucothea, you who dwell
By the immortal sea-nymphs, Nereus' daughters,
Come with the noble mother of Heracles
To the shrine of Melia,
To the treasure-house of golden tripods,
The temple that above all others
Apollo held in honour,

ant. 1 And he named it the Ismenion,
The seat of prophecy that knows no lie.
Daughters of Harmonia, the god now summons
To assemble here that band of heroine women
Who dwelt within this land, that you may sing
In praise of holy Themis
And Pytho, and the centre-stone
Of earth, whose word is justice—here
As evening's shadows fall.

str. 1 *Cadmus:* the mythical founder and first king of Thebes.

Semele and Ino: two of the daughters of Cadmus and his wife Harmonia. The tragic incidents of their lives and death were well-known Greek legends. They were awarded immortality, Semele with the gods on Olympus, Ino with the immortal sea-nymphs, the Nereids. Her second name *Leucothea*, the White Goddess, was a name also applied to several other deities associated with the sea, including the sea-born Aphrodite.

Mother of Heracles: Alcmene, wife of Amphitryon king of Thebes, and mother of Heracles by Zeus.

Melia: the mother by Apollo of Ismenus, who gave his name, as noted in the foreword, to the shrine Ismenion and also to the Ismenus, a river close to Thebes.

ant. 1 *Holy Themis:* the goddess of Right and Justice.

The centre-stone of earth: i.e. the temple and oracle of Delphi. (See note on Pyth. VI. str. 1).

ep. 1 Thebes will you honour, city of seven gates,
And the contest of Kirrha,
Where Thrasydaeus has once more enriched
His father's house with a third victor's crown,
Won in the rich domain of Pylades,
Host of Orestes of Laconia:

str. 2 Orestes, whom, when the murderer's blade
Had slain his father, his nurse Arsinoë
Saved from the dread hand and the grievous guile
Of Clytemnestra; when the maid Cassandra
Daughter of Dardan Priam, felt the edge
Of the bright sword of bronze;
When with the soul of Agamemnon,
To the dark shores of Acheron
That ruthless woman's will

ant. 2 Had sent her hasting down. Whence came this?
Maybe was it Iphigeneia, done to death
Far from her home beside Euripus' banks,
Sparked that harsh-handed rage within her soul?

ep. 1 *The contest of Kirrha:* i.e. the Pythian Games (see note on Pyth. III. str. 4).

The domain of Pylades: this means in fact that Thrasydaeus' victory was won at Delphi. Pylades was the son of Strophius, with whom the child Orestes found refuge, as described in the next strophe, and who lived in Phocis, the district which includes Mount Parnassus and Delphi. Pylades and Orestes were brought up together and became close friends. Pindar's choice of this phrase was no doubt to allow mention of the name of Orestes, to serve as a link—albeit a very brief one, as often in Pindar's Odes—between what has preceded and the myth which follows.

Orestes of Laconia: in this Ode Pindar follows a tradition which placed the home of Agamemnon and Clytemnestra at Amyclae, a city near Sparta in Laconia. Aeschylus placed it in Argos, and Homer in Mycenae, which modern archaeology seems now to confirm.

str. 2 *The murderer:* Clytemnestra.

Cassandra: the maiden prophetess, daughter of Priam king of Troy, brought home as a prisoner by Agamemnon at the end of the Trojan war.

Acheron: the river of the Underworld.

ant. 2 *Iphigeneia:* daughter of Agamemnon and Clytemnestra. When setting out from Greece to start the war against Troy, the Greek forces under Agamemnon were held up by contrary winds at Aulis on the east coast of Greece. Agamemnon was persuaded by the great prophet Calchas that a favourable wind could only be secured if the gods were propitiated by the sacrifice of Agamemnon's daughter Iphigeneia, and this took place.

Euripus' banks: the Euripus is the name of the narrow channel which separates the island of Euboea from the east coast of Greece, where Aulis stands.

Or in thraldom to her paramour's bed, her nightly
Adulterous joy beguiled her?
A sin that is most sorely loathed
By new-wed brides, that can never
Be hid away, the prey

ep. 2 Of stranger's chatter, while the tongues of neighbours
Take joy in tales of evil.
For wealth earns ever an equal toll of envy,
But a man of humble lot may boast unheard.
Thus he died, that heroic son of Atreus,
Returned after long years to famed Amyclae;

str. 3 Who destroyed, too, the prophet maid,
When the city of Troy was burnt in flames
For Helen's sake, and to their sumptuous homes
He had wrought ruin. But his son, yet a child,
Came to old Strophius, to be his guest,
Dwelling beneath Parnassus.
Then, grown in years, with the god of War
Beside him, he slew his mother, and gave
Aegisthus to bloody death.

ant. 3 Look, friends, how on a changing path
Where three ways meet, my steps are whirled about,
Though following a straight road heretofore.
Some gale, is it, has carried me off course,
Like a sea-going bark? Ah Muse, 'tis yours,
If you agreed to hire
Your voice for pay or silver fee,
To praise now one name, then another,
Weaving a mingled theme,

Her paramour: Aegisthus.

ep. 2 *Son of Atreus:* Agamemnon.

str. 3 *The prophet maid:* Cassandra.

Helen: wife of Menelaus, king of Sparta. Her abduction by Paris to Troy was the cause of the Trojan war.

Came to old Strophius: brought there by Arsinoë, his nurse, as described in str. 2.

ant. 3 *Look friends . . . etc. :* see foreword on this passage.

Where three ways meet: this phrase seems to refer to the fact that Pindar has been asked to celebrate three victories in this Ode, one of Thrasydaeus and two of his father.

ep. 3 Whether singing his father's Pythian crown,
Or Thrasydaeus' honour;
For the joy and glory of both flame like a fire.
In days gone by their racing chariot won
At Olympia's far-famed contest a rich glory,
Bright as the sunlight's gleam, with their swift steeds;

str. 4 Then, entering the lists at Pytho
For stripped runners, their swift feet put to shame
The host of all Hellas. May the gods grant me
To love the fair things that their grace bestows,
And strive for that my life's prime can attain.
In the affairs of cities
The greatest blessings flow, I deem,
From the middle stream of men; the lot
Of tyrants I deplore.

ant. 4 On fine deeds for the common weal
My hopes are set; the doom of jealous envy
Is put to naught, if a man gains the heights
And through a peaceful life shuns the fell path
Of pride. His onwards steps will find the verge
Of death's dark day more gracious,
Leaving to his beloved kin
Of all possessions the most blest,
An honourable name.

ep. 3 *Their racing chariot:* in using the word 'their' in this line and also in the second line of str. 4, 'their swift feet', Pindar appears to be attributing these victories jointly to Thrasydaeus and his father, without indicating who was the victor in each. This is perhaps the lack of clear distinction between these successes of which Pindar seems just to have admitted that his poem (the 'Muse') is guilty. See also the foreword.

str. 4 *The host of all Hellas:* competitors from the whole of Greece.

May the gods grant me: see foreword on this passage and on ant. 4, which follows.

And strive for that . . . etc.: i.e. may I not yield to ambitions beyond my best capacity.

ep. 4 This it was spread abroad the wide-sung praise
Of Iolaus' glory,
And of the might of Castor, and your fame
O royal Pollux; you twin sons divine,
Who live today within Therapnae's dwellings,
Tomorrow in the halls of high Olympus.

ep. 4 *Iolaus:* a Theban hero, nephew and charioteer of Heracles.

Castor and Pollux: the famous twin brothers who later became a constellation. Pollux, the son of Zeus, was immortal; Castor mortal. On the death of Castor, Pollux begged Zeus that he would allow them never to be separated. Zeus granted them a future life together, to be spent half below the earth and half with the immortals in heaven. The story is finely told by Pindar at the end of Nemean X.

Therapnae: the burial place of the brothers, near Sparta.

PYTHIAN XII

For

MIDAS OF ACRAGAS

Winner of the Flute-Playing Contest

THIS victory was won at the same Pythian festival, of 490 B.C., as that of Xenocrates, celebrated in Ode VI. That Ode, as has been noted, was written largely as a tribute to the friendship which had sprung up between Pindar and the son of Xenocrates, Thrasybulus, who as his father's charioteer won that victory for him. It seems probable that Midas, whose flute-playing success is here celebrated, was a musician in the service of Xenocrates or his brother Theron at Acragas, and came to Delphi as a follower of Thrasybulus. Very possibly Thrasybulus commissioned this Ode from Pindar on his behalf.

After an invocation addressed to the city of Acragas, and some words of praise for Midas, the Ode turns to the story of Perseus and the Gorgon Medusa, with the connected story of the invention by the goddess Athene of the flute, and of a melody well-known to the Greeks called the 'many-headed tune'. According to Pindar this tune derived from the cries of the three Gorgon sisters as Perseus attacked and beheaded Medusa. This myth occupies the greater part of this short Ode, which concludes with a typical Pindaric warning of the uncertainty of human fortunes.

In telling this story of Perseus, well known to the Greeks, Pindar as often elsewhere does not recount its events in their proper chronological order. The following resumé of the story will help the reader to understand various references in the Ode.

Danaë was the only child of Acrisius, king of Argos, who was warned by an oracle that he would be killed by his grandson. In order to safeguard Danaë from male attentions Acrisius locked her up in a prison. Zeus however contrived an entry by turning himself into a stream of gold, and his union with Danaë resulted in the birth of Perseus. Acrisius, not daring to commit the sacrilege of shedding his daughter's blood, had Danaë and the infant Perseus enclosed in a wooden chest and pushed out to sea. A fisherman of the Aegean island of Seriphos found them and brought them safely to land. They then became the captives of Polydectes, king of Seriphos, who treated them as slaves. Later, intending to marry Danaë, Polydectes pretended that his bride was to be the famous Hippodamia, daughter of Oenomaus, king of Elis (her story is told in Ol. I). He called upon the chieftains of the island to give him wedding presents. Perseus, now grown to manhood, resolved to bring back as his present the head of Medusa, which turned to stone anyone who looked at it. He was helped by Athene, who gave him a burnished shield with which to see the reflection of Medusa without looking at her. He needed also winged sandals, a wallet in which to carry Medusa's head, and a helmet to make him invisible. The whereabouts of these was known only to the Three Grey Sisters, '*the grim offspring of Phorcus*', who had only one tooth and one eye, shared between them. Perseus stole their eye as it was passed from the hand of one to another, and refused to return it to them until they told him where he could find these three things. They did so, and thus armed Perseus completed his task, and returning to Seriphos with Medusa's head, turned Polydectes and the islanders into stone.

str. 1 I pray you, lover of splendour,
Seat of Persephone, fairest of all
Cities of men, high-built upon your hill above
The stream of Acragas, and her rich banks of pasture,
O queen, grant of your gentle heart to accept
This crown of Pytho, Midas' glory, and give him
Goodwill of the immortals and of men;
Welcome him too that he surpassed
All Hellas in the art
That long ago Pallas Athene invented,
Weaving in music's rich refrain
The ghoulish dirge of the fierce-hearted Gorgons.

str. 1 *Seat of Persephone:* the goddess Persephone, daughter of Demeter the goddess of fertility, was the object of special worship by the Greeks of Sicily; and Acragas, one of the largest cities of Sicily, is therefore spoken of as her 'seat'. Zeus was said to have appointed Persephone to be the tutelary goddess of the island (see Nem. I. ant. 1).

The Gorgons: three sisters, Stheno, Euryale and Medusa, were turned into the three Gorgons, monsters with snakes in place of hair, because of a sacrilegious act committed by Medusa against the goddess Athene. Anyone who looked at the head of Medusa was immediately turned into stone.

str. 2 This in their anguished struggle
From those dread maidens' lips was heard streaming,
And from those writhing serpent heads untouchable,
When Perseus o'er the third of those fell sisters launched
His cry of triumph, and brought fatal doom
To Seriphos by the sea—doom for that isle
And for her people. Yes, for he had made blind
The grim offspring of Phorcus, and bitter
The wedding-gift he brought
To Polydectes, thus to end his mother's
Long slavery and enforced wedlock—
That son of Danaë, who raped the head

str. 3 Of the fair-cheeked Medusa;
He who, men tell, was from a flowing stream
Of gold begotten. But when the goddess maid delivered
From these labours this man she loved, then she contrived
The manifold melodies of the flute, to make
In music's notes an image of the shrill
Lamenting cries, strung from Euryale's
Ravening jaws. A goddess found,
But finding, gave the strain
To mortal men to hold, naming it the tune
Of many heads, a glorious grace
For the great contests where the peoples gather.

str. 4 Often its clear call rings
From the light bronze, and from the reeds which grow
Beside the Graces' city, home of lovely dances,
Where the nymph, daughter of Kephissus, has her precinct;
Faithful their witness to the dancers' feet.

str. 3 *Fair-cheeked Medusa:* because she was originally a beautiful young woman.

The goddess maid: Athene. She is often referred to as 'the maiden goddess'.

This man she loved: Perseus.

A glorious grace: this 'many-headed tune' was a popular tune suitable for playing on public occasions such as the 'great contests' i.e. the Panhellenic festivals.

str. 4 *The light bronze:* Greek flutes were made of reed with a bronze mouthpiece, on the lines of the modern clarinet.

The Graces' city: the city of Thebes. Boeotia, of which Thebes was the capital city, was closely associated with the Graces, and at Orchomenus, another Boeotian city, the home of the primeval Minyae, the Graces had been worshipped from the earliest times.

Kephissus: the name of the main river of Boeotia.

Now if a mortal man wins happy fortune
Not without toil shall this be seen: a god may
  Bring it to pass—today, maybe—
    Yes, but the will of fate
None can escape. Soon shall there come an hour
  To strike beyond all expectation,
And give one boon past hope, withhold another.

One boon past hope: early commentators relate these words to a story that Midas while playing in the competition had the misfortune to break the mouthpiece of his flute, but nevertheless continued playing and won the prize. If true, this incident may have suggested these words, but in any case the sentence can bear a wider interpretation and expresses a sentiment often voiced by Pindar.

NEMEAN I

For

CHROMIUS OF AETNA

Winner of the Chariot-Race

CHROMIUS was the brother-in-law and life-long friend in arms of Hieron, ruler of Syracuse and of Gela, the most powerful of the group of rulers of the Greek city states of Sicily and south Italy. At some date after 480 B.C. Hieron transferred the population of Catana to Syracuse and refounded Catana under its new name of Aetna. He appointed Chromius to be its governor.

The opening lines of strophe 2 seem to suggest that Pindar himself was present as director of the chorus by which the Ode was performed. The poet also seems to speak of Chromius as a man with whom he was personally acquainted, and this and other evidence makes it probable that this Ode was written during Pindar's visit to Sicily in the year 476/75, though the date of this victory of Chromius at the Nemean Games is not known.

The Ode seems to have been performed before the house of Chromius on Ortygia, an island converted by the construction of a causeway into a peninsula, abutting onto the city of Syracuse on the mainland of Sicily. The mention, in the opening lines of the Ode, of Alpheus and the goddess Artemis derives from the legend attached to the fountain Arethusa on Ortygia. One version of the legend tells how the young huntsman Alpheus was enamoured of the nymph Arethusa, but she, wishing to escape him, fled overseas from the Peloponnese to Ortygia. Alpheus was turned by the gods into a river, the largest river of the Peloponnese, which flows past Olympia into the Ionian sea. Alpheus then continued his pursuit of Arethusa under the sea to Ortygia where his waters were turned into the fountain Arethusa. Another version of the story is that it was the goddess Artemis whom Alpheus vainly pursued. This version no doubt relates to the fact that the cult of the goddess Artemis was strongly established on Ortygia, having been brought there by some of the early Greek colonists who came to Ortygia from the district of Elis, through which the river Alpheus flows, where the worship of Artemis was one of the leading religious cults.

Artemis, with her twin brother Apollo, was born on the island of Delos. Pindar's phrase referring to Ortygia as 'sister of Delos' implies that the island was so honoured by Artemis as to rank with her native Delos.

Pindar's reference to Ortygia as a 'branch of glorious Syracuse' was no doubt justified in his own times, when Ortygia was only a small part of the very large city which Syracuse had by then become. In fact however the early Greek settlers first made their home on the island of Ortygia and the larger city of Syracuse was a later expansion.

The myth in this Ode, the legend of the infant Heracles and the snakes, was probably chosen by Pindar because Chromius was a member of the Hyllean tribe and thus traced his descent from Heracles, the grand-father of Hyllus.

str. 1 O revered ground where Alpheus
Stayed his pursuit, and Artemis found rest,
Ortygia,
Let thy name, branch of glorious Syracuse
And sister of Delos, prelude my song,
Whose words shall ring sweet to the ear, in praise
Of race-horses swift-footed as the wind,
And in honour of Zeus of Aetna.
For Chromius' chariot and Nemea's contest
Charge me to yoke to his victorious deeds
My melody of triumph.

ant. 1 This the gods founded and inspired
And the supreme valour of the man I praise.
For in success
Breeds the full height of fame, and Poetry
Loves above all to tell of the great games.

str. 1 *Alpheus, Ortygia, Delos:* see foreword to this Ode.
Zeus of Aetna: the chief religious cult in Sicily was that of 'Zeus of Aetna', i.e. of Mount Aetna, a cult established long before the more recent founding of the city of Aetna, with which the name of Chromius is associated in this Ode.

ant. 1 *For in success:* here, as frequently in the Odes, the word 'success' means victory in the Games.

Spread then of glory's fragrance a full measure
To grace this isle, which Zeus, lord of Olympus,
  Gave to Persephone, and ruled
Nodding his flowing locks, that Sicily
Bear on her soil a dower of harvest riches
    First of all fruitful earth,

ep. 1 And her proud crown of glorious citadels.
Bestowed upon her too the son of Cronos
    A people of proud horsemen,
  Wooers of war and bronze-clad might,
Crowned too not seldom with the shining fronds
Of the Olympiad olive. Many a glory
    In truth my arrows' flight shall compass.

str. 2 Now stand I at the courtyard gate,
Singing my lays, where dwells a generous host;
    Friendly the feast
Laid for my welcome, and her thronging guests
Know well these halls of hospitable fame.
And if the smoke of envy's blame arise,
Good friends has he to douse the fire at source.
  Many the diverse arts of men;
Each to his kind, and let him follow straight
The paths appointed, striving with the skill
    That nature's gift endowed him.

ant. 2 For strength of arm plies to its goal
In deed and act; the mind nurtures her harvest
    Of wise counsels—
Whoso the gift inherits to foresee
Things yet to come. Son of Agesidamus,
Both one and the other in your talents lie.
I love not to keep hidden in my house
  Wealthy treasure, but to take joy
Of that I have, and amongst friends be known
Of liberal repute. Like hopes to these,
    In this our life of toil,

Persephone: Queen of the Underworld. Persephone was the daughter of Demeter, goddess of fertility, and was the object of special worship by the Greeks of Sicily.

ep. 1 *The Olympiad olive:* the wreath of wild olive, the victors' prize at Olympia.

str. 2 *Now stand I, etc.:* Pindar wrote this Ode while on a visit to Sicily in the year 476/75.

ant. 2 *Son of Agesidamus:* Chromius.

ep. 2 Every man shares. For me, my eager thought
Clings, on the high peaks of his valorous deeds,
To Heracles, and bids me
Unfold the ancient tale, how he
This son of Zeus—sped from his mother's womb
To the bright light of day with his twin brother—
From childbirth pangs barely was free

str. 3 When Hera from her golden throne,
Failed not to mark him, wrapped in swaddling robes
Of saffron hue,
And the gods' queen with anger in her heart
Sent serpents speeding. Through the open doors
O'er the wide floor came they to the chamber's depth,
Thirsting to fold upon the babes new-born
Their pointed fangs and gaping jaws.
But Heracles, raising upright his head,
Stood to defy them, and then first knew he
The taste of battle's trial.

ant. 3 One to each hand he seized—those hands
Invincible—the necks of the two snakes,
And hanging there
Throttled within his grip, the flying minutes
Strained from these monsters' forms their breath of life.
And a dire terror struck the hearts of all
The maidservants allotted to the task
Of tending to Alcmene's bed.
But she herself leapt from her couch, unrobed,
And ran barefoot, with no thought but to fend
The fierce beasts from their prey.

ep. 3 And the Cadmean chiefs in their bronze armour
Came quickly thronging and Amphitryon
His unsheathed sword in hand,
Torment of fear piercing his heart;
Grief in his own house spells for every man
A bitter load, but for another's sorrow
The heart soon knows relief from care.

ep. 2 *His twin brother:* Iphicles. The mother of the twins was Alcmene wife of Amphitryon king of Thebes.

str. 3 *Hera:* Queen of the gods, wife of Zeus.

ant. 3 *Alcmene:* wife of Amphitryon, mother of Heracles by Zeus.

ep. 3 *Cadmean:* Theban. The legendary Cadmus was the first king and founder of Thebes.

Amphitryon: King of Thebes, husband of Alcmene.

str. 4 And he stood there, a mingled play
Of fear, wonder and gladness in his heart.
For well he saw
The miracle of his son's spirit and strength,
And that the messengers' report stood now
Reversed by the immortals' will. He summoned
The peerless prophet of the most high Zeus,
His neighbour, the seer of true vision,
Teiresias; who then declared to him
And all the gathered host, what chance of fortunes
Heracles should encounter;

ant. 4 Of monsters merciless how many
On the dry land, how many on the sea
He should destroy;
And of mankind, whom bent upon the path
Of pride and treachery he should consign
To an accursed death. This too he told:
When that the gods join battle with the Giants
On Phlegra's plain, then shall his bow
Speed forth a gale of shafts to quell their might,
And the fair glory of their gleaming locks
Lie sullied in the dust.

ep. 4 And he in peace for all time shall enjoy,
In the home of the blessed, leisure unbroken,
A recompense most choice
For his great deeds of toil; and winning
The lovely Hebe for his bride, and sharing
His marriage feast beside Zeus, son of Cronos,
Shall live to grace his august law.

str. 4 *Teiresias:* the legendary prophet of Thebes, who played a prominent part in the tragedy of Oedipus.

ant. 4 *Phlegra's plain:* a Thracian plain on which the Giants, in their revolt against Zeus and the other gods, were defeated. Heracles was largely instrumental in securing the victory of the gods in this battle.

ep. 4 *In the home of the blessed:* on the death of Heracles he was awarded a place amongst the immortals on Mount Olympus. The goddess Hera released him from her long-standing animosity, and her daughter Hebe, the goddess of Youth and Beauty, became his wife.

NEMEAN II

For

TIMODEMUS OF ACHARNAE

Winner of the Pankration

TIMODEMUS was an Athenian, belonging to the district of Acharnae. His family, the Timodemid clan, appear to have inhabited the island of Salamis, and as is clear from the Ode had won a large number of victories at the Pythian, Isthmian and Nemean Games as well as in athletic contests held in Athens. This Nemean victory of the young man Timodemus was his first. The Ode would seem to have been sung at Athens on the winner's return home, probably in the triumphal procession of welcome, for which its metrical construction, a series of identical strophes, makes it suitable. The date of the Ode is uncertain, perhaps 487 or 485 B.C.

The pankration was a combination of boxing and wrestling, probably with a wide licence of rules.

str. 1 Like to those woven strains of song,
Wherein the Homerid bards are wont to offer
Invocation to Zeus, here too I praise
One who has his foundation laid
Of victory's honour in the sacred games,
First in the precinct, famed in song,
Of Zeus of Nemea.

str. 2 If too, propitious destiny,
Guiding him in his fathers' path, has granted
That he shall be the glory of great Athens,
Well may it prove, not once or twice
Timonous' son shall cull the fairest flowers
At the Isthmus, and in the games
Of Pytho too. For near

str. 1 *The Homerid bards:* the Homeridai, or 'Rhapsodists', a feature of literary interest in Athens, were professional orators who gave public recitals of poetry, particularly of Homer.

str. 2 *Timonous' son:* Timodemus.

str. 3 The Pleiades, those mountain maids,
Needs must Orion follow close behind.
And Salamis, need I tell, can nurse a man
Of warrior breed. Hector in Troy
Heard Ajax challenge, and for you, Timodemus,
The stern Pankration's proof of valour
Raises high your renown.

str. 4 For men of noble name, Acharnae
Down the long years is known; and in the games
The Timodemid clan has supreme honour.
First by Parnassus lordly height
In four contests their athletes won the prize,
Then in the vales of noble Pelops
Eight times the men of Corinth

str. 5 Crowned them ere now: seven at Nemea
Where Zeus presides, in their own city more
Than man may count. To Zeus then, countrymen,
Sound your triumphant hymn, to honour
Timodemus as he rides home to fame.
Strike up, and let your voices ring
Rich melodies of song.

str. 3 *The Pleiades:* they are referred to as 'mountain maids' because they were the daughters of the giant Atlas, who held the sky aloft, and became Mount Atlas, standing as he does today at the western boundary of the Mediterranean in North Africa.

Orion: the great constellation of Orion appears in the sky near the star-cluster of the Pleiades, which it appears to follow. The Nemean victory betokens a greater one to follow.

Salamis: this was the home of the Timodemid clan, and also of the Homeric hero Ajax, one of the greatest of the Greek warriors in the Trojan war.

str. 4 *Parnassus:* the mountain which lies behind Delphi.

The vales of noble Pelops: the Peloponnesus, within whose boundaries lie both Corinth with its Isthmian games, and Nemea.

NEMEAN III

For

ARISTOCLEIDES OF AEGINA

Winner of the Pankration

EXCEPT from what may be gathered from this Ode, nothing further is known of Aristocleides and his family. As we see from the concluding line of the Ode he had gained victories at the minor local games of Epidaurus and Megara as well as at Nemea, but he does not appear to have been a prominent athlete or to have belonged to a family of any athletic distinction. This may account, in the parts of the Ode normally devoted to praise of the victor and his family, for the greater emphasis given to the glories of Aegina and her mythical heroes than to Aristocleides himself.

We have no evidence by which the date when this Ode was written can be fixed with any certainty. We learn however from the concluding lines that it was written at some interval of time after the victory which it celebrates. Lines in the fourth antistrophe which seem to reveal discreetly that Aristocleides was no longer a young man when the Ode was written suggest that the interval was a lengthy one, because the pankration was not a contest for anyone past the prime of his physical activity. There is nothing in the Ode indicative of Aegina's troubles with Athens and it is unlikely therefore to have been composed later than 466 B.C., but probably belongs to one of the earlier peaceful intervals. Some close analogies with the group of Odes written in honour of Sicilian victors in 476–75 B.C., when Pindar paid a visit to Sicily, make it very possible that this Ode was written near to that time, perhaps shortly after Pindar's return to Greece. There is no evidence to show the date of the actual victory at Nemea.

The arrangement of the Ode follows the normal pattern. Before the myth proper, which begins in antistrophe 2, and tells of the adventures of Peleus and Telamon (sons of Aeacus), and of Achilles (son of Peleus), there is a digression in strophe 2, for which Pindar apologizes, on the exploits of Heracles. This may have been occasioned merely by the mention of the name of Heracles in the last line of the preceding epode—Heracles, whose birthplace was Thebes, Pindar's own city, was a favourite subject for his eulogies. Possibly however, if this Ode was written, as has been suggested, shortly after Pindar's return from his visit to Sicily in 476–75 B.C., the passage may have some connection with differences which are believed to have arisen at that time between Pindar and citizens of Thebes, when Pindar was anxious to show his loyalty to his native city and to pay compliments to her traditional heroes.

Other short digressions from the main theme, 'asides' of a general nature which, as has been noted in the Introduction, are a common feature of Pindar's Odes, occur in epode 2 and in the fourth strophe and antistrophe. In epode 2 the passage beginning 'By worth of inborn talent' expresses a favourite theme of Pindar, the superiority of natural genius over acquired or instructed skill. These lines may have been intended merely to enhance the picture he draws of the warlike merits of Telamon in the preceding lines, and of Achilles in the lines that follow. If so, they are not inappropriate in this context. Their wording however is equally applicable to the skill of poetic composition and it may be that they should be considered in conjunction with the lines in the final epode of the poem, in which Pindar is openly claiming the superiority of his own art to that of his rivals. Pindar's handling of the mythical stories in his Odes seems to have been a special target for jealous criticism by his rivals. Something in the story of the Aeacid heroes, into the middle of which these lines are rather suddenly interpolated, may have suggested to Pindar that this was an appropriate point for an attack on his critics. The terms of contempt used by Pindar in this passage and in the final epode are paralleled by several similarly biting comments on his rivals in other Odes, e.g. Ol. II. str. 5 and Nem. IV. str. 5.

In the passage in strophe and antistrophe 4 beginning 'By proof of deed' Pindar seems to be politely marking the fact that Aristocleides is no longer a young man, but also suggesting that the fine qualities which he demonstrated in his youth in his Nemean victory continue to be matched by qualities of a kind appropriate to a man's later years. The notion that each age of human life has its own virtue, on the same principle as Shakespeare's description of the seven ages of man, was of course a common one. Pythagoras divided virtue into four species, assigning one to each of the four ages of life. But Pindar here mentions three ages only and in the ensuing sentence adds a fourth virtue of his own 'To hold the moment's task steadfast in mind'. This is a brief expression of a favourite theme of Pindar found in many of his Odes, usually less curtly stated. Here in its narrowest sense it can be taken to mean, coming from a superb craftsman such as Pindar, that the first principle of good workmanship must be to keep one's mind on the job, or 'one's eye on the ball' as a modern player of games would put it. But as we know from similar passages, less briefly expressed, the wider implications of the theme are the condemnation of excessive ambition and pride, the extolling of modesty and a just appreciation of one's own talents and responsibilities. 'Seek not to become Zeus' as Pindar says to another Aeginetan victor (Isthm. V. ep. 1).

str. 1 Muse whom I worship, mother of my spirit,
I beg thee come, this festal month of Nemea,
To the Dorian island, thronged with many a guest,
To Aegina come.
For by the water of Asopus waits
Young manhood's choir, triumphant architects
Of songs of revel,
Longing to hear thy voice.
One venture thirsts for this,
And one for that. An athlete's victories crave
Song above all,
Fit servitor of his crowns and valorous deeds.

ant. 1 Of song grant, of my skill, full measure. Strike,
O daughter of the lord of cloud-capped heaven,
Chords to his honour; mine to wed them with
The youthful voices

str. 1 The *Muse* invoked, as we see from the final lines of the Ode, is Clio, one of the Nine Muses, the patron goddesses of literature and song. In course of time, when special attributes came to be assigned to them individually, Clio was regarded as the Muse of History.

Dorian island: Aegina became the home of many of the early 'Dorian' invaders of Greece, and her citizens, like those of Sparta, were proud to claim Dorian descent.

The water of Asopus: the well known Asopus river is in Boeotia, whose capital city is Thebes, where Pindar wrote this Ode. In asking his 'Muse' to come to Aegina, in the opening lines, Pindar means that the theme of this poem will be Aegina. The young men of his chorus however are waiting in Thebes to be trained in its performance. They are 'longing to hear thy voice', i.e. this poem, perhaps because its composition, as stated in the foreword, has been long delayed. Some scholars incline to an alternative view, that the 'water of Asopus' means the sea surrounding the island of Aegina, so called because the river-god Asopus was the father of the maid Oenone who gave her name to the island, later known as Aegina. On that view the young men of the chorus are pictured as waiting on the island for the receipt of the Ode from Pindar.

ant. 1 *Daughter of the lord of cloud-capped heaven:* Clio, daughter of Zeus, lord of Olympus.

And with the lyre. A joyful task have I
To praise this land, where dwelt the Myrmidons
In days gone by.
Now to their meeting-place
Long cherished in old story,
Aristocleides, by thy favour proved,
Brings no disgrace,
Whose strength endured the challenge, and failed not

ep. 1 The Pankration's forceful round. Balm for your hurts
And healing for weary limbs your victor's crown
Brings to you now
In the deep valley of Nemea.
Have you fair looks, and deeds,
Son of Aristophanes, fashioned in beauty's form?
And have you scaled valour's high peaks? No further
Tempt then the uneasy task, beyond the pillars
Of Heracles to sail the uncharted sea,

str. 2 Those famous marks the hero-god set up
To bound the sailor's voyage. And he slew
Huge monsters in the deep, and he traced out
The shoals and eddies,
And journeying to the farthest goal destined
For safe return, made plain the ends of earth.
O heart of mine
To what far foreign headland
Lead you my sail astray?
Aeacus and his race are my ship's burthen
The word attesting,
The flower of truth, which bids 'Praise noble men';

The Myrmidons: the earliest inhabitants of Aegina. There was a legend that in order to supply Aeacus with a people, Zeus turned ants (Myrmikes) into human beings.

ep. 1 *Son of Aristophanes:* Aristocleides.
The pillars of Heracles: Mount Atlas and the Rock of Gibraltar on either side of the straits.

str. 2 See foreword in reference to this digression on Heracles.
The shoals and eddies: probably a reference to the Syrtes, the shoals and shallows off the north coast of Africa.
Aeacus and his race: for the family tree of the Aeacid clan see Introduction. (Aeacus was the first mythical king of Aegina.)

ant. 2 And strangers' cargo brings a man small profit.
Search nearer home. There you have fitting glory,
Rich theme for song. For in great deeds of daring
Long years ago
Peleus rejoiced, who cut the giant spear,
Whose single hand unaided took Iolcus;
And Thetis too
The ocean maid, he held
Struggling in his strong grasp.
And Telamon, that man of mighty strength,
Staunch friend-in-arms
With Iolaus, felled Laomedon.

ep. 2 When too the bronze-bowed Amazons to encounter
Iolaus led him, their man-devouring dread
Could never dull
The sharp blade of his soul. By worth
Of inborn talent a man
Wins rich repute. Whose art is but instructed,
An obscure feather-brain he, now here aspiring
Now there, and steps with no sure foot, essaying
A thousand valorous deeds to no avail.

str. 3 Fair-haired Achilles dwelling in Philyra's halls,
While yet a child made mighty deeds his play;
Many a time his hand brandished the short
Tipped javelin,

ant. 2 *The giant spear:* Peleus, son of Aeacus, cut down a fir tree to make a spear for Heracles.

Iolcus: a city of eastern Thessaly, the modern Volos.

Thetis: the immortal sea-nymph, promised by Zeus to Peleus as his bride. Thetis, unwilling, turned herself, when in Peleus' arms, into fire and various kinds of wild beast, but Peleus held on to her until she surrendered, and the marriage took place, attended by all the gods. Thetis became the mother of Achilles.

Telamon: son of Aeacus and brother of Peleus. Iolaus was the charioteer of Heracles. It was Heracles, according to the legend, who accompanied by Telamon attacked and overthrew Troy in the generation before the Trojan War, and killed Laomedon, king of Troy, in revenge for his failure to pay the agreed reward for the help Heracles gave in destroying a dragon which was ravaging the country. Pindar omits the name of Heracles here, presumably so as not to diminish the lustre of Telamon, the Aeacid.

ep. 2 *Amazons:* here again according to legend it was Heracles, accompanied by Telamon, who fought with the Amazons, in order to carry out one of his twelve labours, which required him to get possession of the girdle of Hippolyta, queen of the Amazons.

str. 3 *Philyra:* the mother of Chiron the Centaur.

Like to the wind in speed, and with wild lions
He fought, and dealt them death. Boars too he slew,
Whose panting frames,
The first in his sixth year
And then through all his days—
He brought to the Centaur, Cronos' son. Astonished
The divine eyes
Of Artemis and bold Athene saw him

ant. 3 Slay without help of hound or artful net
The stag his fleet foot mastered. This tale too
Of men of old have I. Wise-hearted Chiron
Nursed the great Jason
Under his roof of stone, and to Asclepius
Taught the soft-fingered skills of medicine's lore.
For Nereus' daughter
Glorious in her fruit,
He set the marriage feast,
And reared her peerless son, and taught him all
The crafts of battle,
Stirring his eager soul to high endeavour.

ep. 3 Till that the winds of the high sea should send him
To Troy, to meet the Lycian lances ringing
Their shrill war-cry,
And Phrygian and Dardanian foes;
And with the Ethiops' spears

The Centaur: Chiron, immortal and benevolent figure, lived in his cave in the forests of Mount Pelion. Many young mythical heroes including the three mentioned here, Achilles, Jason and Asclepius the founder of medical art, received from Chiron education appropriate to their heroic function.

ant. 3 *Nereus' daughter:* Thetis, whom Peleus married.
Glorious in her fruit: i.e. as the mother of Achilles.
The marriage feast: of Peleus and Thetis, which Chiron arranged on Mount Pelion, and which was attended by all the gods.

ep. 3 *Lycian, Phrygian:* peoples of Asia Minor, allies of Troy in the Trojan War.
Dardanian: another name for Trojan. Dardanus was an ancient king of Troy.
Ethiops: the Ethiopians under their leader Memnon, whom Achilles killed, were also allies of the Trojans. 'Ethiopia' was a name somewhat loosely applied by the Greeks to any country to the east or south of Egypt, and sometimes to Egypt itself.

In close combat, fronting them hand-to-hand,
He pledged his heart, their chieftain, great Memnon
Fiery cousin to Helenus, should travel
His homeward road no more. Far-flung the light

str. 4 That shines thenceforth for the sons of Aeacus.
Zeus, thine their blood and in thy honour the contest
For which the voice of youth this hymn is chanting,
Proclaiming joy
To the land that bred them. For Aristocleides' crown
Ring out a cheer, for on the page of glory
His brave exploits
Have writ this island's name,
And her revered College
Of priests of Pytho. Now by proof of deed
Is the issue plain
Where a man shall reveal his gifts excelling,

ant. 4 A boy amongst young boys, man amongst men,
Elder with eld, each in each tripart age
Of this our life. Yet, to four virtues heir,
Our mortal span
This too enjoins, to hold the moment's task
Steadfast in mind. In these you have your share.
Friend, fare you well;
I send you now this gift
Of milk and honey blended,
And the cream of the mixing crowns the bowl,
A draught of song
Borne on the breath of flutes of Aeolis,

Helenus: a son of Priam, king of Troy.

str. 4 *Thine their blood:* Aeacus was the son of Zeus by Oenone who gave her name to the island later called Aegina.

In thy honour: the Nemean Games were part of the religious festival held at Nemea in honour of Zeus.

College of priests of Pytho: there was at Aegina a college (thearion) and order of priests of Pytho (Delphi) for the worship of Apollo. It is very likely that the festival at which this Ode would be sung was held in the college precincts.

ant. 4 *Flutes of Aeolis:* the music which accompanied this Ode was in the Aeolian mode.

ep. 4 Though it comes late. Yet of all birds on wing
Swift is the eagle, from the deep sky afar
Spying his mark,
Lo, suddenly hath he seized, swooping,
His tawny-dappled prey.
But chattering daws have a lowly range.
In your honour then, if high-throned Clio wills,
For your proud spirit of conquest, from Nemea
From Megara and Epidaurus the light has shone.

ep. 4 Pindar's apology for the late arrival of this Ode takes the form of this fine metaphor in which he identifies himself, with his rivals, not for the only time in his Odes, as an eagle with lesser birds. For the connection of these lines with the passage in epode 2 see the foreword.

Megara and Epidaurus: Aristocleides appears to have won victories at the minor games of Megara and Epidaurus as well as at Nemea.

NEMEAN IV

For

TIMASARCHUS OF AEGINA

Winner of the Boys' Wrestling-Match

TIMASARCHUS was a member of the Theandrid family with whom, as we may judge from the references to several of its members both past and present, Pindar had a close acquaintance. The references to their musical and poetical skill suggest, as does a line in Nemean VII referring to Aegina as 'a city of music lovers', that there was a close community of artistic interest between Pindar and citizens of Aegina.

The opening strophe pays tribute to the power of songs (the daughters of the Muses) and is expressed in phrases which can easily imply that in winning his victory the boy Timasarchus had to surmount a long and probably painful struggle against his competitors. This implication is further supported in strophe 4 where, in the story of the giant Alkyoneus, Pindar is at pains to make clear the redoubtable resistance he offered before he was overcome by Heracles and Telamon. The second half of the strophe points in the same direction and in particular the sentence 'Deeds done, he only who has dared them knows What cost the doing' has little relevance if not to the same implication. The mention of Heracles here may be a point of evidence in regard to the date of this Ode, see below in this foreword.

In strophes 2 and 3 the Ode follows the normal pattern, after the initial invocation, of praise of the victor and his family, and refers to other victories won by Timasarchus—his 'chain of crowns'. With strophe 5 and the opening lines of strophe 6 comes an interruption to the main theme. Here Pindar after a reference to his affection for Aegina and his determination to contribute to her festival, held at the time of the 'new moon', makes a spirited defence of his poetry against the 'fell intent' and 'envy' of his critics and rivals, and expresses his confidence that its merits will eventually 'bring it to the end ordained'.

Then follows the myth devoted to heroes of the clan of Aeacus and in particular to Peleus and his marriage with Thetis. Strophe 9 onwards returns to eulogy of the victor's family and we learn from strophe 11, 'that which his own eyes have seen', that Pindar had been present at Nemea to witness Timasarchus' victory. The Ode concludes with a happy tribute to the victor's trainer Melesias, who is mentioned in other Odes and was an Athenian.

In regard to the date of this Ode, Pindar's defence of his work against his jealous critics probably implies that this Ode was written before his poetry had become known and recognized at its true worth, i.e. in the earlier rather than the later years of his career. The victory which Timarsarchus gained in Athens, recorded in strophe 3, together with Pindar's complimentary reference to that city, and the fact that Melesias, an Athenian, was Timarsarchus' trainer, indicate that his Nemean victory was won at a time when hostilities between Aegina and Athens were not acute, that is not after the year 466 B.C. at the latest. On the other hand the mention in strophe 6 of Cyprus, where Teucer, of the clan of Aeacus and so a Greek, 'rules afar off', would probably not have been made by Pindar if he was writing before 478 B.C. when an expedition under Pausanias, king of Sparta, brought Cyprus under Hellenic dominion. The reference to Heracles in strophe 4, though it comes naturally enough after the mention of Timasarchus' victory and entertainment at Thebes, may be connected, as was the similar digression on Heracles in Nemean III (see foreword to that Ode), with differences Pindar is believed to have had with citizens of Thebes about the year 475/74. It is a fairly safe conclusion that this Ode was written not very long after that date.

str. 1 For toils that fall to man's accomplishment
Best of all doctors is a cheerful heart.
  But the wise daughters of the Muse
  Bring too their healing balm, the soft
    Embrace of song.
Nor can the warmth of water soothe more surely
  The body's pain, than will the praise
Of high desert tuned to the lyre. For words
  Live longer down the years than deeds,
If that a man may with the Graces' favour
  Haply bring forth the heart's deep mood
To live upon the tongue. May it be mine

str. 2 Such prelude to my songs of praise to render,
Honouring Zeus, Cronos' son, and Nemea,
And Timasarchus' wrestling-bout;
And may the race of Aeacus
Give it acclaim,
Whose high-towered stronghold like a beacon stands
For the just dues of every guest.
Could but Timocritus, your father, still
Know the sun's warmth and healing rays,
How many a note would he have plucked, linking
His lively lyre with this my song,
To praise the victor and his chain of crowns

str. 3 Won at Cleonae's contest, and from Athens,
City of noble name and sunlit splendour,
And Thebes ringed with her seven gates,
Where by Amphitryon's glorious tomb,
With willing hands
The men of Cadmus' line crowned him with flowers,
For Aegina's sake. For as a friend
Received by friends he found a generous welcome,
Though in a city not his own,
In that rich house, the hall of Heracles.
It was that hero who of yore,
Allied with Telamon's great might, laid low

str. 4 The walls of Troy, and slew the Meropes
And that great man of war, giant of terror,
Alkyoneus; yet not before
With rocks his only weapon, he felled
Twelve four-horsed chariots,

str. 2 *The race of Aeacus:* Aeacus was the first mythical king of Aegina. For the family-tree of his clan see the Introduction.

High-towered stronghold, etc.: Aegina had a high reputation for dealing equitably with strangers.

str. 3 *Cleonae's contest:* Nemea was close to the small town of Cleonae, whose citizens provided the local management of the Nemean festival and the judges for the Games until the year 460 B.C. when this privilege was usurped by Argos.

Amphitryon: a mythical king of Thebes, husband of Alcmene, who was the mother by Zeus of Heracles.

Cadmus: the mythical founder of Thebes.

str. 4 *The walls of Troy:* the overthrow of Troy by Heracles and Telamon was in an earlier generation than that of the Trojan War. See note on Nem. III. ant. 2.

Meropes: inhabitants of the Aegean island of Cos, against which Heracles made an expedition.

Alkyoneus: in the battle of the gods against the giants on the plain of Phlegra, Heracles played a decisive part in the defeat of the latter.

And the men who bestrode them twice the number,
Proud horsemen all. Untried were he
In battle's storm, who could not understand
What lies within this brief-told tale.
Deeds done, he only who has dared them knows
What cost the doing. Long is the story,
To tell the whole my Music's rule forbids

str. 5 And time pressing apace. For with a spell,
A love-charm, the new moon draws on my heart
To grace her festival with song.
How then: what though the deep sea's tide
Hold thee waist-high,
Strain, O my soul, against its fell intent;
Our ship all eyes shall see, riding
In the broad light of day, victorious
Over the foe, safely to shore.
Another man with envy in his eye—
Vainly his empty thought rolls round
To fall in darkness to the unheeding soil.

str. 6 For me, whatever share of excellence
The throne of Fate endowed, I know full well
That Time, although his foot be slow,
Shall bring it to the end ordained.
Sweet lyre of mine,
Strike up then, and forthwith, to weave the song,
In strains of Lydian harmony,
Dear to Oenone's heart and to Cyprus,
Where Teucer, son of Telamon,
Rules afar off: and Salamis Ajax holds
His patrimony; and Achilles
That sunlit island in the Euxine sea.

str. 5 *Her festival:* the festival of Aegina at which this Ode would be sung was held in honour of Apollo at the time of the new moon, in the month called Delphinios in the Aeginetan calendar.

The deep sea's tide, etc.: see foreword on this passage.

str. 6 *Lydian harmony:* the music of this Ode was written in the 'Lydian' mode.

Oenone: the mother by Zeus of Aeacus; she gave her name to the island which was later called Aegina.

Cyprus: see foreword.

Salamis: Telamon son of Aeacus, after his departure, with his brother Peleus, from Aegina (see Nem. V. ep. 1 for the story) settled in Salamis. Ajax inherited the island from Telamon his father.

Sunlit island: the island of Leuce in the Black Sea off the mouth of the river Danube. There was a cult and a temple of Achilles here, very possibly established by Aeginetan sailors.

str. 7 Thetis rules Phthia; Neoptolemus
In far-flung Epirus, where soaring headlands
And pasturing folds fall proudly down
From high Dodona's range, to meet
The Ionian wave;
And Peleus' warring arm beset Iolcus
By Pelion's height, and gave the city
To be the servant of the Haimones,
When he had foiled Acastus' bride
Hippolyta and her treacherous guile. Then sought
Pelias' son, stealing his sword
The blade of Daedalus' magic, to contrive

str. 8 His death by ambush; saved by Chiron's hand,
The fate destined by Zeus he made his own:
Devouring flames, and the sharp claws
Of fearless lions, and tearing teeth
Safely endured,
His Nereid bride he won from her high seat,
And saw, round him enthroned, the gods

str. 7 *Phthia:* a city of central Thessaly where Peleus found a home after leaving Aegina. It thus became the home of Thetis after her marriage to Peleus.

Neoptolemus: son of Achilles. After his return from the Trojan War he went to *Epirus* in N.W. Greece but shortly afterwards met his death at Delphi. (See Nem. VII for further details.) His family remained rulers of Epirus.

Dodona: there was a temple and oracle of great antiquity at Dodona, in a mountain valley of Epirus, some miles south of the present town of Joannina. There was also a large amphitheatre which can be seen today, little damaged, and is used for occasional productions of ancient Greek plays, or concerts.

Peleus' warring arm, etc.: Peleus was the guest of Acastus, the *son of Pelias*, and king of eastern Thessaly and its capital city *Iolcus*, the modern Volos. *Hippolyta* the wife of Acastus, enamoured of Peleus who spurned her advances, accused him to Acastus of trying to seduce her, and also sent a message to Antigone, Peleus' wife in Phthia, that Peleus was about to marry someone else. On hearing this Antigone killed herself. Acastus took Peleus out hunting on Mount Pelion, stole and hid his invincible sword and left him to be killed by the savage Centaurs. Chiron rescued Peleus and returned his sword to him. Peleus then captured Iolcus and put Hippolyta to death. Then followed his marriage to Thetis.

The Haimones: the people of central Thessaly.

Daedalus: the great craftsman, of magic skill, who made Peleus' sword.

str. 8 *The fate destined by Zeus:* that he should become the husband of Thetis; she turned herself into fire and wild beasts in order to escape from Peleus, but he held her firmly and the marriage took place. (See also Nem. III. ant. 2 note.)

Of sky and sea proffer their gifts, foretelling
  The kingdom he and his race should rule.
Westwards beyond Gadeira none may pass:
  About, my ship: to Europe's mainland
Turn once again your sail; of Aeacus' sons

str. 9 All the full tale I may not here unfold.
But for Theandrus' line am I come, ready
  With songs to herald the contests
  Where strong young limbs enrich their pride;
    The songs I pledged
For Olympia, for the Isthmus and Nemea,
  From whence, their worth by trial proved,
They homeward came bearing the fruits of glory,
  Their victors' crowns. Thus it befalls,
Your father's clan has honour, Timasarchus,
  —So the word runs—high above all
In victory's hymns of triumph. Do you bid me

str. 10 For Callicles your mother's brother, too,
A pillar build whiter than Parian marble?
  Gold in the smelter's hand throws forth
  Its clearest gleam, but song praising
    His noble deeds
Marks out a man to be the peer of kings.
  So may the music of my tongue
Sound in the ear of Callicles, telling
  By Acheron where he dwells, how once
The contest of the Wielder of the Trident,
  God of the sounding seas, proclaimed him
Victor, and crowned him with Corinthian parsley.

Gadeira: the modern Cadiz, where there was a temple of Heracles. Pindar says it is time for the poem to return from mythology to its main subject.

str. 9 *Theandrus:* ancestor of Timasarchus and his family.
Olympia: members of the family had gained victories at the Olympian and the Isthmian as well as at the Nemean Games.

str. 10 *Acheron:* the river of the Underworld. Callicles was no longer alive.
The Wielder of the Trident: Poseidon, to whom the Isthmian Games held near Corinth were sacred.
Parsley: the victors' prize at the Isthmian Games was a wreath of wild parsley.

str. 11 His praise your father's father Euphanes
Was glad, my son, to sing in years gone by.
But to each his own age-fellow;
And that which his own eyes have seen,
A man may hope
In telling it to win the highest prize.
So—if Melesias praise he sings,
His words will strive, matching the wrestler's limbs,
To weave their rhythmic harmony,
Songs that shall never to the dust be thrown,
Of kindly sooth to brave endeavour,
But to rebellious strength a stern taskmaster.

str. 11 *His own eyes:* it seems that Pindar was present at Nemea when Timasarchus won his victory.

Melesias: the trainer of Timasarchus. This tribute to him makes free use in the original Greek of the terminology of the wrestling-ring.

NEMEAN V

For

PYTHEAS OF AEGINA

Winner of the Youths' Pankration

THE opening lines of this Ode comprise an appropriate tribute to the eminent place achieved by Aegina in the field of early classical or 'archaic' sculpture, amply confirmed by modern archaeology, and to her importance on the high seas and in maritime commerce.

Pytheas, as we see from the last two lines of the opening strophe, had not yet reached manhood when he won this victory, which must have been in the class of events for adolescents, or 'beardless' athletes as they were called. The date of this victory and of this Ode was probably 489/88 B.C. Menander, the trainer of Pytheas, mentioned in epode 3, was an Athenian. Open hostilities between Aegina and Athens broke out in 488 B.C. and lasted until shortly before the battle of Salamis against the Persians in 480 B.C. It is therefore likely that this victory and Menander's contribution to it took place before 488, although the reverent respect accorded by all city-states of Greece to the national Games and to the athletes who took part in them makes it possible that Menander might none the less have been a visitor to Aegina later than 488/87 in spite of the existing state of war with Athens. We have definite evidence from other Odes, Isthmian V and VI (see notes to those Odes), which record victories gained by Pytheas' younger brother Phylakidas, that the Nemean victory must have been won some time before 480 B.C.

The myth is devoted to the sons of Aeacus, Telamon and Peleus, and particularly to the marriage of Peleus and Thetis and to Peleus' difficulties with Hippolyta and her husband Acastus. This Hippolyta (also called Astydamia) is not to be confused with Hippolyta queen of the Amazons, whom Theseus married and whose son Hippolytus is the subject of the tragedy 'Hippolytus' by Euripides.

str. 1 No sculptor I, to carve an image standing
Idle upon its step. But upon every craft and sail
Speed, lovely song, from Aegina
To tell abroad that Lampon's son,
Broad-shouldered Pytheas,
Has won at Nemea the Pankratiast crown,
Though not yet on his cheek is seen the dower
Of rich-flown summer, mother of the vine-bloom.

ant. 1 The clan of Aeacus, warrior heroes sprung
From Zeus and Cronos and the glorious Nereids, share his honour,
And his own motherland, those meadows
Loved by her guests. That she might breed
Brave men and noble ships
A prayer went up long since beside the altar
Of Zeus Hellenius, where the far-famed sons
Of Endais stood and stretched their hands to heaven,

ep. 1 With Phocus in his lordly might,
Whom divine Psamatheia bore
Beside the crested wave.
Of a dread act, a deed maybe
Unrightly dared, my heart forebodes to tell,
Wherefore these warriors left this famous isle,
What fate of heaven drove them from Oenone.
Be still my tongue: here profits not
To tell the whole truth with clear face unveiled.
Often is man's best wisdom to be silent.

ant. 1 *Cronos:* father of Zeus who was the father of Aeacus.
Nereids: sea-nymphs, daughters of Nereus, a sea-god. Thetis wife of Peleus and mother of Achilles was one of them.
Zeus Hellenius: a cult of Zeus under this title is believed to have been set up by the Myrmidons, the earliest inhabitants of Aegina.
Sons of Endais: Telamon and Peleus, sons of Aeacus by his wife Endais.

ep. 1 *Phocus:* son of Aeacus by Psamatheia, a sea-nymph.
A dread act: owing to jealousy of their half-brother Phocus, who was the favourite son of their father, Telamon and Peleus killed him while they were practising hurling the discus. For this the two brothers had to leave Aegina. Telamon went to Salamis and Peleus to Thessaly. Pindar's language in these lines, part of a passage devoted to the praise of the clan of Aeacus, seems to aim at not incriminating the brothers too deeply. Phocus was killed by a blow from a discus, and one version of the story is that it was an accident.
Oenone: the original name of the island of Aegina. Oenone was the mother of Aeacus by Zeus.

str. 2 But if of fortune's wealth my praise is due
Of strength of hand or armoured war, rake a long landing-pit
Straightway for me; my limbs can muster
A nimble spring; even o'er the main
Eagles can wing their way.
Yet for these men the Muses' peerless choir
Glad welcome sang on Pelion, and with them
Apollo's seven-stringed lyre and golden quill

ant. 2 Led many a lovely strain. To Zeus a prelude,
Then sang they first divine Thetis, and Peleus, whom with guile
Fair-faced Hippolyta, Cretheus' daughter,
Sought to ensnare, as helpmate duping
Magnetes' chief, Acastus
Her husband, with deceit-embroidered counsel,
And false-wrought tales, that Peleus made to force her
There in her marriage bed. False tale indeed!

ep. 2 For it was she conjured and begged him
With many a full-hearted prayer.
Her reckless words but chafed
His wrath, and he fearing the Father,
Protector of the law of host and guest,
Straightway denied her. Then from heaven beholding
The king of the high gods, cloud-gathering Zeus,
With nodding brow forthwith ordained
A sea-nymph of the golden-spindled Nereids
His bride should be, and to accept this kinship,

str. 2 *Landing-pit:* metaphor from the long-jump, which was a regular athletic event.

Eagles: by a quick change of metaphor, Pindar identifies himself or his art as often in other Odes with an eagle, the king of birds.

These men: Telamon and Peleus.

Pelion: Mount Pelion, where the marriage feast of Peleus and Thetis was held, attended by all the gods (see Nem. III. ant. 2 and 3, and Nem. IV. str. 8).

ant. 2 *Magnetes:* the tribe inhabiting the area of Mount Pelion and Mount Ossa in eastern Thessaly where Acastus was king.

ep. 2 *The Father:* Zeus. A breach of the laws of hospitality was regarded as a serious sacrilege, as it still is in Eastern and near-Eastern countries.

Golden-spindled: an epithet applied more than once to the Nereids by Pindar. Its origin is perhaps that, as the Nereids moved about the sea, their spindles, used as they are today by the peasant women of Greece as they go about the country-side, were seen as the whirling spray of the sea-waves. Unbleached wool has a golden tinge in Greece, but this Greek epithet can equally well mean glorious-, bright- or shining-spindled.

This kinship: the wife of Poseidon was Amphitrite, also a Nereid, so that Peleus on his marriage to Thetis would become the brother-in-law of Poseidon.

str. 3 'Listed Poseidon's favour, who from Aigae
Not seldom journeys to the far-famed Dorian Isthmus. There
The flute's high note and joyful throngs,
With bold contests for strength of limb,
Receive him as their god.
His inborn fate decrees each man's achievement.
For you, Euthymenes, at Aegina
The goddess victory opened her embrace

ant. 3 And touched your ears with fine-wrought melody.
Now as you, Pytheas, tread your uncle's steps, his honours grace you
And every kinsman of your stock.
Nemea and Aegina's own month,
The feast loved of Apollo,
Brought you to fame; youth's challenge you o'erthrew
At home and in the glade by Nisus' hill,
And glad am I that every city strives

ep. 3 For noble ends. Yet mark, Menander
Gave you success, happy respite
From toil—fitly from Athens,
True craftsman of athletic skill.

str. 3 *Aigae:* the mythical home of Poseidon, in Achaea.

Dorian Isthmus: these lines, referring to the Isthmian Games held in honour of Poseidon, seem at first sight out of place in a Nemean Ode, but Pindar no doubt included them to suggest that Pytheas might soon win an Isthmian victory as he may well have hoped to do, and as in fact his younger brother Phylakidas did, twice within the next few years, victories celebrated in Isthmian Odes V and VI.

His inborn fate: the merits of natural talent are a common theme for Pindar's 'asides'.

Euthymenes: Pytheas' maternal uncle, who seems to have won a prize at Aegina's own athletic contests.

ant. 3 *Aegina's own month:* the month Delphinios in the Aeginetan calendar, in which the athletic contests took place, or in which the festival in honour of Apollo was held at which the Odes in honour of the victors were chanted.

Nisus' hill: a hill near Megara, where it appears Pytheas had won a victory in their local games, as well as at Nemea and Aegina.

Every city: the mention of the Megara games prompts Pindar to express his satisfaction that the cities of Greece were following the example of the four great national Games in establishing their own local games, as had Epidaurus, Sicyon and other places mentioned in Pindar's Odes.

ep. 3 *Menander:* Pytheas' trainer. See foreword to this Ode.

Comes now Themistius in your path of praise?
Hence chill reserve; sing out full-throated, hoist
Your sail to the mast's topyard, cry him for valour
  Twice crowned at Epidaurus, boxer
Pankratiast, and at Aeacus' city gate
Wreathed with fresh flowers, gift of the fair-haired Graces.

Themistius: Pytheas' grandfather.

Fresh flowers: on his return to Aegina from his victories at Epidaurus, Themistius seems to have been welcomed with 'wreaths', perhaps floral wreaths, but possibly—'gift of the fair-haired Graces'—poems in his honour.

NEMEAN VI

For

ALCIMIDAS OF AEGINA

Winner of the Boys' Wrestling-Match

ALCIMIDAS belonged to one of the leading families of Aegina, the Bassid clan. This victory, as Pindar says (ant. 3) is the twenty-fifth victory won by members of this family at one or other of the Panhellenic Games, successes which appear to have fallen to them in alternate generations. The Ode is built round the idea of the instability of human fortune, that both strength and weakness, success and failure, are part and parcel of our mortal lot.

There is only a brief myth in this Ode, referring to the glories of the clan of Aeacus and the victory of Achilles over Memnon, leader of the Ethiopians, who were allies of Troy in the Trojan War. The brevity of this in an Ode in honour of an Aeginetan victor is noteworthy, and may indicate that the fortunes of Aegina were no longer free from the severe threat of the power of Athens. The date of the Ode cannot be definitely fixed, but was probably in the region of 470 B.C.

str. 1 The race of men and of the gods is one.
For from one mother have we both
The life we breathe.
And yet the whole discrete endowment
Of power sets us apart;
For man is naught, but the bronze vault of heaven
Remains for ever a throne immutable.

str. 1 The first lines can also be translated 'There is one race of men, one race of gods. But from one mother, etc.' The other version however seems more in keeping with Pindar's way of thinking on this subject.

One mother : Mother Earth was, according to common Greek belief, the mother of gods and men.

Nevertheless some likeness still
May we with the immortals claim, whether
Of mind's nobility or body's grace,
Though knowing not to what goal
Has destiny, by day or through the night,
Marked out for us to run.

ant. 1 Here too Alcimidas gives ready proof
Of natural heritage resembling
The harvest fields,
Which changing year by year, today
From their broad acres yield
Abundant livelihood for man, tomorrow
They take their ease and strength again recapture.
For from Nemea's lovely games
Here has come home a boy, bred to the contest,
Who trod the destined way ordained of Zeus,
And has revealed himself
Now, in the struggle of the wrestlers' ring,
A huntsman well requited.

ep. 1 Thus followed he the road
Where trod his grandfather Praxidamas
True scion of this stock;
For he, victorious in Olympia's field,
First to the clan of Aeacus brought home
The wreath that Alpheus' banks bestow:
And five times crowned at Isthmus' games
And at Nemea thrice,
The faded memory of Socleides' name,
First of the sons of Agesimachus,
He brought once more to honour.

ep. 1 *Alpheus:* the river beside Olympia.

Socleides: father of Praxidamas, and not, apparently, an athlete. The name of Theon, the father of Alcimidas, is not mentioned in this Ode, in spite of the fact that it is almost *de rigueur* in Pindar's Odes for the father of the victor to be included in the eulogy of the victor's family. He was clearly no athlete, and Pindar no doubt felt that in view of the emphasis he gives to the successes of other members of the clan and to the principle of alternating generations, the omission of Theon's name was excusable and indeed tactful.

str. 2 For the three others, athletes crowned, of all
Who have tasted the toils of contest,
Won to the heights
Of brave renown. Thus with heaven's aid
No other house they proved
In all the folded vales of broad Hellas
Has in its treasures more crowns laid away
For victory in the boxer's ring.
Bold boast: I doubt not, like an archer's arrow
It hits the mark full-square. For this great clan, then,
Come, Muse, strike up, and breathe
A gale of noble praise. For those who see
The light of day no more

ant. 2 It is by song and on the tongues of men
Their noble deeds live down the years.
And no short measure
Of fine deeds has the Bassid clan:
Their race is old in story,
Their ships ride home the burthen of their praise,
And to the ploughmen of the Muses' meadow
Rich store they can provide, for song
To honour proud achievement. Came there not
In holy Pytho once to victory,
His hands bound in the thongs,
A man of the same blood, who won the favour
Of the children of Leto,

ep. 2 Goddess of the gold spindle?
Callias his name, and by Castalia's fountain
As evening fell, his glory
Flamed with the Graces' song. And by the bridge
That spans the restless sea, Creontidas

str. 2 *Three others:* we do not know the names of these three brothers of Socleides, or what victories they won, except that they were boxing successes.

ant. 2 *Pytho:* i.e. at the Pythian Games at Delphi.

The thongs: leather straps, bound round the boxer's hands, took the place of the modern boxing-glove.

The children of Leto: Apollo and Artemis. A Pythian victory implied the favour of these deities, particularly that of Apollo. The epithet 'of the gold spindle' is regularly applied in Homer to Artemis; here Pindar applies it to her mother.

ep. 2 *Callias and Creontidas:* ancestors of Alcimidas; their exact relationship does not appear.

Castalia: the well-known spring, still in existence close to Delphi.

The bridge: the Isthmus of Corinth.

Found honour, in Poseidon's precinct,
At the feast of the neighbouring people,
Where bulls are sacrificed,
Their two-year ritual. The lion's herb, too,
By the primeval hills of shady Phlious
Graced his victorious brow.

str. 3 Wide are the roads from every side, that lead
The voice of chronicle to adorn
This island's fame.
For by their deeds of valour proved
The sons of Aeacus
Raised high their destined glory, and o'er land
And far across the sea flies forth their name.
Even to the Ethiopian race,
When mighty Memnon came not home again,
Their fame took wing; for dire strife fell upon them
When great Achilles stepped
Down from his chariot to the ground, and slew
The son of shining Dawn,

ant. 3 With his fell-pointed spear. In these great deeds
The bards of old found for their songs
A broad highway;
And I, too, at the self-same call
Follow my art's resource.
Yet, as they tell of ships that ride the storm,
That wave which each moment threatens most nearly
The straining hull, breeds in all hearts
The sharpest breath of fear. Now I right gladly
Bending my shoulder to a two-fold burden,
Come as a messenger
To sing, Alcimidas, your proud success,
The five-and-twentieth now

In Poseidon's precinct: i.e. at the Isthmian Games, sacred to Poseidon, held every two years.

The lion's herb: a name given to wild parsley, a wreath of which was the prize at the Nemean Games.

Phlious: a place near Nemea.

str. 3 *Memnon:* the Ethiopian leader whom Achilles killed in the Trojan War.

The son of shining Dawn: Memnon was the son of Tithonus and Aurora.

ant. 3 *Yet, as they tell, etc.:* in different words, Pindar is repeating the comment made in Nem. III. ant. 4 and elsewhere in the Odes, that the task in hand must have a man's first attention—that it is time, here in fact, to return to the main subject of the Ode.

Two-fold burden: praise of Alcimidas and of his trainer Melesias.

ep. 3 Earned by your famous race,
At the contests which men entitle sacred.
And two more prizes still,
The wreaths of victory at Olympia,
In the precinct of Zeus, the son of Cronos,
The chance fall of the lot denied
To you and Polytimidas.
Now to the dolphin's speed
Through the sea-foam, Melesias let me liken,
Skilful master of hands and supple strength,
A most wise charioteer.

ep. 3 *The chance fall of the lot, etc.*: it is unusual for an Ode to end with the mention of unsuccessful attempts, even though the loss of the two prizes seems here to have been due to luck of the 'draw' rather than to lack of skill. But this ending is in keeping with the prominence given in the Ode to the changing vicissitudes of human fortune.

Polytimidas: a relation of Alcimidas, probably brother or cousin.

Melesias: the trainer, also mentioned in Ol. VIII and Nem. IV.

Charioteer: in the sense of guide and adviser.

NEMEAN VII

For

SOGENES OF AEGINA

Winner of the Boys' Pentathlon

This Ode contains much which can only be understood in the light of the circumstances in which the poem was written. These remained for long obscure, until in recent years the discovery of Pindar's Paean No. 6, which is mentioned in ancient commentaries but of which we had hitherto no text, provided a key to the puzzle.

In this Paean, written for a religious festival at Delphi, Pindar refers to the story of Neoptolemus, the son of Achilles, after the fall of Troy. It was Neoptolemus who killed king Priam, when he had taken refuge at the altar of 'Zeus Herkeios', protector of the sanctities of the home. For this sacrilegious act, Apollo vowed vengeance upon him; and when after his return to Greece Neoptolemus came to Delphi in order to make an offering to Apollo to commemorate the victory won at Troy, a quarrel arose between him and the priests of the temple because of his refusal to hand over the flesh of the sacrificed animals normally allotted to them. In the fight which ensued Neoptolemus was killed.

This legend, which does not reflect great credit on Neoptolemus, was well known to Greeks of Pindar's time and in the Paean written for the priests of Apollo, who would not of course expect that Neoptolemus should be represented as blameless, Pindar does not seem to be concerned to depart from the accepted version of the story. In Aegina however, where the clan of Aeacus, to which Neoptolemus belonged, provided the great national heroes of the island, feelings appear to have been ruffled, and as passages in the present Ode seem to suggest, his rivals and critics, who there is reason to believe were busy enough in Aegina, no doubt played up to the full Pindar's references to Neoptolemus in the Paean, although these are quite brief and not such as would normally arouse objection in Greek minds.

It is clear that Pindar used this Ode as an opportunity to exculpate himself from the charge of having cast a slur on Neoptolemus, and

The Pentathlon: a contest consisting of five events, jumping, throwing the discus, hurling the javelin, a foot-race and a wrestling-match.

to defend his own good intentions and integrity. He was not however in a comfortable position and the construction of the Ode seems to reflect an unhappy and indignant state of mind. The Ode takes some time to reach the point where the 'apology' begins—in the second half of antistrophe 2—and the earlier epode 1 and strophe 2 contain what might seem a digression, the story of the tragic death of Ajax. After the death of Achilles in the Trojan War the Greeks decided to give his golden armour to the warrior adjudged to have fought most gallantly. Ajax confidently expected to receive this award, but the persuasive power of Odysseus induced the Greeks to award it to himself, whereupon Ajax killed himself in chagrin. As Ajax was the grandson of Aeacus his story is not out of place in an Ode in honour of an Aeginetan, but as the main myth of this poem is concerned with Neoptolemus, this passage was perhaps included additionally in order to stress the power of specious misrepresentation, typified by the success of the 'wily Odysseus' over the claims of Ajax. As such it would be a preliminary part of Pindar's vigorous defence of himself and his good intentions expressed later in the Ode. It also appears, from a later passage in epode 3 where Pindar says that he will defend Thearion, the father of Sogenes, from 'dark slander', that Thearion, too, was suffering from misrepresentation or some similar trouble, and this passage on Ajax may also be connected with this.

The Ode then proceeds, in antistrophe 2, to some lines in praise of the power of poetry, with the suggestion that Neoptolemus, whose story now begins, is not unworthy of the deathless renown which poetry can confer. The story in Pindar's present version contains no word at all that would redound to Neoptolemus' discredit, and the quarrel over the 'meats of sacrifice' is represented as a fortuitous difference with a single opponent. The other posthumous honours which accrue to Neoptolemus as he 'lies in Pytho's soil' take the Ode to the beginning of antistrophe 3. A short interlude on the vicissitudes of human life, reflecting no doubt Thearion's troubles or Pindar's own, leads to praise of Thearion and to Pindar's claim (strophe 4) to be a man of moderation and good will. This is followed by Pindar's strenuous assertion that he has never overstepped the bounds or 'cast a sharp-flung word' (antistrophe 4), or that if in a moment of poetic exaltation, 'borne on wings aloft', he 'called a cry too shrill', this cannot affect the honour of Sogenes to which he is now paying due tribute. Then after lines, justly famous, in praise of poetry, there follows a rather lengthy passage, continued almost to the end of the Ode, expressing the hope that good fortune will continue to attend the family, present and future, of Thearion and Sogenes; and the aid of Heracles is invoked to this end. The connection with Heracles is that the house in Aegina in which the family lived lay between two sanctuaries sacred to Heracles.

Then in a line of the last epode Pindar gives vent, surprisingly, and as if dragged out of him by *force majeure*, to a final, brief and direct denial of having cast a slur on Neoptolemus. This and the concluding lines of the poem, excusing himself for so much repetition of the same idea—lines expressed in such light-hearted terms as to seem almost undignified in contrast with what has gone before—leave one with the impression that Pindar suddenly felt tired of the whole sorry business, and that he wanted to suggest to his Aeginetan friends, by a final jocular remark, that they had taken a small matter much too seriously.

No date can be assigned with any certainty to this Ode. It must have been written after, probably not very long after, Paean No. 6. There is evidence in that poem that it was written while Aegina was still a strong naval power, and so not one of Pindar's later poems. But before it was written he had been appointed by Delphi to be their 'proxenos' (representative in another city), and had also been accorded the hereditary right of a place at the Delphic 'theoxenia', a regularly held religious banquet, at which the Paean was to be chanted. Such marks of distinction imply that Pindar had by then advanced some way in his career. Thus the Paean and Nemean VII which followed it seem likely to have been written in Pindar's middle or early-middle age.

str. 1 Goddess of childbirth, Eleithuia,
Maid to the throne of the deep-thinking Fates,
Child of all-powerful Hera, hear my song.
For without thee should we see neither
The light of day, nor know the kindly dark,
Nor win the gift of Hebe, thy sister,
The glorious limbs of Youth.
Yet is the life we breathe not given to all
For a like end. Destiny's bar
Yokes one man to this venture, one to that.

str. 1 *Eleithuia:* this invocation to the goddess of childbirth is suitable in any poem in honour of a boy, but there is also evidence, derived by ancient editors from an epigram of Simonides, now lost, that Thearion the father of Sogenes had to wait many years for a son to be born to him, which makes this invocation the more appropriate.

Hebe: the goddess of youth and beauty.

But with thy favour now
Sogenes, listed on the roll of valour,
Thearion's son, with the Pentathlete victors
Rises to glory on my song.

ant. 1 For his city is one of music-lovers,
The sons of Aeacus, bred to the clash of spears;
And glad are they to embrace a spirit, that shares
Their love of contest. If success
Crowns a man's venture, sweeter then than honey
The theme he pours into the Muses' stream.
But lacking songs to praise them,
The mightiest feats of valour can but find
A sorry grave of deep darkness.
But for fine deeds a mirror to establish,
One way alone we know,
If Memory's shining diadem will grant
Recompense for their labours, in the glory
Of music on the tongues of men.

ep. 1 Wise men are they
Who know the tempest that shall blow
The third day hence,
Whom thirst for profit shall not bring to grief.
Yet rich and poor alike travel the road
That leads at last to death.
Yet I am fain to think
That by the sweet charm of great Homer's word
Odysseus wins a larger fame
Than his proved deeds would grant him.

str. 2 Through false tales and the skilled magic
Of wingéd words, a majesty enfolds him.
The poet's art by his fables deceives us
And leads the mind astray. For blind

ant. 1 *Success:* the Greek word, though it has commonly no more particular meaning than the English 'success', is in Pindar frequently used, as here, to suggest victory in the Games.

ep. 1 *Wise men are they, etc.:* Pindar follows up his preceding lines emphasizing the power of poetry to give immortality to fine deeds, by suggesting that in commissioning this poem on behalf of his son, Thearion is wise not to spare himself the cost of this. The lines also serve as a buffer to lessen the contrast between the high praise of the power of poetry and the warning that follows against the deceits that poetry can induce.

Odysseus: the mention of Odysseus provides a connecting link with the reference in the following strophe to the death of Ajax, and the part played by Odysseus in causing this. See foreword.

Of heart are all the most of men. Never,
Had they but been minded to know the truth,
    Never would mighty Ajax,
In anger's travail for the arms denied him,
  Have plunged his sharp sword through his breast:
Ajax, the mightiest warrior in battle
    Of all, save but Achilles,
Whom on their war-ships, to bring back his bride
To fair-haired Menelaus, the swift breath
  Of straight-flown Zephyrus escorted

ant. 2 To Ilos' city. Yet forget not,
Death's wave comes to all men, falling on him
Who recked not of it, and alike on him
  Who had some foretaste of it. But honour,
Honour is theirs, who win richly from heaven
    Storied renown, so to secure a name
    Deathless even in the grave.
So was it when came to the great centre-stone
  Of earth's broad breast Neoptolemus,
And lies in Pytho's soil—he who laid low
    Priam's city, stern struggle
Where too the Danai laboured. Sailing thence
He failed of Skyros, and far-wandering brought
  His scattered sails to Ephyra.

str. 2 *Ajax:* see foreword.
Zephyrus: the west wind.

ant. 2 *Ilos' city:* Ilium, the ancient name of Troy.
So was it, etc.: i.e. that a 'deathless name' was the reward of Neoptollemus, see foreword. These lines almost suggest that Neoptolemus was the main factor in the capture of Troy, something of an exaggeration, although he was one of the Greeks inside the Wooden Horse.
The great centre-stone of earth: the temple of Delphi. The priestess who pronounced the Pythian oracles was seated, while she did so, on a large stone. Delphi is often referred to in Greek literature as the 'centre-stone' or 'navel' of the earth.
Neoptolemus: see foreword.
Failed of Skyros: Skyros is the island in the Aegean, north-east of Euboea, which was the home of Neoptolemus during his youth until he was summoned by the Greeks to take part in the Trojan War after the death of his father Achilles. In his sixth Paean Pindar tells us that Neoptolemus was fated never to see his mother again or to return to his native land, and that Apollo swore that he should never reach his 'happy home' again, but should die young at Delphi. All this, for the reasons given in the foreword, is toned down by Pindar here to the innocent phrase that he failed to reach Skyros.
Ephyra: a city in Epirus, the district in the north-west of Greece opposite the island of Corfu. The name is applied to other places in Greece, including Corinth.

ep. 2 Then was his kingdom
For a brief time Molossia;
But since that day
His race has held that honoured throne. But he
Departed straight to the god's temple, bringing
The chief spoils of Troy's city
As offerings to Apollo.
There, o'er the meats of sacrifice, a quarrel
Broke with a man who chanced to meet him,
And with a knife-blade slew him.

str. 3 Heavy the grief of those who guard
The rights of Delphi's guests. Yet he fulfilled
The lot of destiny; for it was decreed
That in that ancient precinct, one
Of Aeacus' mighty race should lie forever,
Beside the strong-walled house of the great god,
To dwell, guardian of right
Over the pomps and ceremonies of heroes
With their rich sacrifice. To pay
His name and fame full justice, shall suffice
Three words: where he presides
O'er brave exploits, no false witness could be
A son of thine, Aegina, and of Zeus.
Boldly I this for him proclaim:

ant. 3 The splendour of their valorous deeds
Born of that house's heritage, gives him
A royal path to glory's record. Yet
As all know well, pleasant is rest
In every work of man; there can be surfeit
Even of honey and the lovely flower
Of Aphrodite's joys.

ep. 2 *Molossia:* the name given later to the kingdom of Epirus, derived from Molossus, the son of Neoptolemus and Hector's wife Andromache, whom Neoptolemus brought from Troy as a captive.

The god's temple: Delphi.

A quarrel: see foreword.

str. 3 *Brave exploits:* the Pythian Games, held at Delphi.

A son: i.e. descendant; Neoptolemus was the great-grandson of Aeacus, who was the son of Zeus and Oenone (Aegina). See Introduction for family-tree of the clan of Aeacus.

ant. 3 *Pleasant is rest, etc.:* another way of saying that life has its 'ups and downs', as had Neoptolemus and, apparently, Thearion. This passage also serves as a short interlude to ease the transition from the Neoptolemus story to the praise of Thearion.

By our inborn talent find we each one
The different path of life we tread,
One here, one there. But what can never be
Is that one man should win
A life entire of blessings. I know no man
To whom Fate gave this lot abidingly.
But you, Thearion, she grants

ep. 3 No grudging share
Of happiness, courage to dare
Deeds of high mettle,
And lessens not your heart's good understanding.
I am your guest. From dark slander shall I
Defend you, as a friend
Brings to a friend a draught
Of purest water, to your true renown
Giving due praise. For men of worth
This is the fit reward.

str. 4 Should an Achaean from his home
Above the Ionian sea, be near me now, no
Blame shall he voice. In his land, in my title
Of Proxenos I have full trust;
On my own folk I look with serene eyes,
Moderate in all I do, guarding my steps
From every violent act.
And may my days to come follow a like
Path of good will. Who knows me well
Shall say if shafts of slander on my tongue
Come with their jarring note.
Son of the house of Euxenos, Sogenes,
Ne'er, as an athlete whose foot faults the line,
Launching his bronze-tipped javelin,

ep. 3 *For men of worth, etc.:* as well as applying to Thearion, Pindar perhaps means this sentence to apply to himself, thus making an easy link with the vigorous defence of himself and his character which begins in the succeeding strophe.

str. 4 *An Achaean:* Epirus borders the Ionian sea. The term 'Achaean' was the name applied most commonly, in Homer and later writers, to all Greeks generally. Here Pindar means not an original Epirote, but a descendant of Neoptolemus or his followers, i.e. someone who might have taken offence at the story given in the Paean.

Proxenos: many city-states appointed as proxenos a citizen of another city-state, to look after their interests and to be available to help their citizens when visiting his city—work of the kind done by a present-day ambassador or consul. It was a mark of trust and distinction.

On my own folk: i.e. at Thebes.

Euxenos: the ancestor from whom the family of Sogenes was descended.

ant. 4 Have I so cast a sharp-flung word.
To you I swear it, who from the wrestlers' ring,
Its struggle and sweat, and from the sun's hot ray
Kept your strong limbs and shoulders free.
If it were toil, greater the joy thereafter.
But this: to pay grace to the victor's honour,
If, borne on wings aloft
I called a cry too shrill, no churlish heart
Is mine, not to subscribe it fully.
Weaving of wreaths is a light task: strike up:
The Muse makes gifts of gold
And of white ivory together mingled,
And, gleaming like the lily's flower, can steal
The clear spray from the deep sea's wave.

ep. 4 Bear Zeus in mind
Chanting your notes of song widespread
For Nemea's honour;
And peace be in your hearts. For it is fitting
That on this soil voices of gentle measure
Should celebrate in song
The almighty King of gods.
For it was he, so runs the tale, begot
Great Aeacus to be his son
Within a mortal womb,

str. 5 And to be ruler of his country
Of splendid name, and to you, Heracles,
To be a kind and loyal host, and brother.
For of all gifts exchanged of man
No greater taste of joy should we adjudge,
Than if a neighbour shall befriend a neighbour
With steadfast loyalty.

ant. 4 *The wrestlers' ring:* of the five events which made up the pentathlon the wrestling-match took place last. We have no certain knowledge of the rules which governed this contest, but it is clear that, if a competitor achieved a winning score before the fourth or fifth event, he was excused the last one, or two, events. As we see from this passage, Sogenes was in this way exempt from the wrestling-match and possibly from the fourth event as well.

If it were toil: most of Pindar's Odes contain some reference to the hard work entailed in winning a victory at the Games, and the previous training involved was no doubt also in mind.

Weaving of wreaths: i.e. the victor's wreath is of small account as a prize compared to an Ode in his honour.

If too a god allow us such relation,
With you, great conqueror of the giants,
In friendship's tie so bonded, Sogenes
Would deem his life well-blessed,
With tender spirit cherishing his father,
To hold in sacred trust the well-found homestead
By his forbears bequeathed to him.

ant. 5 For he lives in your holy precinct,
As if beneath a four-horsed chariot yoke,
Binding on this hand and on that, the house
Wherein he dwells. O blessèd one,
Your task it can well be to win for him
Propitious grace from Hera's husband, and
The grey-eyed goddess maid.
Not seldom is it in your power to grant
To mortal souls, strength to withstand
The toils that baffle them. May you for these,
Father and son, accord
A life of steadfast strength, that fortune's blessing
Cleave to them both, in youth and sunlit age.
And may their children's children ever

ep. 5 Preserve these honours,
And achieve fortune happier still
In years to come.
But shall my heart never admit that I
With words none can redeem smirched Neoptolemus.
Yet to repeat the same
Saying three times or more,
Argues a wit helpless and weak, as one
Who to his babes mumbles the tale
'Corinth the son of Zeus'.

str. 5 *Conqueror of the giants:* Heracles, another reference as in Nem. IV. str. 4 to the battle of the gods against the giants in which Heracles played a decisive part.

ant. 5 *In your holy precinct:* the house in which Sogenes lived was situated between two sanctuaries sacred to Heracles, which Pindar compares to the double yoke of a four-horsed chariot.
O blessed one: Heracles.
Hera's husband: Zeus.
The grey-eyed goddess maid: the goddess Athene.

ep. 5 On this final reference to Neoptolemus see foreword.
Corinth the son of Zeus: this is thought to be a proverbial phrase, indicating a much-used story or possibly a nursery tale.

NEMEAN VIII

For DEINIS OF AEGINA

Winner of the Foot-Race

We may judge from the opening lines of this Ode that Deinis, to whom the poem is addressed, was a young man in the prime of his youth. His father Megas, no longer alive, was also it appears a Nemean victor, and the wording of two passages in the Ode suggests that both Megas and Deinis had each won two victories in the foot-race.

The myth in this Ode is a further reference to the story, given more briefly in the preceding Ode VII, of Ajax and Odysseus, and emphasizes even more vigorously the evils done by envy and misrepresentation.

Some commentators have been inclined to see in these passages a parallel with situations arising during the long antagonism between Aegina and other cities of Greece, particularly Athens, which produced many occasions when bitter aspersions against Aegina were no doubt rife. If so the references in epode 1 to Athens and Sparta as having been in the times of Aeacus willingly subordinate to his power, might have been intended by Pindar as a comforting reminder to the Aeginetans of the high position their island enjoyed in ancient times.

There are however so many similarities in this Ode to the preceding Nemean VII as to make it more likely that, in repeating the story of the death of Ajax and the strong condemnation of 'treachery's tongue' (epode 2), the poem is continuing Pindar's defence of himself against the allegations of his enemies. After the story of Ajax, it contains in strophe 3, as does strophe 4 of Nemean VII, a strong defence of his own integrity and outlook, and it is difficult not to conclude that this Ode was written shortly after the other one and with a similar underlying purpose. In contrast however with Nemean VII there is every indication in the happier tone and easy expression of the poem that Pindar had recovered from the anxious *malaise* and indignant temper which make themselves felt in the previous Ode. It seems quite probable that that Ode had had the desired effect in mollifying the hurt feelings of Pindar's Aeginetan friends, and that he can now address them in an easier frame of mind.

If this assumption is correct this Ode would date itself shortly after Nemean VII, which probably belongs to Pindar's middle or early middle age.

str. 1 O sovereign Youth, herald of Aphrodite
And her sweet passions born of heaven,
Whose wing lights on the eyes of youth and maid,
And whose constraining hands
On one with kindly touch, but on another
All too ungently fall—
Happy is he who in his every act
Fails not the moment due, and can prevail
The noblest loves to master.

ant. 1 Such loves were shepherd to the bridal bed
Of Zeus and Aegina, to bring them
The Cyprian goddess' gifts. And there was born
A son, king of Oenone,
Peerless in counsel and in might of hand.
Many, and oft, would plead
His audience, for the flower of warrior pride
Dwelling in lands nearby, were glad unbidden
His sovereign laws to obey,

ep. 1 Those who in Athens' rock-built city marshalled
The people's host, and the great line
Of Pelops' sons, rulers in Sparta.
A suppliant now come I,
To embrace the knees of Aeacus, long revered,

ant. 1 *The Cyprian goddess:* Aphrodite. Her home was at Paphos on the island of Cyprus.
A son: Aeacus.
Oenone: the original name of Aegina.

ep. 1 *Pelops' sons:* descendants of Pelops included Menelaus king of Sparta and his brother Agamemnon king of Mycenae, both cities of the Peloponnesus, a name which means the island of Pelops.

Bringing for his dear city, and for these
His citizens, a Lydian circlet, richly
With fluted notes embroidered, glory's prize
  For Deinis and his father Megas,
    Victorious in the foot-race
  Twice on Nemea's field. True is it,
Good fortune founded with the help of heaven,
Lasts for mankind far longer down the years.

str. 2 Such was it loaded Kinyras with riches
  In sea-girt Cyprus long ago.
Look, on feet lightly-poised I stand, to take
    New breath before I speak.
Story is vast in range: new ways to find
    And test upon the touchstone,
Here danger lies: words are rich food for envy,
Who lays her hand ever upon the noble,
    Striving not with lesser men.

ant. 2 She it was devoured the son of Telamon,
  His body pierced with his own sword.
A dauntless heart having no able tongue,
    Howsoe'er fierce the battle,
Lies hid, forgotten; but the highest prize
    For shifty craft lies spread.
The Danaans' secret votes courted Odysseus,
But Ajax, cheated of the golden arms,
    Wrestled with bloody death.

Lydian circlet: the music for this Ode was written in the 'Lydian' mode.

Glory's prize: this Ode.

str. 2 *Kinyras:* a legendary king of Cyprus, a priest of Aphrodite and a favourite of Apollo. Mentioned here as typifying the 'good fortune' that can derive from the 'help of heaven'.

To take new breath: Pindar pictures himself as poised to embark on an important theme for which all his resource is needed. In most of the Odes, as here, Pindar devotes the central part to ideas to which he wants to give special significance.

New ways: Pindar's handling of his myths is believed to have been the chief target for his critics' attacks. The way he tells the legendary stories is certainly not conventional, but characteristic of his original methods.

ant. 2 *The son of Telamon:* Ajax. In Greek legend and literature he is represented as the warrior of superb fighting qualities and gigantic stature, but not blessed with much eloquence.

Danaans: the name, like 'Achaeans', used in Homer and other early writers for the Greeks generally.

Odysseus and *Ajax:* see foreword to Nem. VII, fourth paragraph.

ep. 2 Unlike indeed, those other wounds they struck
And cleft the hot flesh of the foe,
Beneath their fence of serried spears
Bearing the brunt of war;
Whether beside Achilles newly slain,
Or whatsoever toll of ills filled full
Those crowded days of death. Yet even of old
Treachery's tongue, breeder of hate, was known,
Close companied with tales of guile,
False-hearted to the core,
She sows the evil seed of blame,
Violates true merit's lustre, and exalts
The worthless man's unsavoury repute.

str. 3 Such thoughts, great Zeus, never may it be mine
To foster, but of life to tread
The simple paths, and dying leave my children
No ill-engendered fame.
Gold is for some their prayer, for some wide acres;
My trust shall be to dwell
Beloved of friends, till earth shall shroud my limbs,
Praising where praise is due, on evil-doers
Sowing widespread rebuke.

ant. 3 Midst poets and just minds true excellence
Reaches full height, as trees refreshed
By fruitful showers spread to the moistening air.
For many a diverse cause
A man needs friends: under the toils of contest
Most need of all; and joy
Seeks too to see clearly before her eyes
The sign of trust. To bring your spirit, Megas,
To earth again, lies not

ep. 2 *They struck:* i.e. Ajax, Odysseus and the Greeks in their battles with the Trojans.

Beside Achilles: one of the fiercest battles of the war developed for the possession of the body of Achilles.

ant. 3 *The toils of contest . . . and joy* . . . these remarks can be of general application, but are probably also intended to refer to the hard work entailed in an athletic contest and to the victor's pleasure in having won it. It seems possible that Pindar also intended to indicate in the word 'joy' his own happiness that, as suggested in the foreword, his relations with his Aeginetan friends were again on a friendly footing as the result of his Ode VII: the 'sign of trust' could mean the fact that Deinis or his family had commissioned the present Ode from Pindar. The sentence might then be taken as a graceful expression of Pindar's thanks.

ep. 3 Within my power, and useless is the end
Of idle hopes. But for your race
And for the Chariades to build
A mighty pillar of the Muse,
This task I can, to honour those swift feet
That won the double prize, twice glorious;
And glad am I if I may utter praise
To match the act; for by songs and their charm
A man can draw the pains of toil
Even from weary limbs.
Yes, hymns of revelry were known
Long years ago, e'er yet the strife arose
Betwixt Adrastus and the sons of Cadmus.

ep. 3 *The Chariades:* the name of the clan to which the family of Megas and Deinis belonged.

Adrastus, etc.: the invention of 'hymns of revelry', songs of praise for great events, was attributed by legend to the time of the expedition of the 'Seven against Thebes', organized by Adrastus and six other leaders. Pindar seems to claim an even earlier date.

NEMEAN IX

For

CHROMIUS OF AETNA

Winner of the Chariot-Race

THIS Ode and the two which follow were not written to celebrate victories in the Nemean Games. The reason for their inclusion at the end of the book of Nemean Odes is given in the Introduction.

The Chromius of this Ode is the same Sicilian leader celebrated in Nemean I, who was made governor of the city of Aetna after its foundation shortly before 476 B.C. The present victory was won by him at the minor games held in honour of Apollo at Sicyon, a city on the south side of the Gulf of Corinth. This Ode appears to have been written after Nemean I, probably at some time between 475 and 471 B.C. The date of the actual victory at Sicyon cannot be ascertained, but it is clear that there was a lengthy interval between the victory and the writing of this Ode, and lines at the end of strophe 9 indicate that Chromius had already reached a mature, if not elderly, age when the Ode was written.

The construction of the Ode follows the normal pattern, with rather a longer passage than usual, in its later sections, devoted to the merits of the victor. The myth tells the story of the expedition of the 'Seven against Thebes' led by Adrastus of Argos, and its relevance to this Ode is that Adrastus was according to legend the founder of the Sicyon games. In fact they were founded in the early years of the sixth century B.C. by Cleisthenes, the ruler of Sicyon. As in other Odes addressed to Sicilian leaders, Hieron and his group, there are many passages or phrases which can be interpreted as suggesting the value of moderation and wisdom in government, rather than that of violence and intrigue, of which the history of Western Greece in this period shows only too many examples.

str. 1 Let us now as Apollo bids, O Muses,
From Sicyon lead our chant of triumph
To Aetna, the new-founded city,
And Chromius' house of happy fortune,
Whose doors, flung wide, brim over with the stream of guests.
For him, then, play aloud
The sweet notes of your praise,
For mounted in his victor's chariot
He gives the signal for the song, in honour
Of Leto and her twin children,
Who keep their joint watch over rocky Pytho.

str. 2 There is a saying on the lips of men
That no deed nobly done should lie
Hidden in silence 'neath the ground,
Whose fit reward is divine song,
Proud poetry's praise. Then let the sounding lyre ring out,
And the flute's note, to honour
The greatest of all contests
Of horsemen's skill, which for Apollo's glory
Adrastus founded by Asopus' stream;
These shall my song now call to mind,
And crown that hero with illustrious honour.

str. 3 He the enthronéd king then of that land
Made known his city's name and fame,
With his new festivals, and contests
For strength of limb and richly-carved
Chariots, sped on their rival course. For he had fled
From bold Amphiaraus
And bitter civil strife,
Driven far from his father's halls, and far
From Argos city; and Talaus' sons were kings
No more, enforced by war's fell fury.
For men of power tread down the older right.

str. 1 Pindar is picturing the procession of the chorus which will chant the Ode. Its arrangement in a succession of strophes, instead of the usual triads, is better fitted for the accompaniment of a march.
As Apollo bids: Apollo was the patron god of the Sicyon games.
Leto: the mother of Apollo and Artemis.

str. 2 *Asopus' stream:* not the Boeotian Asopus but a river near Sicyon.

str. 3 *Amphiaraus* usurped the throne of Argos from Adrastus, who retired temporarily to Sicyon.
Talaus: father of Adrastus.

str. 4 But when in marriage to this son of Oikleus
They gave, as for a pledge of faith,
Eriphyle, who was to prove
Her husband's slayer, they became
The greatest captains of the fair-haired Danai.
And on a time they led
Their soldier host against
Seven-gated Thebes—a road that won no sign
Of happy omen, but the lightning flash
Of Zeus bade not their hot-head madness
Lead forth from home, but to renounce their march.

str. 5 But to a fated end clearly revealed
The host sped forth upon its way,
Clad in their brazen mail and trappings
Of horsemen's gear. But their fond hopes
Of sweet return were sundered on Ismenus' banks,
And their young limbs fed fat,
With smoke white-billowing,
Seven burning pyres; but for Amphiaraus
Zeus with his thunderbolt's consuming might
Cleft open the deep-breasted earth,
And hid him from man's sight, horses and all,

str. 6 E'er that the spear of Periclymenus
Should pierce his back, and that in shame
His warrior heart should meet its end.
For even the children of the gods
Take flight in terrors sprung from heaven.—O son of Cronos,
If it can be, would that
This test of warrior worth,

str. 4 *The son of Oikleus:* Amphiaraus.
Eriphyle: the sister of Adrastus. By her marriage to Amphiaraus, the quarrel between these two was made up. She became responsible for the death of Amphiaraus, because when he was hesitating to join the expedition of the 'Seven against Thebes', having foreseen through his prophetic powers that it would meet with disaster, Eriphyle persuaded him to join it, having been suborned to do so by Polyneices, one of the 'Seven'. Polyneices was the son of Oedipus, and had been exiled from Thebes by his brother Eteocles.

str. 5 *Ismenus' banks:* a river near Thebes.

str. 6 *Periclymenus:* one of the defenders of Thebes.

This trial for life or death, against the host
Of the Phoenician spears, I might delay
For many a day. Great father Zeus,
I beg thee grant the sons of Aetna's city

str. 7 Long share of wisdom's rule, and that this people
May be full partners in the glories
Their city shall reveal. For here,
Be sure, are men who love full well
A horseman's skill, and hearts that reck not of possessions,
Hard to believe. For Honour,
Who brings men high renown,
By hope of gain in secret is perverted.
Had you been shield-bearer to Chromius, battling
On foot, on horse or on the sea,
You would have judged, facing the conflict's din,

str. 8 That under stress of war it was that goddess,
Honour, that bred within his heart
The warrior mettle to fend off
The havoc of Mars. Few men there are
Who have the strength of hand, or heart, to devise plans
To turn the cloud of bloodshed,
Threatening their very door,
Onto the ranks of their dread enemies.
Hector's renown found its full flower, they say,
Beside Scamander's stream, and here
Near to Helorus' steeply-riven banks,

Phoenician spears: the Carthaginians. They had been heavily defeated by the Greeks of Sicily and south Italy at the battle of Himera in 480 B.C., the year of the defeat at Salamis of the Persians, with whose invasion of Greece the Carthaginian attack on Western Greece was timed to coincide. They remained however a menace, as these lines, written a good many years after Himera, suggest.

str. 8 *Hector* was a young man, as was Chromios at Helorus.
Scamander: the river near the battlefields of Troy.
Helorus' banks: a river in Sicily, where in the battle of Helorus, about the year 492 B.C., Hippocrates, tyrant of Gela, defeated the Syracusans. His sons Gelon and Hieron, and Chromius their friend, assisted at this battle. Chromius must at this date have been a fairly young man. The many subsequent struggles between the city-states of Sicily, in which Chromius as the friend and brother-in-law of Hieron must have taken part, and also possibly the naval defeat of the Etruscans at the battle of Cumae in 474 B.C. (if this Ode was written after that date) are reflected in strophes 7, 8 and 9.

str. 9 Whose name men call the ford of goddess Rhea,
There shone forth a like gleam of glory
To light Agesidamus' son,
In his first years of young manhood;
And many another day of his deeds could I tell
Braved on the dusty land
Or on the neighbouring sea.
But from the dangers which beset our youth,
If rightly met, comes to our elder years
An age of peace. Then let him know
That heaven has given him blessings beyond count.

str. 10 For if, together with possessions rich,
A man wins glorious renown,
Achievement has no higher peak
For mortal footsteps to attain.
Peace and the banquet like each other passing well;
And victory flowers anew
In the sweet chant of song;
While by the wine-bowl can the singer's voice
Be more courageous yet. Then let the draught
Be poured and mixed, that sweet and rich
Proclaimer of the songs of revelry.

str. 11 And let the strong child of the vine be served
In silver goblets, which his steeds
For Chromius won, and which with wreaths
Woven as Apollo's rite demands,
They brought from holy Sicyon. Father Zeus, I pray thee,
May the song that I sing
To praise this deed of valour,
Be by the Graces blest, and may our voices
More than all others, honour his victory.
For that I set my arrow's aim
As near as may be to the Muses' mark.

str. 9 *Agesidamus' son:* Chromius.

str. 10 The procession is now over and the banquet can begin.

str. 11 *Silver goblets:* these were the prizes of victory in the Sicyon games, as well as the usual wreaths.

NEMEAN X

For

THEAIUS OF ARGOS

Winner of the Wrestling-Match

THIS Ode is written partly in praise of Theaius and the several athletic victories he had won, and partly as a panegyric of the city of Argos and her legendary heroes. Although a Nemean victory is mentioned amongst the other successes of Theaius, no special emphasis is laid on this, and the poem is not a Nemean Ode. (For its inclusion, with Nemean IX and XI, in this book, see Introduction.)

The first part of the Ode is devoted to the praise of Argive heroes, the central part to the athletic victories of Theaius and his family and of other citizens of Argos, and the last section to the myth, in which Pindar tells the story of Castor and Pollux, the brothers who eventually became the well-known constellation.

The people of Argos were especially devoted to the worship of Hera, the divine patroness of their city, and their chief religious festival, mentioned in strophe 2 of this Ode, was in her honour. (The remains of the extensive temple of Hera, the Heraeum, can be seen today a few miles from Argos.) It is clear that this Ode was written for performance at this festival, which included athletic contests, and the victory of Theaius in one of these is mentioned in the Ode amongst his other successes.

Though redeemed by its fine ending, this Ode is not one of the more attractive of Pindar's poems, suffering somewhat, as some readers may consider, from the lengthy and detailed references in the earlier sections. Though its date is uncertain, if it was one of Pindar's earliest compositions, as some editors are inclined to think, one is reminded of the remark said to have been made to him in his younger days by the poetess Corinna, his fellow-student, that 'You should sow with the hand, not with the whole sack'.

str. 1 Of Danaus' city, and his fifty daughters
On their resplendent thrones, sing, O ye Graces.
Of Argos sing, the home of Hera,
Abode worthy a god. This city's name
A thousand deeds of her bold sons
Light with the flame of valour.
Long is the tale of Perseus and the Gorgon
Medusa: many the cities that the hands
Of Epaphus founded
In Egypt: nor does Hypermnestra fail
Of glory, who alone of all, kept hid
Her sword within its sheath.

ant. 1 To Diomede a god's immortal power
The grey-eyed goddess gave, fair-haired Athene;
And once in Thebes the earth, sundered
By lightning bolts of Zeus, engulfed the seer
Son of Oikleus, storm-cloud of war.
Adorned with beauty's tresses,
Her women of old brought Argos fame, and Zeus
Paying court to Alcmene and to Danaë,
Gave proof of this.

str. 1 *Danaus:* a legendary king of Argos.

Perseus: grandson of Acrisius, another legendary king of Argos.

Epaphus: ancestor of Danaus. He was the son of Zeus and Io, a priestess of Hera at Argos. Zeus made love to Io, and in jealousy Hera transformed her into a heifer and drove her from Argos. She came to Egypt, where Zeus restored her to human form, and she became the mother of Epaphus who remained in Egypt.

Hypermnestra: one of the fifty daughters of Danaus. After a quarrel with his brother Aegyptus Danaus migrated to Argos. To resolve the quarrel Aegyptus proposed that his fifty sons should marry the fifty daughters of Danaus, and the sons arrived at Argos. Danaus, who did not agree, treacherously arranged that the marriages should take place all on the same day, but that each daughter should arm herself with a sword and kill her husband on the marriage night. All did so except Hypermnestra who spared her husband Lynceus and helped him to escape.

ant. 1 *Diomede:* one of the Greek heroes of the Trojan War.

Son of Oikleus: Amphiaraus. The story of his death after the defeat of the 'Seven against Thebes' is told in Nemean IX.

Alcmene: the mother by Zeus of Heracles. Her husband Amphitryon was an Argive by birth but migrated to Thebes.

Danaë: Acrisius, her father, having been warned by an oracle that he would meet his death at the hands of a son of Danaë, shut her up in a bronze tower. But Zeus changed himself into a shower of gold in order to visit her, and their son Perseus was born. On returning to Argos after killing the Gorgon Medusa, Perseus accidentally killed his grandfather Acrisius with a discus which he was hurling during the games held in his honour.

And for Lynceus and for Adrastus' father
She set within their hearts the fruit of wisdom
Linked with unswerving right.

ep. 1 She bred that warrior soul
Amphitryon, whose race received the god
Of strength supreme, when in bronze arms he slew
The Teleboai; for great Zeus
Taking his likeness, brought the seed
Of Heracles the dauntless to his chamber;
Who now upon Olympus dwelling,
Has to his wedded wife,
Beside her mother, guardian of marriage, Hebe
Fairest of all the goddesses.

str. 2 My tongue lacks time the long tale to unfold
Of noble deeds sprung from that sacred land
Of Argos, and harsh the penalty
For wearying men's ears. Yet come, strike up
The lyre's melodious chords, and let
Your inward vision scan
The wrestlers' ring. The games and their bronze prize
To the Sacrifice of Oxen call the people,
To honour Hera,
And the contest's decision. Twice victor there,
Oulias' son, Theaius, may forget
The toils he braved so well.

Lynceus: husband of Hypermnestra. According to one version of the myth he returned to Argos and killed Danaus, and became king of Argos.

Adrastus' father: Talaus, another king of Argos. Adrastus organized the expedition of the 'Seven against Thebes'. The tombs of Lynceus and Talaus are said to have been next to one another in the market-place of Argos.

ep. 1 *Amphitryon:* it was during the absence of Amphitryon from Thebes, fighting against a tribe called the Teleboai, that Zeus visited Alcmene.

The god of strength supreme: Heracles.

Hebe: the goddess of Youth and Beauty, whom Heracles married, was the daughter of Zeus and Hera. The worship of Hera was closely associated with the sanctity of marriage and the rights of women.

str. 2 *Bronze prize:* a bronze shield was the prize at these athletic contests at Argos.

Sacrifice of Oxen: the festival in honour of Hera, the Heraea, at which cattle were sacrificed.

ant. 2 Once, too, he overcame the host of Hellas
At Pytho, and by happy fortune won
Crowns at the Isthmus and Nemea;
Three victories for the Muses' plough to till,
Won beside Ocean's gates, and three
Within the sacred field
Where king Adrastus set the games. Ah, Zeus,
His thought may dream dreams though his tongue be silent;
With thee, great Father,
Lies every issue, but well tried in toil,
And with a brave heart in his breast, he begs
No favour undeserved.

ep. 2 Clear are the words I sing
To Zeus, and whosoever braves the struggle
For the supreme prize at the greatest games—
That highest glory held by Pisa,
The games founded by Heracles.
Yet twice, at Athens' feasts, sweet revels rang
As for a prelude, when Theaius
The fruitful olive's oil
In richly figured urns, fresh from the kiln,
Brought home to Hera's lordly people.

str. 3 Comes to you too, by favour of the Graces
And of the sons of Tyndareus, no less,
The glory of the contests won
By that renownéd race, your mother's kin.
Had I the blood of Thrasycles
And Antias within me,

ant. 2 *At Pytho:* at the Pythian Games.
Ocean's gates: the Isthmus of Corinth.
The sacred field: the Nemean Games, founded, according to one version of the legend, by Adrastus.
Ah Zeus, etc.: Pindar means that Theaius is hoping for the highest of all athletic distinctions, a victory at the Olympian Games, whose presiding deity was Zeus.

ep. 2 *Olive's oil, etc.:* a jar of olive oil was the prize at the Athenian Games.

str. 3 *The sons of Tyndareus:* Tyndareus was a legendary king of Sparta, husband of Leda. Castor was their son, a mortal; Pollux was immortal, being the son of Leda by Zeus who visited her disguised as a swan. Sisters of the two brothers were Helen, the cause of the Trojan War, and Clytemnestra, wife of Agamemnon. For the connection of the brothers with Theaius see note to ep. 3 below.
Thrasycles, Antias: ancestors of Theaius' mother.

Proud should I be to hold my head on high
Before the eyes of Argos. Many a crown
Has Proetus' city,
Famed for its heroes, won—four victories
At Corinth in the Isthmus vale, and four
Won from Cleonae's judges.

ant. 3 From Sicyon too, loaded with silver cups
To grace their wine, and from Pellene's city
They homeward came, mantled with robes
Of woven wool. But for the numberless
Prizes of bronze, that lengthy count
No leisure were enough
For me to tell: for Cleitor and Tegea
And the Achaeans' lofty citadels,
Lycaeon too
On the race-course of Zeus, set them on high,
Endowed with strength of arm or speed of foot
To gain their victories.

ep. 3 Since Pamphaes gave welcome
Within his house to Castor and to Pollux,
No wonder if his kin inherit inborn
The talent of the athlete's prowess.
For the two brothers, at the games
Of Sparta's wide-built city, joint patrons
With Hermes and with Heracles,
The presidency share.
And due regard have they for men of justice.
Truly the gods are faithful friends.

Proetus: brother of Acrisius and joint ruler with him of Argos, until a quarrel resulted in Proetus establishing himself as king of nearby Tiryns.

Cleonae: a town near Nemea, which provided the local administration of the Games and the twelve judges.

ant. 3 *Sicyon:* silver wine-cups were the prizes at the local games of Sicyon.

Pellene: woollen cloaks were the prizes at the local games of Pellene, a city of Achaea in the north central Peloponnese.

Cleitor, Tegea, Lycaeon: other cities of the central Peloponnese. At Lycaeon, on a mountainous position in Arcadia, there was an important temple of Zeus.

ep. 3 *Pamphaes:* a distant ancestor of Theaius, who was reputed to have entertained Castor and Pollux, noted in legend for their fine physique and their horsemanship.

str. 4 Now, each alternate day they change their dwelling,
One day beside Zeus, their belovéd father;
Then in the valley of Therapnae
Within the earth's deep folds, these brothers share
Their common destiny; for so,
Rather than be for ever
A god and dwell in heaven, Pollux chose
For both this twofold life, when Castor fell,
Laid low in combat.
For Idas, in hot anger for the cattle
Stolen from him, with his bronze-pointed spear
Dealt him a grievous wound;

ant. 4 When Lynceus, who of all mankind possessed
The sharpest eye, as he kept widespread watch
From Mount Taygetus, had spied him
Sitting within an oak tree's hollow trunk.
And the two sons of Aphareus
Came upon racing feet
Straightway, and swiftly planned and wrought upon him
Their sinful deed. But from the hands of Zeus
Dire chastisement
Fell on them too; for straight came Leda's son
In hot pursuit, till by their father's grave
They stood and turned to face him.

ep. 4 Then seizing from the tomb
A polished stone, ornament to the dead,
They hurled it at Pollux, but could not crush him
Or stay his course; but springing on them
He drove his swift bronze javelin

str. 4 *Therapnae:* a city near Sparta, overlooking the left bank of the river Eurotas.

Idas: brother of Lynceus (ant. 4) who is not the same person as Lynceus the husband of Hypermnestra. Pindar follows the version of the myth which attributes their quarrel with Castor and Pollux to a dispute over the division of a herd of cattle. Another version gives the reason as rivalry for the daughters of Leucippus, whom Castor and Pollux abducted from Idas and Lynceus.

ant. 4 *Mount Taygetus:* the highest mountain in the Peloponnese to the west of Sparta.

Aphareus: father of Idas and Lynceus.

Leda's son: Pollux.

In Lynceus' flank. And Zeus upon Idas
Launched his fire-wrought consuming bolt,
And the two burnt together,
Friendless, upon one pyre. Hard is it for men
To strive against a mightier power.

str. 5 Then swiftly ran the son of Tyndareus
Back to his warrior brother, and he found him
Still living, but within his throat
Death's rattle sounded. Then with hot tears streaming
And bitter groans, he cried aloud:
'O Father, son of Cronos,
What release shall there be from sorrows? Grant
That I too with my brother here may die,
Great king, I beg thee.
For glory is departed from a man
Robbed of his friends, and under stress of toils
Few mortals will abide

ant. 5 Faithful companions to share in the labour.'
He ended, and Zeus came and stood before him
And spoke these words: 'Thou art my son;
But after in thy mother's womb was set
The mortal seed of this thy brother,
Sprung from her hero husband.
But see then, none the less this choice I give thee:
If freed from death and the harsh years of age,
It is thy will
To dwell beside my throne upon Olympus,
Companion to Athene and to Ares,
God of the shadowing spear,

ep. 5 This choice is thine to take.
But if, in thy heart's travail for thy brother,
Thou art in mind to share all things alike
With him, then half thy days shalt thou
Beneath the earth draw breath, and half
Within the golden citadels of heaven.'
He spoke, and Pollux had no thought
But for the single choice;
And Zeus made free the eye, and then the voice
Of Castor of the brazen circlet.

ep. 5 *Of the brazen circlet:* the traditional epithet attached to Castor's name.

NEMEAN XI

For

ARISTAGORAS OF TENEDOS

Prytanis

THIS Ode does not celebrate an athletic victory but was written for the inauguration of Aristagoras as prytanis, that is president or chief magistrate of the governing body of the Aegean island of Tenedos, an annual appointment. This ceremony included a religious festival and a banquet, as we see from the first antistrophe.

The Ode also refers to Aristagoras as having been an athlete who had won many victories at local games. This is perhaps the reason for the inclusion of the poem, in early manuscripts, with the book of Nemean Odes. Its structure is less complex, and it is written in a quieter tone of voice, than most of the Odes in honour of athletic victors. Its date is not known, but it is probably one of Pindar's later compositions.

str. 1 Daughter of Rhea, guardian of parliaments,
Hestia, sister of all-highest Zeus,
And of Hera who shares his throne,
Welcome with goodwill to your sacred hall
Aristagoras, and his fellows with goodwill,
Beneath your glorious sceptre.
For they in honouring you keep watch and ward
On Tenedos island and secure her weal.

ant. 1 First of all other gods they worship you
With many a gift of wine and many a victim,
And the lyre sounds for you, and song.
And at their well-spread tables, never bare,
The rites of Zeus, the hospitable father,
Receive their due. And now
May Aristagoras enjoy, with glory
And an untroubled heart, his twelve-month rule.

str. 1 *Hestia:* the guardian goddess of the Hearth or Homestead.

ep. 1 Of such a man I happy deem
Firstly Agesilas his father,
Then his own proud-built body, and heritage
Of dauntless courage. But let him
Who enjoys wealth, and beauty beyond others,
And in the athlete's field has shown his strength,
Remember that this body's fine array
Is mortal, and that at the last
The earth will be his vesture.

str. 2 But now his citizens with words of honour
Must praise him, and with song sweeter than honey
Make his name rich. For in the contests
Of neighbouring cities, Aristagoras
And his renownéd clan have won the crown
At sixteen victories;
A glorious toll, gained in the Wrestlers' ring
And the Pankration's great-hearted struggle.

ant. 2 Too fearful for his youthful years, his parents
Forbade him try his strength on Pytho's field,
Or in Olympia's contest. Yet
By the god of True Speech, I am of mind
That by Castalia and the tree-clad hill
Of Cronos, had he ventured,
His homeward way had been more richly honoured
Than of all those who strove to meet his challenge,

ep. 2 Had he but kept the fourth-year feast
Of Heracles, its revel and song,
And with a gleaming wreath bound up his hair.
But in this life one shall we find
Whom vain and empty-headed boasts will rob
Of his success; another, his own strength
Too much mistrusting, sees his hand held back
From the rewards which are his due,
By a too fearful heart.

ant. 2 *Pytho's field:* the Pythian Games at Delphi.
Castalia: the well-known fountain at Delphi.
Hill of Cronos: Olympia.

ep. 2 *Feast of Heracles:* the Olympian Games, founded by Heracles, held every four years.
Gleaming wreath: the victor's wreath of olive.

str. 3 Yet was it easy to forecast in him
Peisander's blood from ancient Sparta, who
Came with Orestes from Amyclae,
And hither led the Aeolian bronze-clad host;
And from his mother's stock from Melanippus,
Descends the ancient line
That once was blended by Ismenus' stream.
For valour's heritage from years of old

ant. 3 Now to this generation, now to that
Alternately gives to the race its vigour.
As the dark furrow may not yield
Its fruit unceasingly, nor will the tree
Through all the passing years give of its flower
The same sweet-scented wealth,
But waits the changing time, so too, for men,
Our mortal destiny shares the same law.

ep. 3 But to mankind is given of Zeus
No sign of clear import; and yet
Do we on our proud-hearted schemes embark,
And many a deed we meditate,
Our limbs bound fast to hopes untamed, foreknowing
Never what may betide. But we must seek
Only for modest gain: from those desires
Which cannot be attained, there springs
The sharpest of all madness.

str. 3 *Peisander:* a legendary figure from whom Aristagoras traced his descent.

Orestes—Amyclae: one version of the legend of Orestes, son of Agamemnon, places their home at Amyclae, a city south of Sparta.

Led the Aeolian host: this refers to the colonization of Tenedos at an early date by Aeolians from the mainland. Pindar's allusion differs slightly from the more usual tradition that the colonization was led by Penthilos, the son of Orestes.

Melanippus: an ancient Theban hero.

Ismenus' stream: the river near Thebes.

ISTHMIAN I

For

HERODOTUS OF THEBES

Winner of the Chariot-Race

THIS Ode has an unusual opening which provides some indication in regard to its possible date, which is not known with certainty. Pindar had been commissioned by the inhabitants of Carthaia, a city of the Aegean island of Keos, to write for them a Paean in honour of Delian Apollo. In the opening section of the present Ode Pindar addresses a request to the island of Delos (in effect to Apollo or to the citizens of Carthaia) to be forgiven if in virtue of his loyalty to Thebes he gives precedence to the composition of this Ode in honour of his Theban compatriot Herodotus. He promises at the same time not to neglect the task he owes to the islanders of Keos. The Paean, of which a good deal has come down to us, is Paean No. IV. Carthaia was the native city of the well-known poet Simonides, an older man than Pindar, who was his great rival. It is extremely unlikely that the citizens of Carthaia would have asked Pindar to write the Paean for them until after the death of Simonides, which occurred in 468 B.C. A later date for the victory of Herodotus, and this Ode, can thus be regarded as virtually certain.

Ten years afterwards in 458 B.C. Thebes and Sparta were on the point of entering into the alliance which found them in 457 fighting side by side against the Athenian army at the battle of Tanagra. It seems very probable that the lengthy passage extending from epode 1 to epode 2 in which Pindar links together the praise of Castor and Iolaus, who were traditional heroes respectively of Sparta and Thebes, is an echo of the political situation of 458. If so, that year would be the date of the victory of Herodotus and of this Ode. The Isthmian Games were held in April or May, and if the Ode was composed in the early summer of that year, it gives additional point to the hopes expressed by Pindar in epode 4 that Herodotus may be successful in the Pythian Games, which were due to be held in August of the same year. The hopes expressed by Pindar extend also to the possibility of an Olympian victory—the next Olympian Games were due in 456. The entry of Herodotus for the Isthmian chariot-race may well have been in preparation for the sterner contests at Delphi and Olympia.

There is no myth in this Ode. Its place is taken by the eulogies mentioned above, of Castor and Iolaus. At the close of that passage Pindar turns in epode 2 to a passage recalling the fortunes of Asopodorus, the father of Herodotus. This Asopodorus is almost certainly the leading Theban of whom the historian Herodotus records that during the Persian invasion, when Thebes was found on the side of the Persians, Asopodorus was in command of the Theban cavalry at the battle of Plataea in 479. Though the Persian army was decisively defeated by the Greek allies, the squadrons under Asopodorus made a successful charge and killed six hundred of the troops provided by Megara and Phlious. He appears to have escaped the punishment meted out to Theban leaders by Pausanias, the commander of the Greek forces, and fled into exile, subsequently finding a home, as stated in this ode, at his family seat at Orchomenus.

In the third antistrophe and epode Pindar discourses, as often elsewhere, on the hard work and expense needed as a preliminary to competition in the Games, and on the distinction accorded to the winner. The fourth triad, after the conventional tribute to the tutelary deity of the Games, Poseidon, records the various places on whose race-courses Herodotus had won other successes. His skill as a charioteer appears to have been considerable. The family of Asopodorus and Herodotus was wealthy and held a leading place in Thebes. The concluding lines of the Ode contain a typically Pindaric warning against failure to make generous and friendly use of such a position.

str. 1 City beloved, my mother,
Thebes of the golden shield, my debt to you
Shall I set higher than all other need
That would my leisure steal. O rocky Delos,
Be not then wroth with me, who to your service
Have given my heart in pledge.
Is there a loyalty more dear
Than good men treasure for their parents' love?
Grant me my plea, isle of Apollo, and I
To honour Phoebus of the flowing hair,

str. 1 *O rocky Delos:* the Aegean island of Delos was the birthplace of Apollo and closely connected with religious rites in his honour. See foreword on this opening passage.

ant. 1 Shall with heaven's help not fail
To seal with song my dues to beauty's grace,
For both these vows, stirring the dancer's footstep
Both 'midst the sailor folk of sea-girt Keos,
And on the ridge that bars the ocean's tide,
The Isthmus' rising plain.
For to the men of Cadmus' line
Six crowns she gave of victory at her contests,
Triumphant glory for their fathers' city,
Where once Alcmene bore that dauntless son,

ep. 1 To whom long since the fierce hounds of Geryon
Yielded in trembling terror.
But I now for Herodotus would fashion,
And for his four-horsed chariot, this meed
Of praise, and that brave talent,
Which with no other hand beside him plied
His horses' reins, would marry to the strain
Of Castor or of Iolaus;
For they of all heroes of Thebes and Sparta
Were born the greatest in their mastery
Of the chariot-driver's skill.

str. 2 And in un-numbered contests
They strove with rival athletes in the Games,
And decked their home with many a prize, with tripods
And bowls and drinking-cups of gold. Rich was
Their taste of glory from their victors' crowns,

ant. 1 *Sea-girt Keos:* see foreword.

Men of Cadmus' line: the Thebans. Cadmus was the mythical founder and first king of Thebes.

She gave: i.e. the Isthmus. Wishing to emphasize the close relation between Thebes and the Isthmus, Pindar recalls that six victories had been won by Thebans at the Isthmian Games.

That dauntless son: Heracles, son of Zeus and Alcmene, the wife of Amphitryon king of Thebes. As elsewhere (cf. Nem. III. str. 2) when paying compliments to Thebes, Pindar makes mention of Heracles, the city's greatest mythical hero.

ep. 1 *The fierce hounds of Geryon:* one of the twelve Labours of Heracles was to bring back to Greece from Spain the cattle of the monster Geryon, which were guarded by the two-headed dog Orthrus.

Of Castor or of Iolaus: Castor was the son of Tyndareus king of Sparta, and Leda his wife. He and his half-brother Pollux, son of Zeus and Leda, were noted athletes in mythical story, particularly as horsemen, charioteers, and boxers. Iolaus, a Theban, was the nephew and charioteer of Heracles. See foreword on the eulogy accorded to them jointly in this passage.

And clearly can be seen
The light of their brave excellence,
Whether in the one-stade course for stripped runners,
Or in the race for full-armed fighting men,
That echoed with the thunder of their shields;

ant. 2 Or when with strong young hands
They launched the pointed javelin, or hurled
The discus with its heavy weight of stone.
For the Pentathlon was not then devised,
But each of the five contests then was given
Its own appointed right.
From these full many a time these heroes,
With many a garland braided on their hair,
Were hailed as victors near the springs of Dirke
And in the land beside Eurotas' stream,

ep. 2 That son of Iphicles born of the race
That sprang from the Sown Men,
And the son of Tyndareus, who 'midst the Achaeans
Dwelt in Therapnae's height above the plain.
To those heroes, farewell.

ant. 2 *The Pentathlon:* a contest consisting of five events. (See Introduction.)

The springs of Dirke: i.e. at Thebes. The Dirke was a river close to Thebes.

Eurotas' stream: the river of the Peloponnese which flows close to Sparta.

ep. 2 *That son of Iphicles:* Iolaus. Iphicles was the son of Alcmene and Amphitryon, and half-brother of Heracles.

The Sown Men: when Cadmus was about to found the city of Thebes he killed a serpent which had destroyed some of his followers. The goddess Athene ordered him to sow the serpent's teeth in the soil, and from these sprang up the 'Sparti', or Sown Men, fully armed. Through fighting with one another their number was reduced to five men. These offered their services to Cadmus and became ancestors of the Thebans.

The son of Tyndareus: Castor.

The Achaeans: this name is used by Homer as a general name for all Greeks, but particularly for the Peloponnesian Greeks of Sparta and Argos. Pindar uses it here to mean the Spartans.

Therapnae: a city lying on a high plateau above the left bank of the Eurotas, overlooking the lower ground on which Sparta is situated. There was a temple at Therapnae of the Dioscuri (sons of Zeus), the name commonly applied to Castor and Pollux.

Now as I cast the mantle of my song
Upon Poseidon and the sacred Isthmus
  And on the lake shores of Onchestus,
I shall amidst my victor's honours praise
The glorious fortune of Asopodorus
    His father, and the fields

str. 3 Of his ancestral homestead
Near to Orchomenus, where he found harbour,
When, as if shipwrecked in the unmeasured deep,
He struggled to withstand the bitter chill
Of dire misfortune's blows. Now once again
    The fate that gave his race
  Their heritage of happiness
From days of old, grants him a sunlit sky.
But he whose heart has known of pain and labour,
Has learnt to see with the clear eyes of wisdom.

ant. 3 If ever a man strives
With all his soul's endeavour, sparing himself
Neither expense nor labour to attain
True excellence, then must we give to those
Who have achieved the goal, a proud tribute
    Of lordly praise, and shun
  All thoughts of envious jealousy.
To a poet's mind the gift is slight, to speak
A kind word for unnumbered toils, and build
For all to share a monument of beauty.

ep. 3 Dues for work done are prized by all, one this
    One that, to each his choice,
Whether he be shepherd, ploughman, or fowler,
Or from the deep-sea's harvest fills his table;
    Yet the chief aim of each,
To ward his belly from pernicious hunger.
But he who wins the rich delight of fame
  In the Games or in the ranks of war,
Receives that welcome, most exalted prize,
The widespread praise of citizens and strangers
    Flowering upon their tongue.

Onchestus: a city by Lake Copais, on the northern boundary of Boeotia not far from Orchomenus, which appears from the following strophe to have been the ancestral home of Asopodorus the father of Herodotus. Onchestus was traditionally regarded as one of the dwelling-places of Poseidon.

str. 3 *As if shipwrecked, etc.:* see foreword.

str. 4 Now must we raise our voices,
Making requital of his favours given,
To praise the son of Cronos, the earth-shaker,
Our neighbour and the chariots' good protector,
And guardian of the flying horses' course.
And must we too proclaim
Your sons, Amphitryon, and praise
The vale of Minyas, and Demeter's precinct
Of glorious name Eleusis, and Euboea,
Each city where the curved race-course is set.

ant. 4 You too, Protesilas,
I would invoke, and praise your holy shrine
In Phylake, built by Achaean men.
Yet to tell all the glories that were given
By Hermes, lord of contests, to your steeds,
For this, Herodotus,
The measured moments of my song
Have all too brief a span. And yet indeed
Often enough deeds that no lips have praised
Earn for reward a larger share of joy.

str. 4 *The earth-shaker:* Poseidon, god of the sea and of subterranean movements. The Isthmian Games were held in his honour. He was traditionally associated with horses, and horse and chariot racing. The term '*our neighbour*' is probably used because of the tradition which placed one of his homes at Onchestus, not far from Thebes.

Your sons, Amphitryon: this refers to Heracles the stepson, and Iolaus the grandson of Amphitryon. The Heracleia and the Iolaia were two important Theban festivals. Pindar is recording here, and by the names of the various cities given in the lines which follow, the places at which Herodotus had won chariot-racing victories.

The vale of Minyas: Orchomenus. The Minyans, with Minyas their mythical king, were early inhabitants of Orchomenus and the surrounding area.

Eleusis: the well-known city not far to the west of Athens, famous for the Eleusinian Mysteries connected with the worship of Demeter.

Euboea: at which particular city or cities of Euboea Herodotus won a chariot-race is not known.

ant. 4 *Protesilas—Phylake:* Protesilas is recorded in Homer (*Iliad* ii. 702) as the first Greek who leapt ashore at Troy from the ships which carried the Greek army to the Trojan War. He came from the Thessalian city of Phylake, where a temple in his name appears to have been built by the Greeks.

Hermes: the messenger of the gods, regarded as the tutelary deity of all skilled accomplishments, including those of athletes.

ep. 4 May the sweet-voiced Pierides raise high
Your name on wings of glory;
And once again your hand be strung with garlands
From Pytho's vale, and with those wreaths most choice
Of Alpheus and the field
Of great Olympia, to bring new honour
To seven-gated Thebes. Now should a man
Store hidden wealth within his halls,
And upon others fall with mocking laughter,
Little thinks he his soul shall fare to Hades
With not a shred of glory.

ep. 4 *The Pierides:* another name for the Muses.
Alpheus: the river that flows beside Olympia.

ISTHMIAN II

For

XENOCRATES OF ACRAGAS

Winner of the Chariot-Race

XENOCRATES was the brother of Theron, ruler of Acragas in Sicily, and the Isthmian victory here celebrated is mentioned in Pindar's second Olympian Ode, written for Theron's victory at Olympia in the year 476 B.C. It must therefore have been won before that date, very possibly in 478, though the present Ode in its honour was not written until some years afterwards. An earlier victory had been won by Xenocrates in the chariot-race at the Pythian Games of 490 B.C. We know that the 'official' epinician odes both for the Pythian and for this subsequent Isthmian victory were commissioned from the poet Simonides, though these two poems have not survived. Pindar nevertheless wrote his sixth Pythian Ode for the first victory of 490 B.C. and the present Ode for the later Isthmian. Both Odes are in fact addressed to Thrasybulus, Xenocrates' son, who is believed to have been the charioteer in the Pythian race of 490 when Pindar, then aged twenty-eight, was present at the Games and formed a warm friendship with the young man. The informal and friendly tone of these Odes suggests that they were written mainly as a personal tribute by Pindar to Thrasybulus and his father Xenocrates. It is clear from the third triad of the present Ode, where Pindar uses the past tense in speaking of Xenocrates, that the Ode was written after his death. The date of this is not certain, but the final epode reflects the disturbed times in Acragas which followed upon the death of Theron in 472 B.C., when his son Thrasydaeus proved incompetent and unpopular, quarrelled with Hieron of Syracuse and was forced into exile. A more democratic type of government was installed in Acragas, and these events must undoubtedly have had an effect on the position in Acragas of Thrasybulus, as a nephew of Theron. We have no exact knowledge of what transpired, but the words of epode 3 show that Pindar was aware of the position, and that these events were of quite recent occurrence. The date of this Ode can thus be put at 472 B.C. or shortly afterwards, and the death of Xenocrates probably not long before.

In the opening section of this Ode Pindar comments on the

practice, by his time well established, for poets to receive payment for their work, in contrast with earlier times when poems, he says, were launched 'lightly' and without thought of gain. It is clear from the third line of epode 1, which ends the passage, that Pindar intended it to have a hidden meaning which would be clear to the good sense of Thrasybulus. Pindar's purpose has been a puzzle to editors both ancient and modern. Some have adopted the rather cynical view that Pindar is referring to, or complaining about, the salary paid, or perhaps still waiting payment, for his poems in honour of Xenocrates. Another view, no doubt more agreeable, is that for Pindar to devote this quite lengthy opening section of an Ode, with the emphasis which this position gives, to a passage having this underlying intention, is out of keeping with the good manners which his Odes show to those to whom he gave his services; and out of step too with the fact of his warm friendship with Thrasybulus, which had lasted by the time this Ode was written for eighteen years. The wording of the opening strophe can be thought to reflect the affectionate ties which developed between Pindar and Thrasybulus after their first meeting in 490 B.C., and might seem inappropriate as an introduction to a claim for money. The passage could be interpreted as a 'dig' at Simonides and the fees he no doubt demanded for the two Odes, mentioned above, which he wrote for Xenocrates. It was common knowledge in ancient times that Simonides had a keen eye for his own monetary interest. If so it could be that Pindar is making the point that in contrast with Simonides he has made a free gift of Pythian VI and the present Ode as a mark of his friendship with Thrasybulus and Xenocrates. A compromise view might be, and is in keeping with the wording of the Ode, that Pindar made no charge for Pythian VI, but now, an older man, less able to disregard business considerations, he is making in a friendly and half apologetic tone a request for payment for the present Ode; or perhaps, having been offered payment for the present Ode, he is saying politely that on this occasion he won't refuse it. What the true meaning of the passage is must remain unsettled.

After this opening section the Ode pays a warm tribute to the qualities of Xenocrates, refers to his Pythian victory celebrated in Pythian VI, and to a victory by him at the Athenian games. His charioteer on that occasion was Nicomachus, who was also a winning charioteer, as the Ode records, at Olympia, at some date not shown.

str. 1 In days gone by poets who mounted, Thrasybulus,
The chariot of the golden-crested Muses,
Saluting them with the proud-sounding lyre,
Would lightly launch their songs sweeter than honey
In praise of youth, wherever beauty's form,
Robbing rich summer of her fairest wealth,
Made suit to dreams of high-throned Aphrodite.

ant. 1 For then the Muse had not yet bowed to love of gain,
Or made herself a hireling journeyman;
Nor in the market clad in masks of silver
Did honey-tongued Terpsichore barter
Her gentle-voiced and sweetly-sung refrains.
But now she bids us pander to that word
The Argive spoke, too sadly near to truth:

ep. 1 'Money, money makes man' said he
By goods and friends alike deserted. No,
For you, friend, have a wise heart. Not unknown
This Isthmian chariot victory that I sing,
Which to Xenocrates Poseidon granted,
And sent to him to bind upon his brow
The crown of Dorian parsley,

str. 2 Honouring thus a master of the chariot's grace,
The glory of the Acragantine people.
And in Krisa the god of endless power
Apollo saw him, and bestowed there too
The light of fame upon him. And he won
The glorious favours of the Erechtheid people
In radiant Athens, where no fault could mar

ant. 1 *Terpsichore:* one of the nine Muses.
The Argive: a man called Aristodemus, whose saying, here quoted, became proverbial.

ep. 1 *Poseidon:* the god in whose honour the Isthmian Games were held.
Dorian parsley: the victor's prize awarded at the Isthmian Games was a wreath of wild parsley. It is not certain why Pindar refers to it here as Dorian parsley.

str. 2 *Krisa:* i.e. the Pythian Games. See note to Pyth. III. str. 4.
The Erechtheid people: the Athenians. Erechtheus was an early king of Athens.

ant. 2 The hand that steered the car and primed the horses' speed,
Bearing on every rein at the just moment—
Nicomachus, whom the heralds of the season
From Elis, the truce-bearers of great Zeus
Knew well, remembering his friendly service.
And with glad words of welcome they received him,
When golden Victory nursed him on her bosom

ep. 2 In their own land, the land they name
The precinct of Olympian Zeus. Of honours
That cannot die Aenesidamus' sons
Were there made free. For indeed, Thrasybulus,
No stranger is the palace of your sires
To the lovely refrains of victory's revel
Or to sweet songs of triumph.

str. 3 For no cliff-track or steep road need he climb, who brings
The honours of the maids of Helicon
To dwell with famous men. Now let me launch
A far-thrown javelin, to match its flight
With the rich charm beyond all other men
That graced the temper of Xenocrates.
The greetings of his citizens acclaimed him

ant. 3 A man revered; the racing steeds bred in his stable
Honour his care for Panhellenic rite;
And to all banquets of the gods he gave
A zealous welcome; for his guests no breath
Of storm could force his hospitable sail
To slacken, but his voyage plied to Phasis
In summer, and in winter to the Nile.

ant. 2 *Nicomachus:* the charioteer in Xenocrates' victory at the Athenian games. *The heralds of the season:* it was the practice, as noted in the Introduction, for the territory of Elis in which Olympia lies, to send out heralds to all states of Greece before the Olympian Games, every four years, announcing a sacred truce.

His friendly service: we do not know what service Nicomachus rendered to the heralds. Possibly they met him in Athens before he came to Olympia to drive the winning chariot there.

ep. 2 *Aenesidamus' sons:* Theron and Xenocrates. Theron won the chariot-race at Olympia in 476 B.C., celebrated in Pindar's Olympian Odes II and III.

str. 3 *The maids of Helicon:* the Muses. Mount Helicon in south-east Boeotia not far from Mount Parnassus was known as the chief dwelling-place of the Muses.

ant. 3 *Phasis . . . the Nile:* the district of Phasis at the eastern end of the Black Sea was considered the farthest point to which Greek sailors could take their ships in summer, and the Egyptian ports of the Nile the farthest possible in winter. The phrase became a commonplace to denote the utmost possible achievement in any undertaking.

ep. 3 Then, though the hopes of jealous envy
Spread mischief through the minds of men, let not
Your tongue cease to proclaim your father's honour,
Or these songs in his praise; I made them not
To lie in idle silence. Take, then, and render
This message, Nicasippus, to my friend
Whose love I hold in honour.

ep. 3 See foreword on this passage.
Nicasippus: nothing is known of Nicasippus except that he was to be the messenger entrusted with the delivery of this Ode to Thrasybulus.

ISTHMIAN III AND IV

For

MELISSUS OF THEBES

Winner of the Chariot-Race and the Pankration

IT HAS always been doubtful—a doubt which perhaps cannot be certainly resolved—whether the third and fourth Isthmian Odes are separate poems, or two parts of the same Ode. Of the two ancient manuscripts which survive, one shows them separately, the other as one poem. Both are in honour of the same citizen of Thebes, Melissus, and both are written in the same metre. The latter fact is a strong argument for their being regarded as one poem, since this is the only case where an Ode of Pindar has not its own separate metre, distinct from that of any other Ode. On the other hand there is internal evidence in the poems which points, though not conclusively, to their having been written for separate occasions. Ode IV can without doubt be regarded as a poem, sufficient in itself, to celebrate the Isthmian victory of Melissus in the pankration. There can also be no doubt that Ode III was composed later than Ode IV, since it refers to the Isthmian victory celebrated in the latter, and Ode IV contains no mention of the Nemean chariot victory also recorded in Ode III. That Ode, short though it is, could be taken as a poem in honour of the Nemean victory, to which it refers with more emphasis than to the Isthmian.

A suggested solution to the question is that there was some delay between this victory of Melissus at the Isthmus and the composition, or performance, of Ode IV; and that meanwhile Melissus won his chariot victory at the Nemean Games, and for this Pindar wrote a short poem (Isthmian III) in the same metre as the other and to be prefixed to it. Thus both poems could be sung to the same music by the same chorus, no doubt at less expense.

Melissus belonged to the clan of the Cleonymides, a wealthy and distinguished Theban family. Both Odes refer to the family's distinction in former years, but indicate that since then they had suffered some eclipse of their reputation. Ode III suggests this briefly in its concluding lines, Ode IV illustrates it at greater length, recalling in epode 1 that the family had in one day lost four of its members in battle but had now recovered from this unhappy blow, and implies in strophe 2 that the present victory of Melissus has restored to them the lustre they enjoyed in former days. The second antistrophe and epode, while praising past successes of the clan at various games rather suggests that sympathy is due to them for not having till now, in spite of their efforts and expenditure, succeeded at any of the Panhellenic Games. The theme that merit can be defeated by the cleverness of the less deserving is illustrated by the briefly told myth of Ajax, robbed by the skilful oratory of Odysseus of the prize for valour, the armour of Achilles, which he had hoped would be his own. This story is also told in Nemean Ode VII and Ode VIII.

The third triad couples one of Pindar's oft-heard tributes to the immortal power of poetry with praises of Melissus, in which his short stature is emphasized. This gives a connecting link with the lines that follow on the conquest of the giant Antaeus by Heracles, who is represented in some mythological versions, and here, as a man of small height. Praise of Heracles continues in strophe 4 and it is clear from antistrophe 4 that the annual Theban festival, the Heracleia, in honour of that hero, is to be the occasion for the performance of this Ode. Epode 4 makes reference to victories won in previous years by Melissus at the games which were part of that festival, including one victory gained by him as a boy; and praise of his trainer on that occasion, Orseas, is included in the final lines.

The date of the victories celebrated in these Odes is not certainly known, but must have been subsequent to the battle mentioned in Ode IV, in which the members of the clan of Melissus lost their lives. This was probably the battle of Plataea, 479 B.C., in which the Theban army, fighting on the side of the Persians, suffered severe losses. If so the victory celebrated in Ode IV may have been won at the Isthmian Games of April/May 478 or perhaps 476, and the Nemean victory of Ode III at the next following Nemean Games of July 477 or 475. In support of these dates it has been suggested that the way Pindar has framed the references in epode 1 and strophe 2 of Ode IV implies that the victories of Melissus came as an early compensation to his family after the losses they had suffered. It has also been thought that the reference in antistrophe 4 to the 'new-built ring of altars' near the Electran gates of Thebes indicates that they had probably been destroyed during the siege of Thebes by the Greek forces under Pausanias, which followed immediately after the battle of Plataea, and they were no doubt rebuilt without delay for the annual festival of the Heracleia. The exact interpretation of this phrase is however disputed, and none of the evidence is certain enough to preclude the possibility of later dates than those suggested above for the two victories and the composition of these Odes.

ISTHMIAN III

For

MELISSUS OF THEBES

Winner of the Chariot-Race

---

str. 1 If any man has won good fortune's prize
Or in the famous Games or in the achievement
Of a rich store of wealth, yet holds his spirit
Free from insatiate pride,
He well deserves that in his ears should ring
The praises of his townsmen. For from thee,
Great Zeus, only may mortal souls be given
Worth of true excellence; and happy fortune
More full and lasting lives with men
Of reverent mind, but for rebellious hearts
No such fair flower dwells with them all their days.

ant. 1 Now to pay grace to glorious deeds our song
Must praise a valiant man, and in triumphant
Revel raise him on high with generous honours.
Not for one contest only
But for two triumphs may Melissus now
Refresh his heart with the sweet taste of joy;
For in the lowland valleys of the Isthmus
He won the victor's garlands, and within
The hollow glen that bears the name
Of the deep-chested lion, his chariot,
Victorious on the racecourse, gave to Thebes

ep. 1 The glory of the herald's proclamation.
To the prowess of his kin he brings no shame;
You know indeed
The old-time glory of Cleonymus
Won on the chariot's course;

ant. 1 *Two triumphs:* see foreword.
The name of the deep-chested lion: i.e. the Nemean Games. One of the Twelve Labours of Heracles was the destruction of the Nemean Lion.

ep. 1 *The herald's proclamation:* the announcement by the herald of the name of each victor in the Panhellenic Games always included the name of his native city.
Cleonymus: an ancestor of Melissus.

And of his mother's line
The sons of Labdacus begrudged no wealth
Or labour spent amidst the four-horsed teams.
But through the rolling years
The age of man sees many a change;
Only the children of the gods
Are free from wounding blows.

ISTHMIAN IV

For

MELISSUS OF THEBES

Winner of the Pankration

str. 1 A thousand ways, thanks to the gods' goodwill
Open on every side widespread before me.
For you Melissus, at the Isthmian Games
Have for my craft made clear
An easy pathway for my song to render
The glorious valour of your kinsmen's race—
That flowering spirit which with the aid of heaven
Ever endows the sons of Cleonymus
Throughout their mortal span. And yet
Now this way, that way lights on all mankind
The changing gale that drives them on their course.

ant. 1 They then at Thebes are spoken of with honour
From years of old, known as ambassadors
Of neighbouring peoples, men who had no share
In loud-voiced insolence.

Labdacus: an early mythical king of Thebes, grandfather of Oedipus.

ant. 1 *Ambassadors:* it was the custom of the city-states of Greece to appoint a member of another city-state to act as their representative to look after their interests in that city. His title was that of 'proxenos', here translated, not quite accurately though his functions were approximately the same, as 'ambassador'.

And of all testimonies that the air
May carry to man's ears, of the unmatched fame
Of those who live or those who are no more,
Of this they harvest all the fairest fruit.
  Their proud valour is of a temper
To reach from their own homestead to the pillars
Of Heracles, that bound the ends of earth.

ep. 1 Beyond that mark a further excellence
Let no man strive to attain. They became too
      Breeders of horse,
And with Ares, the god of arms, found favour.
    And yet in one brief day
    The harsh snow-storm of war
Bereft their happy hearth of four brave men.
But now for them the dark of wintry months
    Is fled away, as though
  The varied earth's embroidery
  Put forth again her purple hues
    And blossoms rosy-red,

str. 2 As was ordained of heaven. And he who dwells—
The god who shakes the earth—beside Onchestus,
And by the bridge that spans the ocean's wave
    Before the walls of Corinth,
Granting now to their race this song most fair,
Brings from her bed again the praise they won
For deeds of glory in the days of old.
For she lay fallen in the arms of sleep.
  Now, wakening once more, her beauty
Shines forth in gleaming splendour like the star
Of Dawn, beyond all other lights of heaven.

ant. 2 In the lands of Athens too their fame was known,
Proclaimed as victors in the chariot's course;
And in Adrastus' games at Sicyon's city,

The pillars of Heracles: the straits of Gibraltar. The phrase here used was a proverbial one indicating the summit of possible achievement.

str. 2 *The god who shakes the earth:* Poseidon, god of the sea and of subterranean powers, the patron god of the Isthmian Games.

Onchestus: a city beside lake Copais in the north of Boeotia, and one of the reputed homes of Poseidon.

ant. 2 *Adrastus' games:* Adrastus, a mythical king of Argos, while in exile from his native city, was credited with the foundation of games at Sicyon on the Gulf of Corinth, and also of the Panhellenic Games at Nemea, though both events in fact date from later historical times.

Like garlands from the bards
Of those far days crowned them with leaves of glory;
Nor from the peoples' feasts, the Panagyries,
Did they withhold their chariots' curving grace;
And in contest with all the hosts of Hellas,
On horse and chariot they rejoiced
To spend their wealth. Who does not put to proof
His worth, remains forgotten and unsung.

ep. 2 Yet even for those who strive, fortune maybe
Conceals her light, ere yet their steps attain
The furthest goal;
For her gifts render both of good and ill.
And often does the craft
Of lesser souls outstrip
And bring to naught the strength of better men.
Full well you know how in the far-spent night
The blood-stained might of Ajax
Pierced through with his own sword, brought shame
To the sons of Hellas, all who journeyed
Unto the land of Troy.

str. 3 Yet has great Homer set his name in honour
Through all mankind, and on his poet's staff
Has raised aloft his every deed of valour,
In words inspired of heaven
To charm the soul of all posterity.
For this it is gives to the path of song
Immortal life, if on the poet's tongue
Fair praise is fairly set. And far and wide
Over the fruitful earth and o'er
The spreading sea, the fame of noble deeds
Sends forth a ray whose light shall live for ever.

Panagyries: local festivals under this name were widespread in all parts of Greece and are still found today in very many Greek towns and villages.

ep. 2 *Ajax:* the famous Greek warrior in the Trojan War. On the death of Achilles it was decided that his armour should be given to the man who had rendered the best services to the Greeks in battle. The eloquence of Odysseus persuaded the Greek assembly to award this prize to himself, rather than to Ajax who had confidently expected it. In bitter chagrin at this blow to his honour, Ajax killed himself with his own sword.

ant. 3 May it be mine to win the Muses' favour,
When for Melissus too that light is kindled
By this my burning torch of song—a worthy
Garland to crown the brow
Of a pankratiast victor, one who springs
From Telesiades' stock. For in his heart
Is bred the daring of loud-roaring lions
In the brunt of battle, in craft a very fox,
Who lies prone and with spreading feet
Stays off the eagle's swoop. Needs must a man
Devise all means to break the foeman's power.

ep. 3 For it was not his fortune to inherit
The stature of Orion. Slight his frame
To look upon,
But with his wrestling strength to take a throw,
Heavy indeed the fall.
And long since, as we know,
To the house of Antaeus there came a hero
From Thebes of Cadmus race, to Libya's corn-lands,
Small in his body's height
But of a soul indomitable,
Bringing a wrestler's grip to stay him
Who crowned with skulls of strangers

str. 4 Poseidon's holy shrine. That hero it was,
Alcmene's mighty son, who came at last
To high Olympus; he who, searching out
All the far lands of earth
And rock-walled stretches of the foaming seas,
Tempered the rough straits for the seamen's sails.

ant. 3 *In craft a very fox, etc.:* these lines apparently refer to a trick of wrestling used in the pankration. 'Ground wrestling', together with hitting and kicking, was allowed in the pankration, though in the wrestling event proper only 'upright wrestling' was permitted.

ep. 3 *Antaeus:* a giant of Libya, who killed all strangers and placed their skulls on the roof of a temple of Poseidon. He derived his strength from contact with the ground. Heracles by lifting him from the ground in a wrestler's hold thus overcame him.

str. 4 *To high Olympus:* after his death Heracles was given immortality and a home with the gods. Amongst his many exploits he was credited with the exploration of all the seas and lands of the then known world.

Now at the side of Zeus the Aegis-bearer
He dwells, enjoying happiness most fair,
  Of the immortal gods a friend
Held in high honour, lord of golden halls,
Husband of Hebe, son-in-law to Hera.

ant. 4 For him then, we his fellow citizens
Above Electra's gates make ready now
His feast, and on the new-built ring of altars
  Burn sacrifice, to honour
Those eight dead warriors of brazen mail—
The sons whom Megara, Creon's daughter, bore him.
And to their glory rises high the flame
Beneath the setting sun's beshrouded rays,
  Mounting aloft an endless stream
Through the long hours of night, of singeing smoke
In billowing clouds to chafe the vault of heaven.

ep. 4 And on the second morning comes the day
Appointed for the yearly games, where strength
    Strips for the test.
There with the myrtle garlands gleaming white
  Upon his brow, my hero
  Showed himself twice a victor,
And as a boy long since a third he won,
Reliant on the wisdom of the skilled
    Pilot who steered his helm.
  With Orseas then my song of triumph
  Shall link his name, and shed upon them
    Its joyful shower of glory.

The Aegis-bearer: a title applied here to Zeus, and often elsewhere to Athene.

Hebe: the goddess of youth and beauty.

ant. 4 *Electra's gates:* one of the 'seven gates' of Thebes, before which the religious rites of the festival of the Heracleia appear to have been celebrated.

The new-built ring of altars: see foreword.

Eight dead warriors: Pindar tactfully refrains from mentioning that Heracles himself killed these eight children of his as the result of being temporarily driven mad by Hera. Some versions of the myth relate that it was in atonement for this sin that Heracles was required to carry out the Twelve Labours imposed on him by Eurystheus.

ep. 4 *Orseas:* as in several other Odes, praise of a boy-victor's success is accompanied by a tribute to his trainer.

ISTHMIAN V

For

PHYLAKIDAS OF AEGINA

Winner of the Pankration

PHYLAKIDAS was the younger brother of Pytheas, whose earlier victory as an adolescent at the Nemean Games is celebrated in Nemean V. Their father was Lampon, a descendant of Cleonicus, and they appear to have belonged to one of the notable families of Aegina with whom Pindar had close ties. The present Ode makes clear in epode 3 that Pytheas had been the adviser, very probably the trainer, of Phylakidas for this event, and refers in epode 1 to the earlier Isthmian victory of Phylakidas celebrated in Isthmian VI; also to a Nemean victory won by him, and to the above-mentioned Nemean victory of Pytheas.

The reference in the third triad of the present Ode to the battle of Salamis, in which the Aeginetan fleet played a conspicuous part in the defeat of the Persians, is so worded as to make clear that the battle was of recent occurrence, showing that the Isthmian Games at which this victory was won were either those of April/May 480 B.C. just previous to the battle, and that the Ode was written just after it, or those of 478 B.C. Pindar's lines in reference to the battle are brief, and appear to be intentionally cut short by a warning against undue boasting and by words of reminder that all human affairs are governed by the will of almighty Zeus. This no doubt reflects the conflict of loyalties which must have deeply troubled Pindar in this period which saw his native city fighting on the side of the Persians.

This Ode does not contain the normal myth, but its place is taken by general praise accorded in the second triad to the heroes of the clan of Aeacus, particularly to the deeds of Achilles, and in the second antistrophe quotes the names of great men of various other cities whose deeds had provided themes for poetry.

str. 1 Mother of the sun, Theia, goddess of many names,
Thanks to thee men ascribe to gold a strength exceeding
All other powers that are.
For ships that sail the seas in rivalry
And racing chariot steeds
For thy honour, O queen,
Rise to the height of wondrous deeds amidst
The whirling wheels of struggle.

ant. 1 And in the contests of the Games, he reaps that prize
Of glory that all hearts desire, whose strength of arm
Or speed of foot has won
Many a crown to bind upon his brow.
But the gods' will is judge
Of man's prowess. Two blessings
Only can nurse the dearest gift of life
Amidst good fortune's flower,

ep. 1 If a man knows success and hears his glory
Proclaimed abroad.
Seek not to become Zeus. The best is yours
If the hand of fate grants to you these fair things;
For mortals mortal gifts are fitting.
For you, Phylakidas, twice has the Isthmus
Laid to your name the deathless flower of valour,
And at Nemea too, both you
And Pytheas won the crown
Of the Pankration. But my heart desires
No taste of song lacking the praise
Of the sons of Aeacus. For I am come
With the Graces' gift in hand for Lampon's sons

str. 2 To this city of righteous law. Her feet have trod
The clear high-road of deeds inspired of the gods' will;
Then grudge not the proud praise
Fit for a draught of song her toils to honour.

str. 1 *Theia:* a deity not often mentioned in Greek literature. She was the mother of the Sun, the Moon and Dawn, and thus the giver of light. We do not know whether there was a special cult of this deity at Aegina, but she is easily associated with the gleaming brightness of gold, often referred to in the Odes (cf Ol. I. str. 1), and in a passage such as this, eulogizing victory, she is no doubt invoked as one of the deities who grants it.

ep. 1 *Twice has the Isthmus, etc.:* see foreword.
The sons of Aeacus: as in all other Odes in honour of Aeginetan victors, the clan of Aeacus, the first mythical king of Aegina, is extolled.

str. 2 *This city of righteous law:* Aegina had a high reputation for just dealings, particularly with the many foreign traders who visited the island.

Her great heroes of battle
Too, have won fame. Their glory
The rich-wrought harmonies of lyre and flute
Proclaim through the long years

ant. 2 Of countless time. To the resource of poet's skill
By grace of Zeus was given a task by Oineus' sons,
Those mighty warriors worshipped
With flaming offerings by Aetolian men,
And in Thebes Iolaus,
The charioteer, has honour,
Perseus in Argos, Pollux and Castor's spear
Beside Eurotas' stream;

ep. 2 But in Oenone Aeacus and his sons'
Great-hearted courage
Is fitly praised; not without battle, twice
They ravaged the city of Troy, with Heracles
Leading them in the first assault,
And then with Atreus' sons. Now let me drive
My chariot far aloft. Tell me, who slew
Cycnus, who slew the mighty Hector,
And brought death to that dauntless
Commander of the Ethiopian host,
Clad in his arms of bronze, Memnon?
Who with his spear wounded the noble warrior
Telephus, by the banks of Caicus?

ant. 2 *Oineus' sons:* Tydeus and Meleager, famous legendary heroes of Calydon in Aetolia.

Iolaus: the nephew of Heracles, and his charioteer.

Perseus: the famous Argive hero, known particularly for his feat in killing the Gorgon Medusa.

Pollux and Castor: the legendary Twins. Their story is told in Nemean Ode X.

Beside Eurotas' stream: i.e. in Sparta.

ep. 2 *Oenone:* the original name of Aegina.

Ravaged the city of Troy: Laomedon, the king of Troy, failed to keep his promise to Heracles to reward him for killing a monster which was plaguing the land. Heracles in company with Telamon, one of the sons of Aeacus, took Troy and killed Laomedon. In a later generation Ajax and Achilles, descendants of Aeacus, took part in the Trojan War under Agamemnon and Menelaus, the sons of Atreus.

Cycnus, Hector, Memnon: all killed by Achilles. Cycnus was king of a city near Troy, and an ally of Troy in the Trojan War. On his death he was turned into a swan. Memnon was the leader of the Ethiopians, also allies of Troy.

Telephus: king of Mysia in Asia Minor, wounded by Achilles when the Greek army landed in Mysia when on their way to Troy. The Caicus is a river of Mysia.

str. 3 Even these for whom my voice proclaims their land of birth
Aegina's glorious isle; her walls high-built of old,
A tower that valorous venture
Would well despair to climb. Many a song
My tongue could launch swift-spun
To honour them. Yes, now
Could Salamis embattled, Ajax' city
Tell of their sailors' might,

ant. 3 Who saved her in the deadly tempest sent of Zeus,
When slaughter fell like hail upon a countless host.
Yet, let proud boasts be stilled
'Neath the waters of silence. Zeus it is
Bestows both good and ill,
Zeus who is lord of all.
But for the joy of songs of triumph, sweet
As honey to the ear,

ep. 3 Such honours long. Let him contest the struggle
Who has learnt well
Of Cleonicus race their athletes' valour;
The long toil of brave souls has not lain buried
In blind darkness, unseen of men;
Nor has the cost that fell to them destroyed
Their zealous hope. Pytheas too I praise,
Supreme master of movement, teaching
Phylakidas the path
Of true-spent blows, skilled with his hands, in spirit
A stern contestant. Bring for him
The crown, and bring the fillet of fine wool
And send forth upon wings this new-made song.

str. 3 *Salamis:* see foreword.

ep. 3 *Cleonicus:* an ancestor of Phylakidas. This sentence is a compliment to Phylakidas and his brother Pytheas, meaning that only those who can attain the same excellence as these two athletes should dare to compete in the Games.

ISTHMIAN VI

For

PHYLAKIDAS OF AEGINA

Winner of the Pankration

THE victory for which this Ode was written was gained at an earlier date than the later success of Phylakidas celebrated in the preceding Isthmian V, in which reference is made to this success. Though the date of the present victory cannot be fixed with certainty it was probably won at the Isthmian Games of 484 B.C., and must certainly have been won not very long before the Persian invasion of 480 B.C.

The Ode pays tribute not only to Phylakidas but to other members of his family, to Lampon his father, praised at some length towards the end of the Ode, to Pytheas his elder brother and to Euthymenes, his maternal uncle, who may have been the winner of one of the victories mentioned in antistrophe 3. The phrase in the second line describing this Ode as 'a second bowl of song' is clear evidence that this victory was gained after the Nemean victory of Pytheas celebrated in Nemean V, but presumably before the Nemean victory of Phylakidas of which the date is not known, but to which reference is made in Isthmian V. For a family so clearly ambitious for athletic distinction it is not surprising that Pindar includes the wish expressed in strophe 1 that they may gain the final success of an Olympian victory.

As in other Aeginetan Odes, including Isthmian V, the glories of the Aeacid clan are given a prominent place, and the myth tells the story of the prophecy Heracles made to Telamon the son of Aeacus, of the birth of his son Ajax.

str. 1 As when a feast is joined of men in merry revel,
Now do we mix a second bowl of song
The Muses' gift to honour Lampon's clan,
Famed on the athletes' field. They at Nemea first
In thy honour, great Zeus, attained the crowning flower;
And now again, by grace
Of the lord of Isthmus and the fifty daughters
Of Nereus, is the youngest of their sons
Phylakidas named a victor.
May it be ours to offer yet a third
To Zeus the Saviour at Olympia,
And shower upon the isle of Aegina
The honeyed music of our songs.

ant. 1 For if a man rejoicing in expense and labour
Achieves great deeds founded of divine will,
And by the gods' grace there is planted for him
The lovely flower of fame, then in the furthest reaches
Of happy fortune is his anchor cast already
And the gods give him honour.
That such proud-hearted spirit may reward him,
Ere yet his eyes look on the path of death
Or the white hairs of age,
Is the prayer of Cleonicus' son; and I
To high-throned Clotho and her sister Fates
Add this my plea, that they may look with favour
On this dear wish of my good friend.

ep. 1 And for you, Aeacus' sons, riding your gleaming
Chariots, the poet's task I see most clear before me,
As I set foot upon this isle, to shower
My songs of praise upon you.

str. 1 *A second bowl of song:* see foreword.

The lord of Isthmus: Poseidon, presiding deity of the Isthmian Games.

Daughters of Nereus: the Nereids, the fifty immortal sea-nymphs.

Zeus the Saviour: according to ancient commentators it was the practice at banquets to offer three libations, the first to Zeus, the second to Earth and the heroes, and the third to Zeus the Saviour. Here Pindar allots the second, as a mark of honour for Lampon's race and Phylakidas, to Poseidon and the Nereids, and combines the third with a prayer for an Olympian success for the family.

ant. 1 *Such proud-hearted spirit:* presumably the pride that would attend an Olympian victory.

Cleonicus' son: Lampon, the father of Phylakidas.

Clotho: one of the three Fates: Clotho the spinner, associated with birth; Lachesis who allots man's fate through his life; Atropos the Fate that cannot be avoided, the giver of death.

ep. 1 *As I set foot upon this isle:* it appears that Pindar attended the performance of this Ode in Aegina.

For your fair deeds a thousand roads are cut
A hundred foot in span, stretching
Unhindered whether beyond the distant springs of Nile
Or through the Hyperborean lands.
No city is there of such alien mind
Or witless speech, that does not hear
The fame of the great hero Peleus,
That happy man wed to a goddess maid,

str. 2 Or of Ajax or mighty Telamon his father,
Whom once across the sea Alcmene's son
Led forth, an eager ally in the pride
Of brazen-armoured war, with men of Tiryns to Troy,
That city of many a hero's toil, to bring revenge
For his false treachery
Upon Laomedon. And Pergamon
He captured, and with Telamon laid low
The race of Meropes,
And on that shepherd in stature like a mountain,
Alkyoneus, meeting with him at Phlegra,
Heracles spared not of his strength to loose
The sounding music of his bowstring.

ant. 2 But when he came to call the son of Aeacus
To join him in that famous voyage, he found him
At the banquet table seated with all his men.

Springs of Nile . . . Hyperborean lands: traditionally regarded as the most southerly and most northerly parts of the earth.

Peleus: son of Aeacus, brother of Telamon. He married the immortal Nereid Thetis, and was the father of Achilles.

str. 2 *Alcmene's son:* Heracles.

Men of Tiryns: the traditional birthplace and home of Heracles was at Thebes, but according to one legend he was brought up as a child at Tiryns, the city near Argos once ruled by his ancestor Perseus. This would account for his being accompanied by men of Tiryns on his expedition to Troy.

Laomedon: an early king of Troy, father of Priam. See Note to Isthmian V. ep. 2.

Pergamon: another name for Troy.

Meropes: while returning from Troy, Heracles and Telamon landed on the Aegean island of Cos, home of the Meropes, who attacked them. The two heroes defeated them and killed their king Eurypylus.

Alkyoneus: a giant killed by Heracles either at Phlegra in Chalcidice in the battle of the gods against the giants—the version followed by Pindar here—or according to another version at the Isthmus of Corinth, where Alkyoneus attacked Heracles as he was bringing home the cattle of Geryon from Spain.

And as he stood there with the lion's skin upon him—
That warrior of the mighty spear, Amphitryon's son—
The chieftain Telamon
Called to him to pour forth the first libation
Of nectar, and he handed him the wine-cup
Rough with its figured gold.
And Heracles lifted his hands to heaven,
Those hands invincible, and spoke these words:
'If ever thou hast given, great father Zeus,
A kindly ear unto my vows

ep. 2 Now do I beg thee, now with solemn prayer
To grant that a brave son be born of Eriboea
To this hero, to be our host and friend
By the award of fate.
And may his body's frame be no less hardy
Than this wild creature's skin that rides
Upon my shoulder now—the beast I slew long since,
First of my labours, in Nemea.
And may his soul be of a like valour.'
So he spoke and the god sent down
The king of birds, a mighty eagle;
And his heart thrilled within him with sweet joy.

str. 3 And he proclaimed these words as with a prophet's tongue:
'The son for whom you pray, lo, Telamon,
He shall be born to you. And from this eagle
Seen by our eyes, so let his name be made Ajax
The man of might, a most dread warrior to the peoples
Amidst the toils of war.'
He spoke, and on the word straightway was seated.
Too long for me all their great deeds to tell.
For I have come, my Muse,
Steward of revels for Phylakidas,
For Pytheas and Euthymenes, and after
The mode of Argive men, so shall my praise
Even in words most brief be spoken.

ant. 2 *The lion's skin:* Heracles is traditionally represented as wearing the skin of a lion, sometimes said, as here, to be that of the Nemean lion, sometimes as that of another famous lion killed by Heracles on Mount Kithaeron on the borders of Boeotia and Attica.

ep. 2 *Eriboea:* wife of Telamon.

str. 3 *Ajax:* Pindar derives this name, in Greek spelling Aias, from the Greek word for eagle, aietos.

Pytheas and Euthymenes: see foreword.

The mode of Argive men: the brevity of speech of people from Argos was proverbial.

ant. 3 For thrice at the Isthmus the Pankration's crown they won,
And others from Nemea's leafy vale,
These famous young sons and their mother's brother.
Precious indeed this share of song they have endowed
To the clear light of day; the dewdrops of the Graces
They shower in gleaming beauty
On the Psaluchid clan, Themistius' house
Raising to great renown, and this city
Their home, beloved of heaven.
Lampon to all he does brings the resource
Of practised care, this word of Hesiod
Holding in high honour, and to his sons
Declares it and its worth commends,

ep. 3 Bringing a glory shared by all his city.
Well-loved for kindly deeds to strangers, moderate is
The path his mind pursues, and modest measure
Governs his acts, nor does
His tongue outrun his thoughts: amidst athletes
A man whose worth you well might say
Prevails as over all earth's rocks the Naxian whetstone,
That conquers bronze. For him shall I
Pour forth a draught of Dirke's holy water,
The spring which the deep-bosomed maids
Of golden-robed Mnemosyne
Made flow beside the well-walled gates of Cadmus.

ant. 3 *At the Isthmus:* one of these victories being that of Phylakidas here celebrated, it is not clear by whom the other two Isthmian victories were won, unless possibly Euthymenes, mentioned in strophe 3, was the winner of one or both. The later victory of Isthmian V cannot be one of these three.

Their mother's brother: presumably Euthymenes.

The Psaluchid clan: the name of Lampon's family.

Themistius: the grandfather of Phylakidas.

This word of Hesiod: Pindar has taken the preceding phrase from a line in Hesiod's *Works and Days* which can be translated 'taking pains helps the work'.

ep. 3 *The Naxian whetstone:* a reference to emery, a stone worked from a remote period in the island of Naxos for use as a whetstone.

Dirke: a river near Thebes.

Mnemosyne: Memory, who became the mother by Zeus of the Muses, 'the deep-bosomed maids'.

Of Cadmus: i.e. of Thebes, founded by Cadmus, known as the 'city of seven gates.'

ISTHMIAN VII

For

STREPSIADES OF THEBES

Winner of the Pankration

EDITORS have found it difficult to date this Ode with any certainty. In its style and manner there is a good deal to suggest that it was one of Pindar's earliest Odes. A line in antistrophe 3, however, referring to the approach of old age, has been felt to imply that this Ode was written in Pindar's later years. The Ode mentions the death of an uncle of Strepsiades and speaks at some length of the battle in which he was killed, where the Thebans were defeated. Strepsiades too seems to have played a praiseworthy part in this battle, and lines in strophe 3 imply that this Ode was written not long after this event. The date of this battle has been variously placed at dates as far apart as 506 B.C.—with the Isthmian Games of 502 conjectured as the date of Strepsiades' victory and of this Ode—and as late as 456 B.C., when the Thebans lost the battle of Oenophyta. If the earlier date is correct, this Ode must have been written by Pindar at the age of sixteen, which seems unlikely. Since both the two dates suggested offer difficulties, in the absence of clear evidence the question need not be pursued further here.

The Ode contains no myth, and an unusual feature is the lengthy list of mythical Theban glories given in the first triad. After the passage commemorating the victor's uncle and the prowess of Strepsiades, the third triad includes one of Pindar's frequent warnings against over-ambition, and ends with a prayer for success at the Pythian Games, which may indicate that Strepsiades was preparing to attempt this greater distinction.

str. 1 Blest city of Thebes, whence of the ancient glories
Known of your land, springs to your heart
The greatest joy? Was it maybe
When Dionysus of the flowing locks
You brought to the light of day, beside the throne
And clashing cymbals of Demeter? Or
When in the deep of night
You welcomed as a golden shower of snow
The mightiest of the gods,

ant. 1 When by Amphitryon's palace doors appearing
He bedded with his bride, to give her
The seed of Heracles? Or was it
The fame Teiresias' wise counsel won?
Or glorious Iolaus the skilled horseman?
Or the unwearied spears of the Sown Men?
Or when from the turmoil
Of pealing battle-cries you sent Adrastus
Home to Argos, the city

ep. 1 Of horse, of countless followers bereft?
Or when you gave the Dorian colony
Of Lacedaemon's men
Strength to stand up in courage, when Aegeus' sons,

str. 1 *Dionysus:* the son by Zeus of Semele, one of the daughters of Cadmus the founder of Thebes. For her tragic story see Ol. II. str. 2. After her death Dionysus was brought up by Ino, her sister.

Demeter: Dionysus, as the god of wine and protector of the vine, is often associated with Demeter, the protectress of agriculture and the fruits of the earth.

Golden shower of snow: Pindar has here transferred to the story of Zeus and Alcmene, Amphitryon's wife, the legend of his visit in the form of a stream of gold to Danaë, in her prison at Argos, which resulted in the birth of Perseus (see Pyth. XII. foreword).

ant. 1 *Teiresias:* the blind Theban seer of legendary fame prominent in the story of Oedipus.

Iolaus: the nephew of Heracles and his charioteer.

The Sown Men: warriors who sprang up from the teeth of a dragon, sown in the soil by Cadmus, and became ancestors of the Thebans. (See also note to Isth. I. ep. 2.)

Adrastus: leader of the expedition of the 'Seven against Thebes', which was decisively defeated.

ep. 1 *The Dorian colony, etc.:* in its early days the city of Sparta, whose people are referred to here as the Dorian colony because they derived from the Dorian invasions, was not firmly established until the Spartans defeated their opponents in the neighbouring city of Amyclae. To do this they were advised by the Delphic oracle to get help from the descendants of Aegeus (king of Athens and father of Theseus). One branch of this clan

Born of your stock, captured Amyclae,
As Pytho's prophet had ordained?
Yes, but the glory of old time
Sleeps, and the minds of men
Remember not,

str. 2 Unless it be that blended in rich streams
Of sounding song, the poet's wisdom
Brings to their ear its perfect flower.
Sound then for Strepsiades too the sweet-sung
Revel of triumph, who wears the Isthmian crown
Of the Pankration; his strength a marvel
To see, beauty adorns
His limbs, and to his body's grace he brings
No lesser share of valour.

ant. 2 The Muses violet-tressed nurse high the flame
Of his renown, and of this flower
He has made free his mother's brother
Who shares his name, to whom bronze-armoured Ares
Brought death. But for the brave is laid in store
The recompense of honour. Let him know well
Whoever in this dark
Storm-cloud fends off from his belovéd land
The blood-stained hail of war,

ep. 2 And brings destruction to the enemy's host,
Such a man shall exalt his city's race
To the utmost of glory,
Both while he lives and when he is no more.
And you, son of Diodotus,
In prowess rivalling the might
Of Meleager and of Hector
And Amphiaraus, you
Breathed forth the spirit

had settled in Thebes (Pindar belonged to the Aegeid clan) and with their help the Spartans took Amyclae and established their supremacy. The Aegeid leader on this occasion, Timomachus, was reputed to have reorganized the Spartan army and put it on the firm basis which was maintained to historical times.

ant. 2 *His mother's brother:* see foreword. His name also was Strepsiades.

ep. 2 *Diodotus:* the victor's father.

Meleager: a legendary hero of Calydon of Aetolia, who took part in the Argonautic expedition and was the hero of the legend of the Calydonian boar.

Hector: the famous hero of Troy.

Amphiaraus: the famous warrior and prophet of Argos who lost his life in the expedition of the Seven against Thebes.

str. 3 Of your fair-flowering prime, fronting the line
Of battle, where brave-hearted men
Bore up on the last slender hope
The strife of war. Bitter the grief they suffered,
Not to be told. But now has the great god,
Holder of earth, granted me summer skies
After the winter's cold.
Songs will I sing, with wreaths my brow adorning,
And may no jealous envy

ant. 3 Of heaven mar whatever taste of joy
Delights each passing day, granting
My onward steps to tread a path
Carefree, to old age and the appointed end.
For all alike we come to death, albeit
With varied fate; whose eyes would peer aloft
To distant realms, too small
Is he to reach the bronze-floored throne of heaven.
Pegasus winging high

ep. 3 Threw down to earth his lord Bellerophon,
Who thought to reach the abodes of heaven, and share
The company of Zeus.
Sweets gained unrightly await an end most bitter.
But for us, Loxias, we pray thee,
God of the golden-flowing hair,
Grant us in thy contest also,
To win the gleaming flower
Of Pytho's crown.

str. 3 *The great god:* Poseidon, god of the sea and subterranean powers. As tutelary deity of the Isthmian Games, by granting this victory he has granted consolation after distress.

ant. 3 *Pegasus:* the winged horse of legend. The story of how Bellerophon mastered Pegasus with the aid of the magic bridle given to him by Athene is told at some length in Olympian Ode XIII. His ambition to reach heaven came to grief.

ep. 3 *Loxias:* another name for Apollo.
Thy contest: the Pythian Games.

ISTHMIAN VIII

For

CLEANDRUS OF AEGINA

Winner of the Pankration

As is clear from the opening strophe, this Ode celebrates victories won by Cleandrus both at the Isthmian and the Nemean Games. The Isthmian success appears to have been the later of the two, and this Ode shows that it was written very shortly after the Persian invasion of 480/479 B.C. It contains in its opening section the clearest and most feelingly stated comment that Pindar has left to us on the subject of the Persian war, an expression both of his joy for the release of Hellas from this threat and of his sorrow for the part played by his native Thebes. This passage must have been written soon after the final defeat of the Persians at the battle of Plataea in 479 B.C., and the Isthmian victory of Cleandrus can thus be placed without much doubt at the Isthmian Games of 478. The date of his Nemean victory is not known, but as the present Ode emphasizes the youth of the victor, it must have been gained not long before. Possibly its celebration was prevented by the war, and combined with this later celebration of the Isthmian victory.

The greater part of this Ode is devoted to the myth. The close connection between Thebes and Aegina is emphasized in the second strophe, and after praise of the clan of Aeacus, usual in an Ode to an Aeginetan victor, the story is told of the quarrel between Zeus and Poseidon for the hand of Thetis, and of how this was resolved by the decision that she should be given in marriage to Peleus the son of Aeacus. The exploits of Achilles, their son, follow as a natural sequel. The final strophe, before returning to its concluding words of praise for Cleandrus, makes reference to an Isthmian victory won by his cousin Nicocles, a boxer, who was no longer alive. Other victories of Cleandrus at Megara and Epidaurus are mentioned before the Ode's closing phrases.

str. 1 Bring for Cleandrus in his pride of youthful years
A recompense of glory for his toils. Young men
Come, to his father Telesarchus take your way,
And by his gleaming doors
Raise up on high your songs of triumph, the reward
Of victory at the Isthmus; and Nemea too
Saw him prevailing in the contests' prize.
For his honour
I too, though heavy grief weighs on my heart,
Am bidden to invoke the glorious Muse.
From great sorrow released let us not languish
Bereft of victors' crowns, nor brood upon our woes.
Let us have done with ills that know no cure,
And send abroad a sweet taste of delight
Even after pain: for now
The stone of Tantalus, hung o'er our heads,
Some god has set aside, that evil

str. 2 Hellas' brave heart could not endure. But now for me
The fear that is gone on its way has made an end
To a cruel load of care. Best is it in all things
To set the task in hand
Clearly before our eyes: treacherous the years that hang
Over our mortal span, twisting the path of life.
Yet even for this, healing is given to men,
If but in freedom
They put their trust. Brave hope then must we cherish,
And a man nursed in seven-gated Thebes
To Aegina must offer the first flower

str. 1 *His gleaming doors:* probably a complimentary phrase indicating that Telesarchus was a man of wealth.

From great sorrow released: a reference to the defeat of the Persian invaders under Xerxes at Salamis 480 B.C. and Plataea 479 B.C.

Ills that know no cure: this no doubt refers to Pindar's distress in regard to Thebes, who fought on the Persian side, and after the battle of Plataea was severely punished by the Greek allies under Pausanias the Peloponnesian leader.

str. 2 *To Aegina:* Thebes and Aegina, both in enmity with Athens, had close ties. Pindar's affection for the island and its people is well known.

Of Beauty's grace; for both were of one father born
The youngest daughters of Asopus' river;
And sovereign Zeus looked upon them with favour.
One of these did he set
By Dirke's lovely waters, to be queen
Of this city of charioteers,

str. 3 But you he carried to Oenopia's isle and wedded.
And there you bore to the loud-roaring god of thunder
Aeacus, a son divine, noblest of mortal men,
Who gave even to the gods
Decision of their strife. Foremost in valour were
His godlike sons and their sons' sons, who took delight
In battle, and to front the ringing medley
Of brazen arms;
Wise too were they and reason ruled their hearts.
These virtues even the gods, in council gathered,
Remembered well, when for marriage with Thetis
There arose strife 'twixt Zeus and glorious Poseidon
When each of the two gods would have her be
His lovely bride, for passion filled their hearts.
But for them did the wisdom
Of the immortal gods not grant this union
Should come to pass, when to their ears

str. 4 Came the prophetic oracle. For in their midst
Wise-counselled Themis told that it was ruled of fate
That the sea-goddess should bring forth a son, of strength
Mightier than his father,
Whose hand should launch a shaft more powerful than the bolt
Of thunder or the fearsome trident, if she wed
With Zeus or with his brothers. 'Cease,' said she,
'From this design,

Daughters of Asopus' river: Thebe, who gave her name to Thebes, and Aegina.

Asopus' river: the largest river in Boeotia.

Dirke's waters: the stream of Dirke was close to Thebes.

This city of charioteers: Thebes. The phrase, literally translated 'a city that loves chariots' is, like other phrases used by Pindar e.g. 'lovers of horses', 'riders of white steeds', a stock phrase implying a compliment to wealth and aristocracy.

str. 3 *But you:* i.e. the maid Aegina.

Oenopia: an early name for Aegina, also known as Oenone.

Thetis: the immortal sea-nymph, daughter of Nereus, the 'Old Man of the Sea'.

str. 4 *Themis:* the deity of lawful Right.

But with a mortal let her bed be blessed,
And let her see her son dying in war—
Like Ares shall he be in strength of arm
And in fleetness of foot like to the lightning flash.
If my word you would hear, grant that her marriage
Be for an honour given of heaven to Peleus,
The son of Aeacus,
Who, so they tell, is of all men most righteous,
Dwelling upon Iolcus' plain.

str. 5 'And to the immortal cave of Chiron let your bidding
Speedily take its way, nor let the ballot-leaves
Of strife be set amidst us twice by Nereus' daughter.
But on the full-moon's eve
Let her for this hero unloose the lovely girdle
Of her pure maidenhood.' Such words the goddess spoke
To the children of Cronos; and they nodded
Giving assent
With their immortal brows. Nor was the fruit
Of these words cast away. For the two gods,
So the tale runs, joined in their honours given
To the wedding of maid Thetis, and the tongues of poets
Have made known the young valour of Achilles
To those who knew it not. For it was he
In vine-clad Mysia
Made the blood flow, and scattered o'er the plain
The darkened gore of Telephus.

str. 6 For Atreus' sons he built a bridge for their return,
And freed Helen, and with his spear cut the great sinews
Of Troy asunder, those heroes who, as he plied
The task of murderous battle

Her son: Achilles.

Peleus: the story of the marriage of Peleus and Thetis is often referred to in the Odes (cf Nem. IV. str. 8 and 9).

Iolcus: the modern Volos in eastern Thessaly. Peleus left Aegina his birthplace (cf Nem. V, ant. 1. ep. 1) and settled in Iolcus.

str. 5 *The cave of Chiron:* Peleus was one of the many heroes of legend who went to be educated by the Centaur Chiron in his cave on Mount Pelion.

The ballot-leaves of strife: in some Greek cities the leaves of the olive tree were sometimes used for recording popular votes of banishment.

The full-moon's eve: the time of full moon was believed to be a favourable moment for marriage.

Mysia: a district in Asia Minor, where the Greek forces landed while on their way to Troy. Telephus of Mysia was wounded by Achilles.

str. 6 *Atreus' sons:* Agamemnon and Menelaus.

Sought to withstand him on the plain, proud-hearted
Memnon
That man of might, and Hector and warriors many another
Noble and brave. For these Achilles' hand
Pointed the way
Down to Persephone's abode, that prince
Of Aeacus' sons, bringing to Aegina
And his own stock the height of fame. Nor even
In death was he of songs forsaken, but the maids
Of Helicon stood by his pyre and grave,
And poured o'er him their dirge in chorus. Thus
Even the immortals ruled
That to a brave man, though he be no more,
The songs of goddesses be given.

str. 7 Now too that word holds, and the Muses' chariot
Speeds forth to praise the memory of Nicocles
Of boxing fame. Honour him then who in the vale
Of Isthmus won the crown
Of Dorian parsley. Like to those resistless hands
Of old, he too conquered long since and put to rout
The men who dwelt nearby; and to his glory
Brings no disfame
This son of his proud uncle's race. Go then,
Let one of his own age bring to Cleandrus,
For his pankration victory, to bind
Upon his brow, the lovely myrtle's crown; for he
In the games of Alcathous won success,
And young men welcomed him at Epidaurus.
Now must brave souls resound
His praise, who in no corner-hole has hidden
His youth, untried of noble deeds.

Memnon: leader of the Ethiopians, allies of the Trojans.

The maids of Helicon: the Muses. Their traditional home was on Mount Helicon in south-eastern Boeotia.

str. 7 *Nicocles:* a cousin of Cleandrus, who it appears had won a victory in the Isthmian Games but was no longer alive.

Those resistless hands: i.e. of Achilles.

This son: Cleandrus.

The games of Alcathous: the local games of Megara. Alcathous was a mythical king of that city.

At Epidaurus: Cleandrus had also been successful in the local games of Epidaurus.